Destiny Calling:

Twenty Years Living With James

Also by John Ormond

Their Spirits, My Demons

Destiny Calling:

Twenty Years Living With James

By John Ormond

© John Ormond, 2012

Published by Startled Kitten

A CIP catalogue record for this book is available from the British Library.

ISBN 978-0-9566355-1-8

Book and cover design by Clare Brayshaw

Prepared and printed by:

York Publishing Services Ltd
64 Hallfield Road
Layerthorpe
York YO31 7ZQ
Tel: 01904 431213
Website: www.yps-publishing.co.uk

Contents

Acknowledgments

First of all a MASSIVE thank you to Sarah-Charlotte Peace for adding colour and detail to the canvas, it was very much appreciated and I'm eternally grateful for your input, advice and support. I'll make sure you get an extra special selection box for Christmas! A big thank you goes out to the good people of the online James community, what a crazy bunch we are! Dedicated and certainly undermedicated! Thanks once again to the Parry family and the Knight family for the support over the years and putting up with my general weirdness and off kilter sense of humour. And lastly, thank you James for truly being the soundtrack of my life.

I'll see you next time. (Book three may or may not be about those playful little creatures known as Stoats)

For further tomfoolery and rhetoric jot along to www.twitter.com/Sean_Hornby74

Introduction

This is an unauthorised account of my life following James, it has not been endorsed by the individual band members, its management or anybody else affiliated with the Manchester group. I therefore need to mention that the opinions, views and comments within Destiny Calling: Twenty Years Living With James are mine and will not necessarily be shared by others including James and anyone else associated with them. The only exceptions relate to where I've either used a direct quote or have paraphrased a quote, comment or opinion from a direct source.

It's an unusual quirky tale which is reflective of my own personality, I write like I think, slightly chaotic and on the edge of near implosion. Certain members of the James community will make an appearance as the story unfolds, some names have been changed to protect the innocent and the not so innocent. Some content has been blatantly made up particularly in relation to the exaggerated acrobatic skills of keyboard player Mark Hunter.

A nod of thanks goes out to the James community past, present and future, I've met some very interesting people over the years due to our love of the band. Dave Brown's 'oneofthethree' website was also an invaluable source of information which helped jog my memory on a number of occasions, cheers Dave.

And for those of you who only know James because of a certain song then hopefully by the end of the read you'll be tempted to explore their back catalogue further.

John Ormond
March 2012

For

E, D and M

The legend that was 'Mickey B's'

1990

Michael changed my life. Well, maybe that's too strong a statement to make but looking back now it's obvious to me at least that he certainly had a positive influence on my life, more so than any of my school teachers ever did. For just a fraction of my life Michael was like an older brother to me, the brother that I never really had. Michael was handsome, cool, deep and wise beyond his twenty two years of age. He was the kind of man that other men would enjoy going for a beer with, the kind of man that women found to be a bit of a turn on. He was so damn cool that he'd hand painted the iconic image of Kiefer Sutherland from *The Lost Boys* onto the back of his leather jacket. It was magnificent and attracted a lot of attention. He was always being asked if he'd sell it but he always declined. To the outside world Michael came across as being so confident and full of humour when he was actually quite a troubled individual that we'd sadly discover at a later date.

I first met Michael when I was fifteen years of age, I had a Saturday job working in an art gallery and picture framers in the town where I lived and had grown up. To the untrained eye the art gallery side of the job was aesthetically pleasing but behind the closed doors of the workshop I felt like I was gambling with my life each shift I worked. This was the direct result of working with petty thieves, drug users and the odd psychopath. 'Noddy' was a guy who worked alongside Michael and I, he had an unhealthy interest in throwing Stanley Knife blades around the workshop, often at his colleagues which of course included a naive fifteen year old boy with a big bowl hair-cut that still managed to incorporate a rather fetching side parting.

"NEW BLADE!" Noddy would shout with a certain amount of glee before launching one of the sharp pieces of metal in your direction. From experience I can confirm that if the blades hit their target then extreme pain would be experienced but it was kind of funny and the bizarre game would make everyone laugh, all except the individual who was bleeding of course. Noddy asked me, in fact he pleaded with me on numerous occasions if he could cut my fingers off with the circular saw. I declined of course as I had no personal insurance, it was a time before you were bombarded with "no win, no fee" opportunities via day time television and text messages left on your phone reminding you about *"your unclaimed compensation from your recent accident blah, blah, blah".*

John Dope was the proprietor and our boss; he was also a rather unpleasant character. The tight arse only paid me one pound an hour and his favourite word was the 'C' word, and I'm not referring to cancer either. His attire was a bit like how I imagine Alan Partridge's dad would have dressed. John was also an ABBA obsessive back in the days when liking ABBA wasn't something you'd brag or boast about. I once found John's stash of pornographic magazines hidden in a secret compartment underneath his desk side drawers. They were disappointingly a tad tame though, more like lingerie catalogues however the women still had quite attractive heads and arms. I left them relatively untouched but pondered upon the idea of removing them and leaving a piece of paper in their place that said *"naughty, naughty"* on it. I also considered mailing a letter to his wife telling her that she'd find something that might interest her if she looked underneath the drawers, but I didn't want to risk being responsible for a divorce or at the very least a black eye and being sacked.

Michael was fairly normal compared to Noddy and John. Well, apart from the time when I watched him pick up a large hairy spider. Without realising that I was watching him he proceeded to shove the poor beast into his mouth and then he only went and bloody ate it. Then there was the time someone cut themselves on the circular saw and he licked the blood up afterwards. Err, and on another occasion he was drinking from a glass and he decided for some reason or other to take a bite out of it, there was quite a bit of blood to clear up from that incident too but on that occasion we used a cloth instead of insisting that he licked it up himself.

Apart from that Michael was 'The Dude' as far as I was concerned. As I was the youngest in the workshop he kindly took me under his wing. Knowing that I was impressed with his artwork he told me that he'd hand paint a t-shirt for me if I wanted. I suggested the cover to the seven inch vinyl of the Dream Warriors single 'My Definition of a Boombastic Jazz Style'. It was a simple colourful design and it certainly represented where my head was at that particular musical point in my life. Musically I was still pretty naive to be honest. I'm probably being a tad harsh on myself, my first proper purchase music wise was the inimitable *Jeff Wayne's Musical Version of the War of the Worlds* and from there I somehow stumbled into the rather exciting world of Hip-Hop. Whilst I was listening to Public Enemy my school mates were having raging wet dreams listening to the soundtrack to *Top Gun*. Okay, there are some alright tunes on it but it wasn't at all representative of me. I liked 'outsider's music', rebellious attitudes, music that 'certain types' embraced. Music that if you noticed somebody wearing a particular band t-shirt you'd be able to psychoanalyse them immediately as being "a little bit different".

One particular Saturday morning Michael staggered into the workshop with a horrendous limp of unknown origin. Grimacing, he made himself a coffee, lit up a cigarette and then he told me that he had a present for me. I was intrigued. He stumbled across to his *Lost Boys* jacket and pulled out a small plastic package which turned out to be a C90 cassette.

"Here you go lad, hope you like it. It should in theory stop you listening to all of that American crap that you've been listening to".

I held the transparent plastic box as if it was some precious unearthly object. The inlay card had been simply decorated in an array of felt tip colours. In silver ink the words '*Mickey B's*' boldly stood out. When asked Michael wouldn't elaborate what *Mickey B*'s meant, instead he diverted my attention to the track listing which was on the inside of the inlay card.

I nervously opened the case, my brow was damp, my knees knocked violently (I was actually in dire need of using the toilet) and I scanned over the array of unfamiliar and nonsensical words that had been scrawled in black ink. That Petrol Emotion, King of the Slums, Primal Scream, The Soup Dragons, James, Bridewell Taxis, Inspiral Carpets. I knew they were band names, but the majority of them sounded, well, rubbish.

"Let me know what you think won't you?" said Michael, I promised him that I'd listen to it as soon as possible and then I wandered over to my own jacket and carefully placed *Mickey B's* into the pocket.

"NEW BLADES!" shouted Noddy and we all immediately ducked for cover.

I owned a poor quality stereo that my mum had bought me for Christmas, some unheard of make that sounded extremely puny however it was still my pride and joy, even more so than the telescope my dear departed dad had bought me for my ninth birthday. I opened up the tape deck, slipped in *Mickey B's*, pressed the play button and slouched back onto my sofa bed with a Wagon Wheel and a glass of Ben Shaws Orangeade for comfort. From the off the tape was nothing short of brilliant. The first song was 'Hey Venus: The Mad Thatcher Disease Mix' by That Petrol Emotion, an utterly fantastic song that superbly fused dance beats with guitars, something I'd never really come across up till that point in my life and on top it featured the fabulous vocalist Steve Mack. (I'd later discover that Michael Stipe from REM stated that if he wasn't in REM he'd want to be in That Petrol Emotion). The song set the tone for the rest of the cassette. Moody, edgy and rather groovy! I sat in absolute awe, I didn't move a muscle except when I breathed or burped due to the gassy liquid. Each song was better than the previous one, I waited for a dud but it simply never came. I was edging towards the end of side one when an unusual sounding song made its presence known; it kind of sat awkwardly amongst the other tracks I'd heard so far. The song featured a rather unusual keyboard riff accompanied by what sounded like submarine sonar bleeping and hooting away. Its unusualness certainly caught my attention. The male vocalist then started singing *"I've got the bends from pressure"*. I was convinced that the song was definitely about being stuck on board a submarine or had at the very least an aquatic focus of some description.

The song was 'Come Home' by the Manchester band James. I thought 'James' was a rather lazy sounding name compared to That Petrol Emotion; I naturally assumed that the vocalist was called James and I wondered what his surname was. 'Come Home' certainly struck a chord with me, if you pardon the pun. I quickly came to the conclusion that James the vocalist had a few personal issues. His lyrics rang of self-loathing and regret. 'Come Home' sounded like a regretful sea shanty set to a shuffling baggy disco beat. I was confused but I immediately loved the song, I must have listened to it at least fifteen times in a row, each time the song finished I'd hit the rewind button and listen to it again but by the ninth listen I disappointingly realised that 'Come Home' had nothing to do with submarines. It wasn't until some time later in the future when I discovered that the lyrics had been written at an extremely difficult and emotionally taxing period in the life of the vocalist. (By the way he wasn't called James after all, no he was called Tim.)

I returned to the workshop the following Saturday, the air was heavily polluted with the usual fragrance of overflowing ashtrays, coffee, Calor Gas and wood shavings. It was somehow a rather comforting smell. I was soon greeted by the older gang of misfits and Michael.

"Have you listened to the tape yet?" Michael asked me, his face a picture of pained anticipation.

"Yes Michael, I love it, thanks very much indeed". The look of relief on his face was clearly evident and he made a strange sort of groaning sound.

"So, any favourite songs then?"

"Yes, well, I liked them all to be honest, but I have to say that my favourite song was by James".

"Ah, James, yes, top band, they've been knocking about for a few years now that lot. They're a right bunch of freaks. I've got some more of their stuff if you're interested?" Michael was obviously quite keen to influence me further.

"That would be great! Cheers!"

"I'll warn you now though; their earlier stuff sounds nothing like 'Come Home', in fact it's not far off from being a trippy kind of folk music".

I suddenly had a terrifying flashback regarding some of the awful folk music that I'd been forced to listen to as a youngster by Uncle Jim. I told Michael that I'd leave it. I didn't want to spoil a good thing. He was very understanding and he said he'd lend me the new Soup Dragons album instead. My friend Gavin who was *really* into Hip-Hop laughed at me when I announced to him that I'd gotten into Indie Music. He thought I was nothing short of a Judas to Hip hop, but for me Hip hop was already edging away from political and cultural awareness, it was instead disappointingly heading into a territory that seemed more focused on "guns, bitches and bling". The 'Daisy Age' really was dead......

Life immediately changed for me, with the pittance wage I earned from my part time job I sought out further musical purchases from the local Our Price record shop, my musical taste became baggier, the band members all had massive basin haircuts and the world of Hip hop started to dim in my young life. It transpired that something called 'Madchester' was in full swing and I was soon caught up with the zeitgeist which affected my dress sense, the way I walked, even the way I talked. I soon realised my own bowl hair cut was rather trendy, well once I'd finally lost the side parting that I'd had for aeons and flared jeans were also back in fashion. This is something I'd never dreamt of a few years earlier when I'd been wearing them not out of choice but because all of my clothes came from second hand shops. It was a rather strange thing, the whole 'Madchester' scene had been happening without my knowledge and although I was rather late for the party I realised that it's obviously better to be late than never to turn up to the party at all.

I continued to listen to *Mickey B's* on a regular basis, I even lent it to some of my school mates and they all agreed that it was rather marvellous. Curtis who was in my sixth form class went out and bought the album *Chemicrazy* by That Petrol Emotion after listening to *Mickey*

B's, however he reported back to me that he was rather disappointed when he realised it was simply an album of guitar based songs without any loops or beats. I found out that it was still an excellent album as Michael generously gave me his copy of *Chemicrazy* a few months later. It was the same occasion when he announced he was leaving town as he'd secured a new job in Sheffield, he promised he'd keep in touch with the rest of the guys (barring John Dope) including little old me. We were gutted at the news, I was very sad; it felt like I was being abandoned by another protective male figure in my life however I was pleased that he was happy with the decision he'd made. As well as *Chemicrazy* Michael gave me a number of books relating to the paranormal and the occult, they both featured some very unsettling material and they remained pretty much unopened.

As 1990 turned into 1991 my Saturday job turned into something a bit more than that. I'd go to work after school for a couple of hours, school holidays were a time to earn extra spending money. In truth I loved the job. The sharp missiles that often headed in my direction were a bit of a nuisance but it was generally a good laugh. Michael was sorely missed, he was irreplaceable in fact and John Dope verbally took his frustrations out on the rest of us. The ancient workshop radio that was held together by brown plastic tape pumped out some great music through its single dusty speaker. Radio One featured plenty of guitar based indie dance which kept me happy throughout my time at work. Two songs were on heavy rotation on the radio during the early part of 1991. The first song was by a mysterious singer named Chesney Hawkes, his song was called 'The One and Only'. It certainly caught my attention mainly because it managed to irritate the hell out of me and because Shane, a gangly bleached blond haired guy I worked with thought the song was one of the greatest songs of all time. He was clearly quite insane as his appalling hair and foul smelling clothes had already pointed at. The other song was 'Sit Down' by James. Now, I'd heard 'Sit Down' a dozen or so times at work but had never clocked that it was the same James who'd lit up my musical life the year before.

"And *that* was the fabulous James with 'Sit Down'" squeaked the over excited DJ on Radio One.

"!" I thought.

"James, 'Come Home', submarines, self-loathing, BRILLIANT!!!" I gaily danced around the circular saw whilst my colleagues looked upon me with confused and nervous looks in their eye. Thankfully Noddy wasn't present otherwise blood would definitely have been spilt. I quickly made my excuses, left work and pounded the streets towards Our Price where I managed to find the last 7" vinyl copy of the said record. As I left the shop I held the record tightly to my chest, my eyes rolled in their sockets and my dry mouth mumbled an unintelligible language, passers-by avoided me like the plague, the homeless guy outside the florist left his pitch and ran away too. I then ran home and proceeded to play the song to death. "Oh, I like this song" my mum said to me as she stuck her head into my bedroom, a lit cigarette hanging from the corner of her mouth dropping ash onto my bedroom floor and we listened to it on repeat for an hour or so.

"'Sit Down' that's a puffs song!" Gavin said one evening when I was around at his house. I laughed but was angry with him for saying such a stupid and unpleasant thing.

"Nah, its not. It's a top tune! It's not as good as 'Come Home' but it's still wicked" I said to him defensive in tone and manner.

"'Come Home', hmmm, not sure about that mate" and Gavin then proceeded to mimic and mock the hook line of the song by going "duh, der, der, duh, der der, duh duh, der duh" if you kind of follow what I mean. Gavin soon bored of ridiculing my new favourite band and instead proceeded to spin some Eric B and Rakim on his turntable, we coolly nodded our heads in time to the beat, arms tightly folded imaging that we were the blackest white dudes in town.

It didn't take that long to realise that 'Sit Down' was everywhere; it appeared to be on some kind of a loop, a mantra, a perpetual call out to the weirdoes and outcasts of the world to unify in a big old sitting down session. By all accounts launderettes country wide reported a 75% increase in customers during the songs peak although I could never fathom out why this was the case. 'Sit Down' was one of those songs that pop along once in a while, a song that appeared to connect with everyone, and I was happily swept along with them too.

That Sunday, I headed off to the seaside for the day with my mum and Ernie who was her best friend; we'd taken a coach to a place up north called Whitby. It's a nice enough town famous for its picturesque harbour, Dracula, Goths and the Magpie Restaurant where pensioners happily queue for up to three hours in either the scorching sun or howling rain just to enjoy fish and chips served silver service style. Anyway, a pleasant time was experienced by the three of us even if this meant that the majority of the day was spent sat in a dirty smoky Working Men's club, my teeth slowly disintegrating via a dozen glasses of coke; the passive smoking was a cheap way to enjoy a packet of cigarettes. On the journey home the radio was on and tuned into Radio One, the Top Forty rundown was being broadcast. Throughout the show The DJ made several comments regarding who was possibly going to be Number One on that particular Sunday, he teasingly kept mentioning James and playing a snippet of 'Sit Down'. The song had entered the charts a week earlier at an impressive number seven but I wondered if it could actually achieve the improbable. I was incredibly excited at the prospect that 'Sit Down' could actually be number one; it really felt like something very special was about to unfold in front of me, a landmark moment in pop history.

And then, a devastating blow.

"And it's a sad week for James; this week's number two is 'Sit Down'" the DJ said sounding rather disappointed. My stomach sank; I felt it would have been too good to be true if the song had indeed reached the top spot. Still, hearing 'Sit Down' being played on a coach full of pensioners and single mums with kids still felt like a wonderful moment. The song came to an end, "*Daaaooooowwwwwnnnnnnnn*"....

A radio jingle sparked up, the disappointment that the DJ had previously felt was soon forgotten...

"A sad week for James maybe but it's a great week for Chesney Hawkes who's this weeks number one with his smash hit 'The one and Only'".

The horrible guitar riff started up and Chesney's song farted into life. I bit my lip in disgust and tasted my own boiling blood. Then, as if that wasn't bad enough some bloke who was sat by himself started to sing along whilst playing the air guitar. It felt like such a personal attack, I was paranoid as hell that he was trying to wind me up, I wanted to point out to him what a horrendous song it was; instead I stared sadly at the blurred scenery as we charged down Sutton Bank at 85 mph. (It was more like 37mph but that's a boring speed hence the slight exaggeration).

The only saving grace was after the chart run down had finished an amazing sounding psychedelic song blared out of the speakers. It was called 'I Am The Walrus' by a little known band from Liverpool called The Beatles. It was such a great tune that I seriously questioned why this band had never been successful. I'm guessing that in a parallel universe The Beatles became massive and made an enormous cultural impact upon our little world. Of course, in that same universe 'Sit Down' would have been number one for twenty seven weeks and would spend the next five years hovering around the top twenty, a bit like the song Elton John sang about a dead princess, (that particular song apparently stayed in the Canadian Top Twenty for about five years but I digress). And that was that. Little did I know that 'Sit Down' would become one of the most famous number two songs of all time, it would be the true start of a love affair that would carry me through highs and lows, relationships and breakups, deaths, births, marriages and hair loss.

As a footnote to the first chapter I must give Michael a mention. After he left town for the industrial city of Sheffield Michael fell on very hard times. His job never really worked out, within a few months he'd lost his girlfriend, his home and he ended up being detained under the Mental Health Act for quite a long time. I know all of this because I met him by chance some years later. He was hollow, his personality had disappeared, the bright sparkling eyes that once lit up his face were dulled and from our too brief conversation it was apparent that he was a lost soul. I never saw Michael again, to some it may seem like he plays such an insignificant part in my story but for me he was one of the most important people in my life, one I'll never forget. God bless you Michael.

Tim the Enchanter

1991

Obviously I really liked James but in reality it was probably nothing too disimilar to the feelings I'd had for The Wombles when I was a wee lad. I continued to listen to 'Sit Down' and 'Come Home' on a regular enough basis and I eventually became aware that James had released an album that featured not only 'Sit Down' but 'Come Home' too. So, one Saturday after work I decided that I was going to spend some of my hard earned cash and buy the album. I called into Our Price and picked up a cassette version of the album *Gold Mother* as well as an album called *Troglodyte History* by a little known or remembered British Hip-Hop artist called Caveman. *Troglodyte History* had received a great review in *Hip-Hop Connection Magazine*; the monthly read obviously influenced my purchase as the magazine was for me at least comparable to the Ten Commandments minus the doomy and gloomy caveats. With the purchases made I headed back home as fast as my legs would carry me. I was going on yet another day trip to the seaside the following day; the journey was going to be a good opportunity to listen to both of the albums on my cheap but much loved personal stereo.

Upon arriving home I decided I'd have a listen to *Gold Mother*, it was either that or watching *Catch Phrase* hosted by the loveable rogue Roy Walker. A tough decision for anyone to have to make but life is full of them. I nipped into the poorly lit kitchen to grab some crisps and pop to accompany the experience and then dashed up the creaky staircase and slid my bedroom door shut behind me. An air of expectation hung over me. I was about to enter a brave new world of Huxley sized proportions; it was the beginning of a beginning, a leap of musical faith. I held the

Gold Mother album as if I was holding a butterfly, the cover was unusual, unsettling, a bit like a distorted picture of The Mona Lisa that had been submerged in a bath of Brasso, when I inspected the inlay card the aquatic scene of a naked swimming woman chasing an equally naked swimming baby amused me for the briefest moment of time, it certainly wasn't *It Takes a Nation of Millions to Hold Us Back* that was for sure.

I inserted the tape into the player, pressed the play button and sat myself down on the squashy back crippling sofa bed. Predictably enough *Gold Mother* started off on a promising note with 'Come Home' sounding crisper and clearer than the version I'd been listening to on *Mickey B's* which had been a recording of a vinyl version of the song. By then I was so very familiar with the song, but I was equally if not more excited at the prospect of what the next song was going to sound like. 'Lose Control' was a bit of a shock though, it featured a walloping bass and drum line with Tim Booth mournfully questioning *"where is the love?"* whilst a squally sounding trumpet popped its head up from time to time to try and cheer him up. The song was melancholy, mysterious and on the edge yet at the same time it reminded me of 'The Pink Panther' theme tune though for the life of me I've no idea why. I wasn't sure if I liked it or not.

The next song 'Government Walls' confused me even further. 'Government Walls' was another brooding song which marched along in an unstoppable manner. What was clear to me was that it was political in content, pretty obvious from the title I guess. It wasn't what I was hoping or expecting from the album. I was expecting variants of 'Come Home's indie dance that I could swing my hips about to. I scratched my head. What had I bought? The song played out for what seemed like an eternity, violins and trumpets cascading over one another, Tim Booth manic in his medium of communication. A feeling of disappointment crept in and tickled my toes, my pop became as flat as water and the sky turned a black sack cloth colour.

My nerves went into overdrive mainly due to the sudden change in the colour of the sky but probably more so at the prospect of what the next song was going to sound like. The brief silence ended when a sample of an American evangelist started to preach about the hidden truths in rock music, it certainly fitted the Biblical atmosphere that enveloped the land. I seriously considered the possibility that I'd picked up a copy of the album that some religious nutcase had tampered with before returning it to the shop in the hope that the next person who bought it would be brainwashed into thinking that music was evil. My copy of *Gold Mother* compared somewhat to The Ark from that Indiana Jones film, the one with snakes and stuff.

Thunder cracked above the house and a howling wind suddenly picked up. My god, I was seriously confused and scared by this weird album. With trembling hands I picked up *Troglodyte History* and considered putting it on in the hope that order would be restored and the demonic atmosphere would be dampened down, but no, I decided I'd finish what I'd started unless the apocalypse came first. Thankfully the song featuring the American evangelist kicked in proper, the song 'God Only Knows' sounded utterly frantic and rather insane, I leapt into the air when Tim mentioned the "F" word", now THAT I wasn't expecting, and I'd thought Tim had sounded like such a pleasant Christian when he was asking us all to sit down with him. If my mum had heard it she'd have gone mental. She hated swearing unless it was someone she personally knew who was partaking in the act and then it was kind of alright.

Well, I kind of liked 'God Only Knows', it really was like nothing I'd ever heard before. Midway through the song Tim started to really weird me out, he appeared to be acting out the part of the evangelist except his tirade was directed at God and religion, Tim questioned the image of God and all of his or her behaviours and mannerisms. It all sounded rather blasphemous to me and I'm not even religious, my old school headmaster would have found it all rather disrespectful. 'God Only Knows' was a very good song though, when Tim Booth became excited he sounded a bit like Tim the Enchanter from Monty Python's Holy Grail; Tim appeared to be shouting with a bit of a Scottish burr to his voice particularly when he screeched out *"I know where i'yyddd ravvvveerr bbbeeeeeee"*. I guessed that although they were a Manchester band

Tim must have originally come from somewhere north of Aberdeen. The ending of the song appeared to signal an exorcism of sorts, the darkness outside passed and the sun broke through the clouds. The bubbles returned to my glass of pop and there was much rejoicing from the masses.

The final song on side one of *Gold Mother* was 'You Can't Tell How Much Suffering (On a Face That's Always Smiling)'. I listened with intent to the lyrics; they appeared to sum up how I felt in the world at the time. I realised that the song had clearly been written for me, it hadn't of course but whilst I listened to those lyrics I felt like I was tuning into a personal message from James. The song sounded pressured, desperate to finish and deliver its message and that's exactly what it did to the melody of a guitar that sounded like it was being folded up and trampled upon by a rather large hairy beast. Well, to say that I was disappointed would have been a bit of an understatement, but it was more than that. I felt utterly bewildered. I questioned whether I'd wasted my money or not, but when I reflected upon listening to side one the positives had just about outweighed the negatives. Still, it was with a heavy sigh that I ejected the tape, flipped it over and pressed play.

The sprightly intro to 'How Was it For You?' livened things up a tad, its wonderful cowbell and guitar melody carried on with the full steam ahead gung-ho attitude that the previous song had. I felt slightly reassured that things were going to be alright in *Gold Mother* land after all. The song was fairly sassy and sexy and I quickly came to the conclusion that it was a song about, er, sex although not in a vulgar manner. The familiar opening of 'Sit Down' made its presence known like a friendly face in an unfamiliar crowd but by the end of the song I was bracing myself for whatever was going to be thrown at me next by this strange band. A shift in tempo and mood flooded the room, 'Walking the Ghost' washed over and soothed me in a way that the rest of the album hadn't. 'Walking the Ghost' felt like it was wrapping itself around me, its warmth protecting, shrink-wrapping and mesmerising me. As the song built and heaved towards its violin laced finale I realised that I was listening to a very special band indeed. Okay, so the music didn't have the immediate pleasure of say The Happy Mondays or The Charlatans but I knew, I believed that I'd need to stick with it. And then, just to throw a massive curveball the albums title track started up. I was shocked at the chaos that blared from the cheap stereo speakers, my face lit up with a huge smile, I didn't know what the song was about, all I could hear was what appeared to be bizarre random lyrics regarding *"ships in bottles"*, *"purple headed aliens"* and *"meconium"* whatever that was.

The song appeared to be never ending; just when I thought it was about to end the whole raggedy beast would start up again. It was great fun, the serious tone of the majority of the album was broken, the charged atmosphere cleared just like the passing of a summer storm. 'Gold Mother' was as long as an average Hawkwind concert but it eventually faded out leaving a haunting little number called 'Top of the World' to drop the mood back into a somber state of affairs. I didn't really know what to make of it but I knew that De La Soul would never sound quite the same ever again.

That was my first experience of *Gold Mother*, a colossus of Armageddon, sex, politics and insecurity. As a listening experience it had been extremely hard work. I'd had a similar enough experience with The Stone Roses debut album in that I'd expected ten different versions of 'Fools Gold' and was absolutely horrified to find melodic guitar pop instead of groovy beat laced funk. I ejected *Gold Mother* and gently placed it back inside its box and then inserted the *Troglodyte History* into the stereo and pressed play. A horrible warped sound sluggishly emitted from the speakers. Sadly it wasn't the fact that track one was just a bit rubbish, unfortunately it was due to the fact that the tape had instead been chewed up by the stereo and I was sadly never to experience *Troglodyte History*. Maybe the ghost featured in 'Walking the Ghost' was unhappy at my choice of music and placed a hex upon my stereo, probably not but it's quite a nice if a somewhat creepy thought.

As previously mentioned I was off on a trip to the seaside the following day with my mum and my mate Charles, we were heading to Scarborough to spend a day in the amusements playing video games, well, not my mum; she was more into playing Bingo. I simply couldn't wait to play Out Run, Double Dragon and R-Type and drooled at the prospect like a rabid dog. During the journey I lent *Gold Mother* to Charles to listen to whilst he lent me a compilation tape called *Awesome*. Of course Charles knew 'Sit Down' but that was about it. He expressed his disappointment upon listening to *Gold Mother* by stating that he thought it was going to be a hit strewn mega feast of pop magic. Well, he didn't, I've just made that last bit up but like me he thought it was going to be an album of indie dance which he was also a fan of. He asked for his album back from me and he sat back and listened to a selection of lovely cuts by 808 State and the appallingly named The Farm.

Within a week Charles had bought a copy of *Gold Mother* from the local supermarket. He suspiciously stated that he'd actually quite liked the album after all and he'd even managed to learn ALL of the lyrics which he'd sing in front of me although I'm using the word 'sing' in an over generous tone. His knowledge of the lyrics made me feel extremely jealous. He'd even correct me if I ever sang the wrong lyrics! I'd introduced him to the album and now he'd hijacked it away from me! It was imperative that I'd have to increase the amount of times that I listened to *Gold Mother* in a race to learn the songs in ways that only Charles could dream of. It all amounted to an unhealthy sense of paranoia.....

Apart from their beautiful spellbinding music James were making their presence known in other ways. I'd noticed an increasing amount of people wearing James t-shirts. They, (the shirts) all appeared to have simple yet striking imagery. As a newish fan I knew I'd have to invest in a t-shirt to show my loyalty and allegiance. After a Stanley Knife blade free day at work one Saturday I headed towards Our Price and cantered upstairs to where band merchandise could be purchased. A miserable sounding song was playing in the background, the lyrics were mumbled, the guitars sounded like they were completely out of tune. From the tiled ceiling coat hangers supported a range of shirts from the Happy Mondays right through to Senseless Things. I felt like I was in an indie launderette. Intermingled with the rest of the cotton based merchandise was a long sleeved white 'James' shirt. On the front was the word "Come" and on the reverse was the word "Home", on the left hand sleeve was the bands name. Its simplicity was magnificent; I pumped my sweating fist into the air and shouted "YEAH!!!!" which caused those browsing amongst the vinyl film soundtrack section to jump in alarm.

I approached the counter and winked at the pale faced Goth wearing a Sisters Of Mercy t-shirt who was serving before asking her for the shirt. From her blank expression she hadn't appreciated the wink I'd given her and she looked at me like I was a miscreant. It transpired that the shirt on display was the last one in the shop, Goth girl climbed up a set of step ladders and removed the shirt for me and placed it in a bag without even folding it. She didn't offer me any kind of a discount either even though the shirt was an 'ex display' model plus it was rather dusty! I felt rather vexed but said nothing and instead I raced home and burst through the kitchen door excited to show my mum my new purchase.

"Ah, that's lovely!" my mum said sounding quite genuine. I told her it was a 'James' shirt and reminded her of the connection between the band name and 'that song'. The shirt was a size too big for me; it camouflaged my skinny little frame, my poor self-image thankfully hidden under a protective sheet of white cotton. I ended up wearing the shirt for the next couple of days flouting any personal hygiene concerns or issues that others may have had. I was addicted. The following week I went back to Our Price and bought a red short sleeved James shirt which had the letters "Ja" on the front in large black text, "m" on the left sleeve and "es" on the reverse of the shirt. It was magnificent, even better than the 'Come Home' shirt and I ended up wearing the shirts almost religiously, one day it was the 'Come Home' top, the next day the red one and so on. James seeped into my life in ways that other bands hadn't namely via my wardrobe and the washing machine. I continued to listen to *Gold Mother* regularly, the songs became further embedded into my psyche, songs that hadn't immediately done much for me became like sweet close friends.

I went on holiday to the east coast town of Bridlington during the late summer of 1991. Bridlington is a lovely place; it's got sand, sea and amusements, lots of lovely shiny amusements full of exciting video games. Gavin had been invited too. The two weeks with Gavin, Mum, Uncle Wally and myself was utter carnage, the adults were drunk the majority of the time and Gavin and I were allowed to run absolute riot. Each night we'd head across to Makis Night Club and enjoy the ambience of the family friendly entertainment which usually consisted of a kids disco followed by a proper disco afterwards. Each and every night 'Sit Down' would be played and the place would erupt with everyone singing along and with a worrying number of people actually sitting down on the dance floor amongst the broken glass and well trodden bar snacks. I was far too cool and self-conscious to participate in such tomfoolery. I'd instead lurk around the perimeter of the dance floor staring intensely at the pretty women dancing, probably making them feel uncomfortable whilst I rubbed my extremely sweaty palms onto my shell suit bottoms.

One particularly beautiful woman caught my eye; or rather I caught her eye. It was probably the first time that such a thing ever happened to me. I noticed her looking over at me a few times; my heart skipped a beat when she made her approach towards me.

"Nice top" she said to me in a husky manner. I was wearing the white 'Come Home' top on that particular evening.

"Oh, cheers!" I said. I suddenly felt pretty cool and hip. It was the first time anyone had ever made a positive comment about any item of clothing I owned. The purple velvet trousers I'd once worn to school on a charity 'Wear What You Want Day' hadn't done my image or reputation much good and I was still feeling the reverberations of that fateful day due to the fact that I'd been given the nickname of 'Uncle Velvet'.

"I absolutely love James" the pretty woman said to me.

"So do I, so do I!" I cried out sounding slightly desperate.

"Hey, I've got something to show you".

My eyebrows raised and my heart sped up. What was she going to show me? With a quick movement of her wrist she showed me a blue watch, but, it was no ordinary watch.

"I've bought this from the official James fan club, it cost thirty pounds!" she said, I leant in close to her, very, very close in fact and had a proper gander at the watch. Indeed it was a James watch. The distinctive James daisy was on the watch face. Now although I loved the clothing I felt that a watch was a step too far.

"Ha! Wow, a watch! God, you'll be able to buy James condoms next!" I wittily said to her.

"You can" she said to me with a certain look in her eye.

"Er, great, well, very nice to have met you" I said and then I quick marched away with just the slightest whiff of panic wafting away from my non-James underwear. (I was fairly shy and clumsy around girls in those days and the fact that she was showing me a bit of interest, even if it was just because of the James top I was wearing scared me off a bit!) The next night the same girl approached me again to say hello but because I was wearing an A Tribe Called Quest t-shirt she didn't really have much time for me and instead ended up snogging Gavin. I felt a tad jealous but managed to convince myself that she was a bit of a trout. (She wasn't.)

The next day Gavin asked me if he could borrow my copy of *Gold Mother!* Gavin had commented in the past that 'Sit Down' was a "puff's song" but the un-trout like girl had obviously had an effect on him as he listened to it on repeat for the entire day only stopping when the batteries gave up the ghost and conked out. I was doubly jealous when I caught him singing 'God Only Knows' without a slip or a wrong word!

On the same holiday Gavin and I went on a day trip up the coast by train to the pretty picturesque town of Scarborough. Time was spent in the amusements until we bored of playing Bubble Bobble and we ended up staggering into an independent record shop which stocked a smorgasbord of various band t-shirts. Taking up residency was a section devoted solely to James. A large sign stated that the store was a seller of "Official James Merchandise". I decided to make a purchase from the shop; for some reason I ended up buying a The Stone Roses 'What The World Is Waiting For' t-shirt. I could have bought one of those shirts anywhere so why I didn't bother to buy a harder to obtain James t-shirt is still a mystery to me, not a mystery of Agatha Christie type proportions I admit but a mystery nonetheless.

Gavin bought some really dodgy rave mix tapes as his souvenir for the day and I tutted my disproval at him. Whilst browsing the albums that were for sale I happened to pick up *Some Friendly*, the debut album by The Charlatans and I burst out laughing when I saw that one of the song titles was called 'You're Not Very Well'. I showed it to Gavin and we both fell about on the floor laughing our heads off. It was easily one of the funniest things I'd ever seen in my life although looking back some years later I'm kind of confused at what we actually found to be so funny. The song title did however become a catch phrase for us and we'd repeat it at various times, sometimes we'd stop a random stranger in the street and say to them "You're not very well" , and then continue along our way leaving the poor person we'd spoken to looking quite disturbed and worried. Sometimes the people would look at themselves in the nearest car mirror to see what if, in fact anything was wrong with them. Naturally this would make us laugh even more.

By the end of the summer I'd bought another shirt which was a blue 'Sit Down' shirt. It was fairly basic in design and viewed from the front it looked like nothing more than a boring plain blue long sleeved top but cunningly hidden on the bottom of the reverse side of the shirt were the immortal words "Sit Down". Class! My Aunty Kath who was in her seventies and my mums friend Ernie who was also knocking on a bit both commented on separate occasions that there appeared to be a "h" missing from one of the words. I was starting to receive a fair bit of sniggering and name calling from people I knew due to the fact that I was always wearing a James t-shirt a pair of shell suit bottoms and black slip on shoes. I wasn't bothered though, I finally felt part of something huge. I was mindful that the majority of the people who were wearing James t-shirts were wearing them out of fashion only; it was that summer's 'look'. Those people would probably never explore anything further than *Gold Mother* or 'Sit Down'.

After the holiday in Bridlington Gavin soon developed a new bunch of friends to hang around with who were much cooler and trendier than me, Charles also started to drift away with a new clique too. I quickly found I'd been left behind, alone with nothing but an ever growing collection of indie vinyl, James t-shirts and memories of fun times that would be no more. Still, that was the situation we found ourselves in, boys turning into young men. I knew that I too was changing and that old friendships would or had to be left behind and that new friendships would be forged, I hoped so anyway.

In September 1991 I started college undertaking a business and finance course, I was glad to be leaving behind a fairly horrible school life. Prior to starting college I ended up buying yet another James t-shirt. It was a 'Lose Control' long sleeved top, dark blue with "James" all jumbled, stretched and distorted on the front of the top, and on the back was a simple daisy design. I thought that this would probably be the last James item of clothing I'd buy however; this was not to be the case.

Ulrika Johnson's confusion

1991/1992

On a cold drizzly Saturday morning some point during mid autumn of 1991 I called into the shop across the road from where I worked to stock up on several bottles of pop and a few packets of Maynards Wine Gums. I also bought a copy of a music magazine called *Rage* that was edited by the legendary Gary Crowley. *Rage* was an excellent magazine, it was sold on a fortnightly basis which would be its Achilles Heel and the magazine wasn't in print for too long, it folded at some point due to lacklustre sales in comparison to the weekly prints, obviously a fortnightly release meant that news wasn't always bang up to date and instead the magazine had to make do with interesting articles, interviews and features. I remember reading an interview with some now forgotten female musician who declared that she'd been working with Damon Albarn from the then fringe mopped wannanbe rock stars Blur.

"Yer know, Damon's a really clever guy, very talented, I think he's going to surprise an awful lot of people one day" she rather boldly stated.

In the same issue Bobby Gillespie from Primal Scream was asked what he would do if he knew the world was about to end.

"I'd take a load of drugs and die happy".

I was disgusted with his reply, he'd sounded like such a nice man on the song he'd sung on *Mickey B's*. Back to the story, well, on this particular wine gum purchasing magazine week *Rage* featured an ever so brief article regarding James; my eyes scanned the nicely printed words and punctuation. The article focused upon their soon to be released new single which was called 'Sound'.

"It'll be interesting to see how James fares without a big sing-along chorus" ran the article.

I was intrigued, a new song? I wasn't aware that the band had been recording any new material, as far as I was concerned they were still riding on the wave of *Gold Mother* and 'Sit Down'. I'd thought that the band had instead been enjoying a rock and rollers life style in the South of France, rubbing shoulders with Formula 1 drivers, guzzling champagne and snorting cocaine off sofas.

Steve was a new friend of mine from college. He was quite the music fan but was annoyingly stuck in the 1980's regarding his likes, he knew that I was a fan of James mainly because I was habitually wearing my James tops. We'd become quite good mates due to a shared interest in music as a whole. He told me whilst walking home from a day of study that James was going to be releasing a new album early in 1992 and that it was going to be called *Seven*.

"That's because there are seven band members" said Steve whilst holding up seven fingers to reinforce the numerical point. Hmmm, I liked the simplicity of the bands mind-set.

Later in the autumn Radio One started to repeatedly play the new James single. It was certainly very different to their previous 'big hit' singles. 'Sound' was a monstrous, rumbling epic tune that sounded like nothing I'd ever heard before. And as for the chorus, well, you couldn't really sing along to it at all. The only way I could possibly describe it was as,

"Ma Ba Woooooooooooooooooooooooo".

THAT was the chorus! It was very odd but rather lovely all the same. In fact it only took me a couple of listens to realise that it was possibly the greatest song ever written. The opening lyrics, *"Ape, your fathers sins, your mothers mood swings to perfection"* summed up my own thoughts and feelings about where I stood in the world regarding my own parents. Once again I felt touched that the band had sent what appeared to be a direct message to me.

On the day that 'Sound' was released I asked my sister if she'd buy the 12" version of it for me from Woolworths as I was at college all day. I couldn't wait to get home on that Monday afternoon and when home time came I raced to my sister's house with my guts churning and boiling in anticipation. I smashed the door off its hinges upon entering her house and stood there like a mighty leviathan silhouetted in the door frame.

"That's the eighth time this month you've broken that door, why can't you just knock and enter like any other normal person?" she said to me in exasperation.

I apologised and offered to have the door repaired once again. The broken door and frame was soon forgotten though as my sister had indeed made a trip to Woolworths for me and bought the 12" vinyl copy of 'Sound'. I held the sheen covered record sleeve in my sweaty mitts and admired the seven handsome men who were wistfully staring back at me like seven little angels.

"Oh, by the way, I've had a listen to that record of yours, it's bloody awful!" she said.

I felt my stomach go a bit funny, my bowels wanted to open there and then; I wanted to break another door or at least rip up a newspaper. She then proceeded to mimic the chorus before bursting into hysterical fits of laughter whilst brewing up a pot of tea for us. I was angry and hurt, how dare she mock James and their heaven sent song. I knew that she was nothing more than a philistine; she'd once had great taste in music, she'd been listening to U2 before anybody else really knew who they were but she'd sadly ended up being the kind of person who only bought shoddy compilation tapes from ASDA. I gently placed the black vinyl onto the player and dropped the needle into the groove, a few moments of crackle passed by before the familiar intro began to throb and rumble out of the stereos single speaker. My sister was waffling away in the background but I didn't bother to tune into her conversation, instead I was lost in the midst of the song, it felt like a safe place to be, tranquil, powerful and awe inspiring. I wrapped my arms tightly around myself and then fell over onto the floor where I remained rigid for several minutes.

When I came around I had an epiphany that James was definitely my favourite ever band, even better than Public Enemy. Of course it didn't matter that my sister thought the greatest song of all time was rubbish, it really didn't matter that my peers at college laughed at my stained shell suit bottoms and James shirts. I knew James were going to be a part of my life for a long time compared to the people who I knew would come and go, just like fashions that keep changing from season to season. I finally knew I was going to have something in my life that felt true, honest and reliable to hold onto.

'Sound' was a top ten hit. I think it confused and disappointed an awful lot of people. Instead of delivering the obvious James performed a diagonal step forward just to confuse one and all and test the public's loyalty and taste. Sure, it would have been totally amazing if the song had reached the top of the charts, but where would they go from there? No, its chart position in the lower region of the top ten was justice enough. 'Sound' rarely left my turntable, in fact I listened to it so much (twenty plus times a day) that I actually started to get a little bit fed up with it, I'd over played it, I'd done this with countless other songs in the past ('Venus' by Don Pablo's Animals for example) and I knew I needed to give 'Sound' a break for a while.

Christmas came and went, the nights started to lighten and the event that would be the new James album release crept ever closer. The music press announced that a new single was going to be released before *Seven* was set loose upon the land, the single had the wonderful title of 'Born of Frustration'. It really felt like the band was once again trying to communicate with me, this time it was through the title of the song. I obviously couldn't wait to hear it. The memory of the first time I heard 'Born of Frustration' is clear, crystal clear in fact; it was when it was played along with its accompanying promo clip on the breakfast television show *TVAM*. At approximately 07:55 the presenter announced,

"And now, we have an exclusive for you, it's the new song by Manchester band James. They had a big hit last year with 'Sit Down', they've a new album coming out called *Seven* and here's their new single 'Born of Frustration'".

I sat still on the sofa, pyjamas on, a warm cup of tea in my hand and the television volume cranked up to a level known only as deafening. The song and promo began to play....

"Ahhhh, Oh????"

I didn't get it. It really wasn't what I was expecting. Whilst the rest of the world had been waiting for 'Sit Down Mk2' regarding 'Sound', I'd wanted 'Sound Mk2' for 'Born of Frustration' if that makes any sense to you. Don't get me wrong, it was a good song, it just wasn't in the same league as 'Sound'. The chorus was all *"La, la, la, la la's"* too. I was once again rather disappointed.

The promo finished and the presenters were back on the screen smiling their glittering white smiles into the camera with sinister looks in their eyes.

"Well, that was an exclusive to viewers of *TVAM*, James with their new single 'Born of Frustration'. Well, what did you think of that then?" the presenter said to the weather girl who was none other than the rather gorgeous (at the time) Ulrika Johnson.

"Er, I didn't like it to be honest. It sounded a bit like Simple Minds, sorry!" said Ulrika looking a tad uncomfortable as if she'd just urinated herself.

"Oh, okay, well, I think you've probably offended an awful lot of people at home with that remark!" laughed the presenter. "Anyway, how's the weather looking today then?" and Ulrika started to blather on about high and low pressures, isobars and other such weather festooned descriptive words.

The sad and worrying thing was that I thought she was probably right, and I didn't even know who or what Simple Minds was although I hazarded a guess that it might potentially be a society for people who weren't smart enough to join MENSA.

Seven is not a number

1992

The following weekend and I was once again working at the picture framers. It was a day like any other, foul language, violence and slave labour. Noddy had spent the morning growling like a dog, even John Dope appeared somewhat alarmed. The radio was my saviour; it kept me sane when I should have been losing it due to developing a severe anxiety disorder from having sharp blades of metal thrown at me. During the afternoon the radio DJ announced that members of James would be giving an interview later on the show to discuss their new album. I was naturally very excited and I ended up running across the road to the shop so that I could buy some pop and wine gums to enjoy whilst I listened to the interview. Within the hour Tim Booth made an appearance with his softly spoken dulcet tone; I placed my work tools down, slipped a handful of wine gums into my mouth and paid attention to the show. Some small talk ensued between the host and the band, Tim announced they were going to play a brand new song from the album called 'Ring the Bells'. I pulled my ears back as far as I possibly could and used a stapler to pin them to my head so that I wouldn't miss a single note.

A distinctive striking intro flared up and then just as suddenly dropped back down so that only Tim and a lonely guitar could be heard. The noise level and tempo slowly began to rise up again, the song battling onwards in a beautiful desperate manner. The only problem was that I really didn't like it. James was blatantly veering away from the sound that had first captivated me and although I'd initially tagged along the journey I didn't like or know where it was going. It was just too unfamiliar for me, it all sounded so grown up and I still didn't feel mature or ready enough to deal with it.

When 'Ring The Bells' finished the DJ started to sycophantically congratulate Tim and the rest of the band for being so ruddy amazing before asking if the bands song writing style had changed much over the course of the twelve successful months or so that they'd experienced. He also made reference to what he described as "child-like nursery rhyme lyrics" to some of the songs he'd heard in advance of the show, in particular a song called 'Protect Me' with it's *"Oh dear, what can the matter be"* opening line. By this point I'd kind of switched off though. James was a strange beast, perhaps I wasn't in for the long haul after all I thought to myself. I'd gone from thinking the band was the greatest thing since the invention of the wheel to being utterly confused and disappointed. I thoughtfully chomped on the remainder of my wine gums, slurped the dregs from my can of pop and proceeded to assemble some picture frames whilst taking care not to chop off the ends of my fingers on the unguarded machinery in the workshop. I then proceeded to remove the wasted staples from my ears and head, the procedure hurt somewhat.

Seven was released in February 1992. Even though the band had blatantly morphed into something which was quite alien to me I still bought a copy of their new album from Woolworths in Harrogate and I listened to it on repeat that evening. By the end of the evening I'd been won over, *Seven* was a great album. I resigned myself to the fact that I was probably going to be listening to 'mature music' from then on, artists such as U2 and Meat Loaf, I felt a sense of sadness when I realised that my copy of the Dream Warriors *And Now The Legacy Begins* album would probably be played no more. I'd studied the album as much as I possibly could during the evening. The opening salvo of 'Born of Frustration' followed by 'Ring the Bells' was familiar enough. I'd grown to like both songs very much even though they initially hadn't really moved me like their other songs had. 'Sound' was still absolutely magnificent. I'd been on a 'Sound' diet for a while after playing it to death and now I was ready to gorge myself upon the wonderful song once more. However, bloody hell, the next song on the album 'Bring a Gun' almost took my head off with its ferocious demonic sounding rattle. It felt like a big old two fingers to anyone who'd commented that James was either twee, a bit wet or as Gavin had once said "puffs music".

'Mother', was the next song on the album. I thought the opening line to the song was unnecessary and a bit silly. I won't repeat what Tim sang but he did use a swear word that rhymed with "Brotherlucker". There was no need for the language but I guessed that Tim had set his stall up for the rest of the song which was brooding and tackled issues relating to war, death and Saddam Hussein's comment that the Gulf War would be "The Mother of all Wars". 'Mother' was followed by 'Don't Wait That Long' which was a BIG song. It was the kind of song that the NME would probably really hate but I really liked it. It was definitely a song that if I was going to compile a compilation tape for a girl I fancied then I'd have included this song on it, in fact looking back I think I might have actually done this once or twice to little avail.

Side two of the album started with 'Live a Love of Life'. It was another song that sounded fairly defiant in manner and it appeared to be having another dig at religion even questioning whether Jesus had been a human being and commenting upon the fact that prophets apparently struggle to keep their bed linen clean. 'Next Lover' was a gorgeous song, beautiful and unique, nothing more to be said about it. 'Heavens' was a song that I'd first heard when James performed it live on a Channel Four television programme called *Friday at the Dome* a few weeks prior to the album launch. It was a wonderful song, again it was quite full on yet quite dainty at the same time, the song held together by a sense of fragility. 'Protect Me' with its "nursery rhyme lyrics" sounded like a good way to end an album however the album's title track which bookended the album was simply the highlight as far as I was concerned. A gorgeous yearning song, there really wasn't an ounce of negativity interwoven in it; it was bound to be a number one single. Well, overall I was very pleased with *Seven*, I certainly preferred it to *Gold Mother* as far as a first listen was concerned but maybe that was because I was more familiar with the band. Perhaps if I'd listened to *Seven* before I'd heard anything else by James then I'd have really hated it. The album remained lodged in the stereo and I listened to it whilst doing my home work for college each night.

As for reviews of the album, well I was still buying music magazines periodically and the few reviews of the album that I read were mixed to say the least. Most of the trendy magazines slagged it off as *"pompous stadium rock"* (I didn't actually know what this meant at the time) whilst other reviewers gave cautious praise to the band for stretching themselves further than they had in the past. When I look back I guess the thing that made me feel a bit cagey about the band was the fact that they had a trumpet player in the group.

Now, I like trumpets don't get me wrong and the trumpet suited the music. My only criticism is trumpets remind me of royalty, parades, coronations and other such supercilious events. Jazz fans will probably lynch me for this comment, I apologise, and I'm probably wrong and barking up the wrong tree or something. But, as I've mentioned about a million times already my musical background was hip-hop and house music. The trumpets towards the end of 'Protect Me' in particular sounded really over the top to me, but maybe I was just a bit naive and young at the time of listening. Trumpets I can kind of live with but please don't get me started on saxophones.

Seriously, never trust a band with a saxophone player.

Actually and we're veering of course now but I once returned a Stereolab album back to HMV, when asked why I was returning it I said "it just sounds like bad jazz". I also returned a Röyksopp album back to Sainsbury's, when asked why I was returning this particular album I said "well, it's rubbish".

I was in York a few months later and on a rare day out with Charles. We stared hauntingly at the Minister for a while before strolling around The Shambles and calling into HMV. Whilst we were in there I found a basket full to the brim with copies of a James VHS entitled *Seven ... The Live Concert*. I hadn't realised that such a thing was available for sale. I dug my wallet out and bought a copy for only £4. When I returned home I showed my mum my new purchase.

"What on earths that? It looks like a baby's' foot!" she said in a disgusted manner, (she actually quite liked babies).

The cover of the album featured a foetus's lower limbs dangling in embryonic fluid inside its host's womb. I've probably depicted that as sounding totally horrendous and graphic but it's actually a rather wonderful image with beautiful hues of colour. I told her she was right; it was a picture of "a baby's foot", feet to be exact, and legs of course.

"Jeeeeesusss" was all she could manage to say and she lit up a Berkeley cigarette in alarm. Mum's music collection all featured album covers with moronic grinning pictures of Cliff Richard, Elvis Presley and Slim Dusty so she was naturally a tad disturbed at the soothing image the album and video featured. I inserted the video into the VCR later that evening and watched the band perform *Seven* in its entirety. I was rather alarmed that Tim was going to seriously damage his neck during 'Don't Wait that Long' as he started shaking like he was having the mother of all seizures. It was the first time I'd seen the band perform a full live performance. Well, I'd seen them perform the odd song on various programmes such as *Friday at the Dome* but it wasn't until watching the video that I'd realised what an odd looking bunch of men they were. It's not like the band members had two heads or anything, it's just that they looked; well 'different' to other bands I'd seen. I liked Tim's image, his understated casual clothing, no sign of any name brand clothing upon his wiry frame, not that I could really tell for definite mind you, I mean there wasn't any extreme close ups of his attire and I acknowledge it's very possible that he was secretly wearing Calvin Klein underwear.

A few weeks later when I was on one of my lunch breaks from the art gallery/workshop I bought the 12" vinyl versions of 'Born of Frustration' and 'Ring the Bells' from the bargain bin in Woolworths, they were 49p each. I had mixed feelings about the extra tracks that were included but I suppose it's not too often that bands give away their best songs as b-sides but the artwork was worth the money alone. That sounds like a back handed compliment doesn't it? What I mean is that the artwork was amazing and was worth a lot more than 98p. Anyway, I pinned both of the record sleeves to my bedroom wall so that I could admire and respect them on a daily basis. Sometimes tears would be shed when I gazed upon them.

I'd read in an issue of the NME that James were to going be performing a large open air show at the theme park Alton Towers that July. Up till that point I'd never even considered going to see the band live at all. I'd never been to an official gig. My only experience of live rock music was a Canadian Christian rock band called Titus who played a short set at my secondary school (they were actually rather good, the "Jesus, Jesus" chant was a bit weird though, fists pumping the air in time to the chant) but that was it up until then. I was actually off to Alton Towers about a month before the gig with my sister and some mates of hers, on the day itself I'd decided to wear my new James top, this one was a bit more pricey than some of the others I'd already bought as it was more like a proper jumper, the James logo was embroided onto the front of the top in lovely gold coloured stitching. A member of staff at Alton Towers asked me if I was going to attend the James gig the following month. I told him that I wasn't and he looked at me like I was a moron. I knew that I wasn't going to go because if I'd bought a ticket then I'd have ended up going by myself, the event felt like it was all a bit above me, I thought people like me shouldn't or wouldn't ever go to gigs. It was a sign of my own insecurity, the same insecurity which made me warm to James' songs about insecurity. Thankfully the Alton Towers show was going to be broadcast live on Radio One so I resigned myself to listening to the show in the comfort of my own bedroom.

On the Saturday evening of the Alton Towers show I grabbed a packet of wine gums and a bottle of pop, made myself comfy in my bedroom and turned the radio on. In the background the crowd noise and the loud thumping dance music pumped out of the PA system, the music featured remixes of James' songs which were being used to fire up the crowd. The DJ commented that the gig had almost been cancelled due to appalling weather conditions and at one point a large plague of alien locusts had swarmed Alton Towers and destroyed most of the rides. The music stopped, the crowd roared and the DJ handed over to James who'd just made their entrance on to the stage.

"Welcome to Alton Showers, we almost never made it!" Tim's voice boomed out to the crowd.

The air was punctuated by whoops and cheers as if the band were playing at a rodeo show somewhere on the other side of the Atlantic and then the band kicked off with three songs from *Seven*. The music sounded mammoth and the audience were certainly giving it some too, they sounded more like reprobates from a football match rather than what I'd envisaged James fans to be like, quiet, mainly female and very polite and kind to small animals. After the opening salvo of the songs from *Seven* the band proceeded to play material which was unfamiliar to me but the audience lapped it up and I realised that I only knew the tip of the iceberg regarding this strange band.

Tim then briefly spoilt the ambience by having a go at the crowd.

"Stop throwing fucking hard objects at us will you? Someone's going to get hurt" he said due to a number of shoes and trainers that had been lobbed at the band I presumed in a friendly enough manner, although it still kind of confused me. First of all, on a cold wet evening why would you want to make yourself feel even more uncomfortable by throwing away your footwear? And what kind of message are you trying to give the band? If someone threw a shoe at me in any context I'd be pretty narked off and in some cultures it's massively frowned upon. Ask George Bush about that one if you can.

Tim then suggested that if the audience was going to throw items then it should just be clothing and teddy bears. Now again, I was confused. The band couldn't have been so hard up that they needed the audience to provide them with a wardrobe. Plus the band was well known for the supply and demand of band merchandise so in theory each band member could have worn a different item of James apparel for every day of the year. And what about the poor buggers in the crowd who ended up stripping off? Sure, they'd initially be kept lovely toasty and warm by the surrounding bodies but then they'd end up dying from exposure once the audience had dispersed. And as for teddy bears? As mentioned already, the audience had sounded quite wild, a bit like a Leeds United match and the thought of a load of tattooed up skinheads lobbing Teddy Bears at the band was something that I couldn't really envisage.

The set list was peppered with songs I knew however the one song that really stuck with me was a song I'd not heard before called 'America'. Seriously, it was so loud with screaming banshee type feedback that I thought the speakers on my new midi system were going to explode! I was recording the concert onto a C90 cassette and I couldn't wait to play that particular song again, but then, disaster! The tape ended and I had to quickly flip it over and press record again thus ruining the recording of that particular song. I was quite annoyed I can tell you.

Tim apologised towards the end of the show (obviously it wasn't because they'd played 'America' when they had thus ruining my taping opportunity) but due to the fact that he hadn't been singing in tune during the gig. I wasn't aware of such technicalities to be honest and neither were those in attendance from what I could tell. The show finished with 'Sit Down' and a large firework display commenced, not that I could see it but I could certainly hear it. The show was a triumph as far as the DJ was concerned even if a bit of bad language had gotten onto the fussy BBC. I went to bed that night gutted that I hadn't bought a ticket and coach package from Cavendish Travel in Leeds so that I could have attended the one off event. I cried. (I didn't really).

The last single to be released from the album was the beautiful title track. The song had been slightly reworked and in my opinion it wasn't half as good as the album version, for me it had certainly lost some of its impact. Three extra tracks 'Goalies Ball', 'William Burroughs' and 'Still Alive' made up the EP, they sounded quite different to the material from the album, a hell of a lot rawer and less polished, the comparison made me realise that Seven sounded rather slick and over produced. I annoyed Goth Girl in Our Price by asking her if the Seven E.P. was available on 12" format.

"I've already told you twice that it isn't" she snapped at me, so much for her customer service skills! She probably ended up working in a HSBC call centre or something. The single bombed though, it didn't even dint the charts, 'Ring the Bells' had only just scraped to the number 40 position. I came to the conclusion that either enough people had bought the album so therefore didn't feel the need to buy the singles or that people had been side stepped too much by James not following up on 'Sit Down'. A review for James' Alton Towers performance in one of the weekly magazines was favourable but it hinted that James had probably reached their zenith regarding popularity and that they'd have to follow it up with something very special indeed otherwise they'd have an awfully long way to fall. I shuddered at the thought and a sudden chill made itself known.

Footnote time: It transpired that the reason for Noddy's unhinged and worrying behaviour was the direct result of a head injury he sustained when he fell off a rope swing a few years earlier. Prior to this he'd been a fairly normal teenager but had developed a massive personality change following the accident.

Foster and Allen for the Indie Generation

1992

I continued to watch the *Seven* concert video a few times a week, often late at night when my mum has gone to bed. I didn't own many other live concert videos to compare it to although I did own an appalling Happy Mondays video and an uncharismatic Inspiral Carpets video too. The *Seven* video gave me a bit of inkling into the band. Tim Booth's curly locks had been shorn prior to its filming and he danced like a man quite possessed flinging himself around the stage, his megaphone being swung wildly putting Pete Townsends windmill guitar thing to shame. Larry wore a rather fetching hat whilst he played his guitar with hardly a footstep made throughout the concert. Multi-instrumentalist Saul's thick lock of hair often hid his face whilst he appeared to fist his guitar at certain intervals during the show. Jim the bass player didn't really look like a rock and roll star, he looked a bit like Mr Ronald who owned my local newsagents although I guessed Jim probably took more care regarding his personal hygiene. Dave the drummer pummelled away at his equipment appropriately enough, he looked like the kind of man that I wouldn't ever want to upset though, I'm not suggesting that he looked aggressive or violent, he just gave off a bit of an angry vibe. Mark, the keyboard player kept himself to himself. No thumbs up to the crowd as Clint Boon from the Inspiral Carpets might have done, Marks long hair trailed down his back in a Rapunzelesque kind of style. Finally there was Andy the trumpet player. The man was wearing a dress for goodness sake but he still somehow managed to look Über cool with his tight dreadlocked hair.

I definitely had a weird fascination with the band member's hair. To me it was important that rock stars had a good head of hair on them, no 'baldies' please. I thought that if the members of James ever went bald then that would the end of it for me! James appeared mismatched and thrown together however they somehow managed to portray the look of a confident solid unit, a bit like The A-Team, a musical version The A-Team without the machine guns and aiming issues. The audience looked like they'd stumbled out of a James outfitters catalogue as every other audience member was wearing a James top of some description or other. There didn't appear to be too much audience/band interaction but perhaps this was just the way the video was edited, or maybe James had developed a moody coolness which meant that friendly banter was kept to a minimum.

On my eighteenth birthday I popped into Our Price with some of my birthday money. I picked up a copy of the Manga film *Akira* as I'd watched it a few months before, I'd loved its depiction of a post-apocalyptic Tokyo, all garish colours and ultra-violence but as I was scanning the shelves I found another James live video! I'd stared at it for perhaps five minutes whilst making a strange humming sound before I finally grabbed it and examined it in further detail, it was entitled *James – Come Home Live*. Goth Girl served me once again, she looked like she'd been crying as her make-up was a bit of a mess but I kept my mouth shut and didn't bother winking at her either. I simply handed over the cash as if I was mute and before I knew it I was racing home with the said items. Upon arriving home slightly out of breath I opened the fridge, poured myself a large glass of pop, shoved the tape into the VCR and sat back on our broken sofa and let the visual pleasantries present themselves.

Before the actual concert band members including Tim and Jim gave a brief interview where Tim divulged that the band loved all of their songs, "even the really awkward ones", and Jim announced that the band was named after him as he was "the best looking and most talented member of the group".

"With that side parting you're having a laugh mate!" I thought to myself before realising that I too still wore my hair with a side parting from time to time and all was forgiven. The concert itself was stunning even if Tim was wearing a rather suspect jacket, a bit like something my Uncle Wally would wear. As I previously mentioned there were a number of tracks that I'd never heard of before and they were all pretty good although I wasn't too keen on the Velvet Undergrounds 'Sunday Morning'.

Tim made me laugh when during 'God Only Knows' he said something along the lines of,

"If God is infinite, and God is everywhere, then God is in you, God is in me, God is in the Microphone". The microphone then shuddered, creaked and moaned but my laughter soon subsided when a distant crack of thunder sounded and the sky once again darkened......

The "God is in the microphone" comment still makes me laugh to this very day, it sounded like something Jim Morrison might have said, Tim certainly had a bit of Morrison in him with his tussled hair and good looks. Thankfully Tim wasn't eligible to join the '27 Club' as he was at that point already knocking on a bit, well he was into his thirties which is ancient in the world of pop music but he looked fairly lean and healthy plus he was very anti-drugs and was apparently Tee-total, my kind of a rock star! The other thing that made me laugh was regarding how many of the audience members looked 'off their heads'. One lad in particular wearing a white top stood by the barrier caught my attention; I'm guessing he'd consumed certain pharmaceuticals to enhance his experience of the show and I bet he couldn't remember a single second of it the following day. The video remained on repeat play at home which upset my mum somewhat as the electricity bill doubled for that quarter of the year.

The departure of the August bank holiday funfair signalled the true ending of summer, autumn arrived overnight with the promise of Harvest Festivals, Halloween and Bonfires. My new college course studying Travel and Tourism was also due to begin, it promised an exciting future for me within that particular industry. Not much was going on in 'James Land' as far as I was aware. Of course those were the days before the internet where your favourite bands every move, breath and fart can be experienced in the comfort of your own loft. I knew from the Alton Towers set list and the *Seven E.P.* that the band obviously had new material in their possession which was reassuring. I wasn't aware James were at that time slogging it around America on a tour with some old bloke I'd never heard of called Neil Young.

Now, I think that every man, woman and beast hopes to meet a like minded person of the opposite or of course the same sex to share passions and interest with in the hope that something will blossom from it and this naturally included my good self. During early autumn I met a rather fetching woman in a hole of a bar/club that my mates and I used to frequent every Saturday night called Josephine's, a horrible rough old place that when it had first opened had been an exclusive over 25s venue with limo's pulling up outside dropping exclusive VIP guests off. When I started frequenting the place it was in its final ugly death throes and on a Saturday night it was '10p a pint night' with a guarantee to have your nose broken by some drunken fool or other. The only saving grace was that you were guaranteed to be able to dance to 'Sit Down' and sometimes if you were really lucky the DJ would play 'Jump Around' by the House Of Pain although the song would often be cut short due to the roughness of the dance floor as it would suddenly flood with blokes on steroids slapping each other's chests and thighs. I once made the stand in DJ cry one night by simply requesting a song.

"Mate, I can't find ANYTHING let alone a B-side by Gang Starr!!!" he wailed. I'm digressing again, apologies....

Well the nice young lady I'd met who smoked filthy Regal cigarettes was 'a friend of a friend' and she was a HUGE James fan and by that I don't mean that she was nine foot tall. Each and every week she'd be wearing a different James top and we'd obviously always end up talking about the band. She told me, although I'm not sure if this was true or not that the *Seven E.P.* was originally going to be called the *Blow Me Away E.P.* in reference to the opening lyrics of the albums title track. However somebody thought it might be deemed as inappropriate particularly in America.

Then she said,

"So, what do you think of their earlier stuff then?"

"Yes, I really like *Gold Mother*. I was a bit unsure at first, it was definitely a grower".

She looked at me with some confusion.

"Er, no, what about *Stutter, Strip Mine* and *One Man Clapping*? Surely you must have those albums too?" she said with some surprise.

"Ah, right, yes. Sorry. Well I've seen them in the shops but I haven't bought them yet".

"WHAT? Are you serious? You can't call yourself a James fan without having their earlier material! It's not all 'Sit Down' and 'Born of Frustration' you know!"

I was annoyed with her but I knew she was right. However, due to her attitude and the fact that I realised she smoked far too much for my liking I decided that I wasn't going to buy her a drink even if it was only 10p a pint.

The following Monday arrived after a sluggish and hung over Sunday and I cleared my head by strolling into town heading towards Our Price. Sure enough there were the three missing James albums for sale all at £10 each. I only had £20 so I had to carefully decide what to buy. I checked the release dates on the back of the albums and decided to buy their earliest material first as I thought that this material would be harder to get hold of in the future. I'd buy *One Man Clapping* at a later date when I had some more money. I returned home and slipped in the *Stutter* cassette into my stereo and pressed play, accompanied of course by a glass of fizzy orange. MY GOD, I wasn't expecting what I heard is all I can say. If comments regarding their later material lambasted it for being a bit "OTT" then *Stutter* was the polar opposite. Tinny, tiny, reedy, folkie, bobble hat wearing, pipe smoking, slipper obsessing, bird watching music was what it was. Let me explain further.

The opening track 'Skullduggery' sounded extremely peculiar. Its lyrics about insects having a lovely yet sinister party inside a person's head were odd to say the least. 'Scarecrow' confused me just as much as the first song but at least it sounded like a song. 'So Many Ways'

I liked upon its first listen. It was quite catchy but it certainly lacked warmth. Well, any song that featured lyrics about snapping your ankle broken is going to make you feel uncomfortable. 'Just Hip' was over before I knew it, it sped by in a flurry of activity before abruptly ending with the lyric *"Oh this looks curly to me"*. 'Johnny Yen' I liked it instantly. Fantastic lyrics, a jaunty pace, it sounded like it could have been a proper old sing along tune. I didn't know if it had been released as a single or not but I'm guessing that had it have been then it would have been a hit record in some chart or other. 'Summer Song', the last song on the first side of the cassette was pretty gorgeous though. The lyrics appeared to be describing a child entering the world from its mother's womb and I suddenly realised that a fair bit of James' material focused on child birth in some form or other and I wondered why this was the case. Well, as ever with James I was fairly confused at this rag-tag collection of songs but I flipped the tape over and pressed play bracing myself for more hilarity and bemusement.

'Really Hard' was another pleasant song which appeared to feature some lovely yet twee female backing vocals. Having been a big fan of *The Transformers* lyrics about robots were naturally going to appeal to me although the song could have been improved somewhat if Optimus Prime or Megatron had been name checked too. A simple chorus of the songs title worked effectively enough for me to be able to sing along to the song upon its virgin listen. The next song 'Billy's Shirts' sounded like another mad old sea shanty, it appeared to be half a dozen songs all cut and pasted together. The lyric of *"seaman's delight"* made me laugh in a smutty kind of way but I was still fairly young and immature so I can kind of be forgiven. 'Why So Close' sounded like a song that my old headmaster used to play on the acoustic guitar during assembly time. Obviously being a James song it was darker than something that the headmaster would sing to the pupils without causing them to develop any more issues than they were going to do anyway. 'Withdrawn' was fantastic and I came to the conclusion that the song was about somebody with mental health issues of some description or other but I could of course be completely wrong. The song certainly sounded like it was being performed by individuals who were in the hyper manic phase of Bi-polar affective disorder. The final song 'Black Hole' was another disturbing sounding song. Was it about death? It certainly came across that way to me when I studied the lyrics; *"Blasting my flesh to the marrow"* made me shudder and squeak in alarm. A sense of chaos, darkness and claustrophobia enveloped the album and as ever I really wasn't too sure about it. This was a recurring theme though for me in relation to the body of James' work that I'd so far experienced. I was hoping that the album would be another grower.

As unsettled as I was by *Stutter* I decided to give *Strip Mine* a listen to. I cautiously placed the tape into the stereo and pressed play. Argghhhh! I jumped as the opening of the first song 'What For?' leapt from the speakers. The leap from the production quality of *Stutter* to that of *Strip Mine* was akin to taking a running jump across The Grand Canyon. The music appeared to have expanded upon the sound of three blokes banging their instruments and some odd individual singing disturbing yet soulful lyrics, the music appeared to be more layered, it immediately felt like an album I'd be more comfortable playing in public than *Stutter* was ever going to be.

'Charlie Dance' bounded along like an over enthusiastic puppy whilst at the same time appearing to reference the nuclear disaster in Chernobyl. In fact, just to go off on a tangent you never really hear about 'acid rain' anymore. It appears to have been left in the 1980's when the governments had everyone scared silly regarding developing cancer from being caught in the rain and catching AIDS from sitting on public toilet seats. It was such a weird decade. 'Are You Ready' continued in a similar musical theme as the previous songs had, jaunty and uplifting, quite forgettable but a nice experience all the same. And then, just because it was James' last song on the first side of the album 'Medieval' turned the mood upside down like an egg timer. A creepy flute, a sinister marching beat, and the wonderful yet threatening mantra of *"We are sound"* created an eerie ambience throughout the song, I wasn't sure if the song was referencing an imaginary conflict but it certainly appeared to be describing field combat of some sort or other.

Strip Mine was more immediate than *Stutter* that was for sure, it felt lighter in mood and the production was a world away from their debut album. Side two started off with the wonderful 'Not There'. The lyric *"Defects we're born with but poisons we choose"* touched me due to the fact that I'd witnessed a hell of a lot of substance misuse whilst growing up and I'd certainly met people who were "not there" due to the fact that their mental state had been altered by alcohol and illicit drug use. 'Ya Ho' sounded quite similar to 'What For?' which of course isn't a bad thing and as I'm a big fan of spending time on the beach I warmed to the song straight away. Once again though James' apparent Bi-polar disorder took a swing to the low side with the next offering 'Riders', a haunting edgy narrative which appeared to be about succumbing to a potion in order to fulfil a role. Temptation and peer pressure sprang to my mind. I felt sorry for the character in the narrative where they finally give in to the pressure and take the potion only to find that it's more of a poison than anything, something that will blacken their soul and change them forever.

'Vulture' thankfully lifted the mood again. The lyrics didn't make too much sense to me, I couldn't work out if it was about war or fox hunting however 'Vulture' would eventually become one of my favourite ever James songs. The ending of the song was simply majestic; I'd love to have been a fly on the wall in the studio whilst the band had been recording it. The album drew to a close on a fairly positive vibe with 'Strip mining' even if it did talk about "the pain of loss" before an instrumental entitled 'Refrain' closed the album proper. As the final notes of the album faded away I was left with a feeling of warmth as well as unease. Had I been a James fan from the early days and listened to the albums in sequence then I think that by the end of *Strip Mine* I'd have been left with a feeling of loss. I felt that as much as the album was generally uplifting and comforting there was a subliminal feeling of sadness running throughout it.

The following week arrived and I was once again at Josephine's however it was no longer a '10p a pint night' but instead it was a 'free bar'. Seriously, all of the lager and bitter was free. They were relying on enough people to get drunk enough to end up paying £5 to go upstairs into the night club proper. However, the beer was heavily watered down and it tasted pretty disgusting. I met up with the female James fan whose name I've sadly forgotten and I informed her that I'd bought the two albums, she seemed genuinely pleased.

"What do you think then?"

"Yes, not bad to be honest. *Stutter* is a bit weird but it's alright. I'm quite into *Strip Mine*, I've listened to it quite a bit" I said to her feeling like I'd finally entered the world of being a serious James fan rather than a casual late comer.

"Yes, they're quite different to *Gold Mother* and *Seven*. I leant a copy of *Stutter* to a friend who'd only gotten into James through *Seven*; and he absolutely hated it" she laughed.

"By the way, make sure you buy *One Man Clapping*, it's a live album and it's becoming more and more difficult to get hold of". I told her I'd seen a copy earlier in the week in Our Price and I reassured her that I'd pop into town on Monday and buy it. We chinked glasses, said cheers and I told her I'd see her later. Little did I know that the club would close down after that night and it would never re-open. It's now a block of flats, the ghost of 'Sit Down' and 'Jump Around' probably still echo around the flats corridors and staircase when there's no one about. I never saw the girl in the James top's again. She's probably into The Killers these days and works for Swintons Insurance. Nice girl though.

On the following Monday I headed back into town to buy a copy of *One Man Clapping*. I went to the rack in Our Price but was disappointed to see that the cassette version had gone. There was a copy on Compact Disc but as I didn't have a Compact Disc player I didn't bother to buy it. I popped across to Woolworths, again no cassette copy but two copies on Compact Disc. There was nothing at all related to James in WH Smith. I popped down to a second hand record shop called Traffic Records where I regularly bought vinyl from but they didn't have a copy either. Disappointed in not finding a copy I left the shop with a 12" copy of a 900ft Jesus song called 'Truth is out of style' as well as a Public Enemy poster. Oh well, I was sure that I'd be able to find a copy of *One Man Clapping* at some point I thought to myself. (If only I'd known the mileage that this little task would cover then I'd have ran back to the shops and bought every single copy of the album I could on any of the formats!)

Over the next few of months I visited a couple of record fairs that took place in town. Although I wasn't able to find a copy of *One Man Clapping* I managed to find various bits of James vinyl including two different 12" versions of 'Come Home'. I also bought 12" versions of 'Lose Control' and 'How was it for You?' The B-sides were of varying quality. 'Promised Land' from the 1989 release of 'Come Home' was excellent, if I could have played the guitar it would have been a song that I'd have certainly tried to learn. The purple edition of 'Come Home' had an extended version of the track and a live track which was confusingly called 'Stutter' but didn't feature on the album of the same name. I didn't know at the time the significance and importance of the song amongst James' fans and I listened to it only casually. A lovely song featured on the 12" of 'Lose Control' called 'Out to Get You'. It was simply gorgeous although it kind of just bubbled along and could have been such a bigger and better song I thought at the time. I also bought a couple of bootleg James concert tapes from the record fairs, the material focused heavily on the *Gold Mother* and *Seven* era only.

An article in a November edition of the NME mentioned that James would be performing a small tour in December. It would be a one hour long acoustic performance fresh from a large tour the band had been on across the other side of the Atlantic. I was due to go to my first proper live concert (we won't include Titus just to protect the minuscule amount of street cred that I have) in November. Steve and I were off to see the mighty Carter the Unstoppable Sex Machine in York at the Barbican Centre. As Christmas was coming up I asked Steve if he'd buy me a ticket to see James on the acoustic tour as they were set to play the Leeds Town and Country Club which was only about fifteen miles from where I lived. Steve initially refused because he hated James; he said the thought of him spending his hard earned cash on a James ticket made him feel sick. After I pleaded and begged he relented and bought me a ticket from Jumbo records in Leeds on the same occasion that we also bought tickets to see U2 who were due to play Roundhay Park the following summer, but that's another tale for another time.....

Leeds Town and Country Club

1992

Going to see Carter the Unstoppable Sex Machine was a mistake, but my dear friends, this wasn't due to the bands performance on the evening as they certainly "rocked tha' mic", although I have to say that they weren't as good as Titus. The issue was this. I went to the Carter gig feeling quite unwell due to a bad cold I'd developed; some unkind souls might have called it "Man Flu". On that late November evening in 1992 Steve and I caught the train to York to go and see Carter supported by the very ordinary The Family Cat. As it was a cold evening and being full of mucus and with a red raw throat I decided to wear a long sleeved t-shirt, (James) and on top of that I wore a Puma long sleeved thick black jumper. Very sensible you might think. Upon arriving at the venue I was rather excited to see a merchandise stall. In fact I was so excited I ended up standing as still as a statue whilst making a strange humming noise for four minutes. Once this bizarre episode passed I handed my cash over to the aggressive looking man working on the stall and bought a long sleeved black 'Impossible Dream' top and a woolly hat. I then proceeded to sliver the long sleeved top over what I was already wearing; the woolly hat was then pulled over my already sweating brow. I must have looked like an Indie version of the Michelin Man! I then skipped like a big fairy into the auditorium before burrowing myself into the front of the audience with Steve in hot pursuit.

To say that I felt unwell before The Family Cat had finished would be an understatement (and not because of their boring dirge) but by the time Carter had finished their third song I seriously thought I was going to die from heat exhaustion. Plus, having a couple of dozen people crowd surf and land on top of my head was as Michael Jackson may have politely said "Bad". I crawled on my hands and knees to the back of the venue whilst being repeatedly stomped upon by army boots and stripped off my sodden and stretched clothes (although my sweaty and soiled underpants stayed on for the dignity of those in attendance). I was so knackered and groggy that I couldn't even clap. Steve had a great time though and found me at the end of the show being looked after by some kind and concerned Grebo's. He found the fact I couldn't handle the pace and the thrill of the show to be extremely amusing! I'd have the last laugh almost a year later though, in the same venue with a band I loved and he hated.

On the 14th December 1992 I caught the train to Leeds to go to my first ever James concert. I went by myself, no one else wanted to go with me, I didn't really know anybody else who actually liked James apart from the girl from Josephine's who'd now vanished out of my life. Whilst walking from Leeds Train Station to the venue I noticed a few other people wearing various James tops. Even though it was midwinter and the temperature was similar to the Siberian Tundra people were actually wearing t-shirts. I'd wisely decided to wear a James top with a denim shirt over the top of it, plus I'd brought my Carter USM hat too.

I approached the Town and Country Club; it looked a bit like an ugly church. My breathing was heavy and I was sweating with excitement, my first James concert was moments away. I wondered what the band members were up to at that precise moment, I guessed they were probably eating Pot Noodles, playing board games and mediating, possibly all at the same time. Left foot followed right, I approached the bouncer at the venues door and handed over my ticket to him, he removed the stub and handed the remainder of ticket back to me as a souvenir.

"Thank you kind sir!"

"Are you taking the mickey mate?" the bouncer said to me. I realised that bouncers probably didn't enjoy small talk so I just winked at him and brushed past him before I could get drawn into an argument over my weirdness. A narrow corridor led to the auditorium; upon entering I was surprised and quite alarmed to find it fairly empty! I simply strolled up to the barrier and stood stage right and waited whilst listening to the warm up music. Time passed. My initial alarm subsided when it became apparent that the place was filling up nicely, the audience noise built, voices intermingling with one another like insect chatter. After a while two blokes casually walked onto the stage. One of them I didn't recognise and he went straight to his drum stool and plonked himself down behind his kit but the other guy I did recognise. It was none other than Andy Diagram who'd played the trumpet and wore dresses in James. He was no longer a member of James and his band was now supporting them which I thought was rather lovely.

A few cheers and "ANDY!" was repeatedly bellowed towards the direction of the stage.

"Alright Leeds? The rest of the lads will be out a bit later".

A few more cheers were made and then the music started up.....

Andy's band was called Spaceheads. I can't really describe the music but as you can imagine the trumpet and drums were obviously the lead instruments. There was a smattering of weird electronic noise mixed into the smelting pot and Andy did a bit singing like a good front man should. A song called 'Laugh in the Face of Power' was rather excellent and Andy said it was going to be released as a single, (it sadly never was). Although I was enjoying the set I had a feeling the majority of the crowd didn't quite get it. Another song featured samples of monkeys and elephants going absolutely berserk. I quite liked it; the song broke down to a quiet middle section before starting up again. Some lass stood next to me spoke out loud,

"Oh no, it's off again". She definitely wasn't enjoying the rather unusual performance. The set eventually ground to a halt, Andy bid us farewell and the warm up music started once more. A buzz filled the room; the odd impatient whistle pierced the air from time to time. The roadies prepared the stage for James, it was a simple set up with a large screen on each side of the stage with folk art imagery displayed on them. It created an atmosphere and vibe of sorts, simple, understated, just what the acoustic set promised to be I thought. The house lights dimmed.....

The members of James sauntered on stage and merrily waved at us, the place erupted and then this really weird experience happened to me. A large percentage of the audience appeared to be mainly teenage females, Smash Hits readers presumably. As the band made their entrance all of them started screaming. Tim and the boys had obviously become something of a cultish pin up band. The hideous screaming was so loud that my hearing vanished and the place fell silent for about five seconds of my life. It was like someone had turned an internal volume knob down for a few moments before readjusting it so that I could hear perfectly normal again. It frightened me and I've never experienced it since, I'm not sure if it's a common occurrence or what. Maybe it was my brains way of protecting itself in some capacity or other. Anyway, normal service was resumed; I looked attentively at the band and decided to put my Carter USM woolly hat on. Mark the keyboardist who was directly in front of me looked in my direction probably wondering if I was cold and trying to remember if he had some spare Lemsip for the sick audience member, (rightly or wrongly I'd previously heard he was a very kind and forgiving man).

The band members were stood pretty much in a single line, their instruments looked sharp and threatening, Mark was stood like Goliath himself holding a Melodica instead of hiding behind his usual banks of futuristic and exciting Casio's and 303's. Tim's was wearing a massive pair of grey pants and a big old baggy top, his mop of curly hair hung limply over his forehead.

Tim Booth then addressed the audience.

"Thanks for coming, we didn't think anyone was going to fucking turn up!" he said to roars of laughter from the audience. I remembered his foul language from Alton Towers and *Seven* and realised that he was a man who liked a good old cuss.

"We're going to do something a little bit different for you all tonight" said Tim, music began to play that sounded somewhat familiar to me as well as some of the other audience members, I realised it was 'Out to Get You', the b-side to the 12" of 'Lose Control' that I'd only ever casually listened to. It sounded a hell of a lot better than the recorded version;

in fact it was very, very beautiful indeed. Our arms swayed in time to the music, I tried to sing along but didn't really know the lyrics and I felt really paranoid when Mark looked down at me, I thought he might be cross with me for not being too clued up on the song. When the song finished I thought the place was going to erupt from the cheering but before we knew it we were straight into another song that I recognised from the Alton Towers show. 'America' sounded just as powerful in its stripped back form and it really picked up in pace towards the end of the song. Tim Booth would state at some point in the future that the song was actually about performing fellatio on America, how that would ever work I've no idea and it's probably best left as a bit of a pervy mystery. The audience went mental and I was swept along too, I was moved in ways that I never thought music could move me. If I'd been able to I would have cried but I'd cried all of my tears in my younger years. A very different and in my humble opinion much improved version of 'Ring the Bells' continued the set, the whole place was mesmerised by the performance. Bearing in mind that it was supposed to be an acoustic set it was as loud as Carter and Titus put together!

Steve had laughed and mocked me at the prospect of going to an acoustic show stating that it would be "boring" and would probably just feature Tim and Larry in a Boy Scouts kind of campfire sing-along show. How very wrong he was. 'Seven' was performed in a similar stripped back manner to the previous song and was swiftly followed by 'Riders' which appeared to be one of the few occasions when the audience didn't go as bananas as they did for the more well known songs. 'Walking the Ghost' followed, it seemed to suit the acoustic set very well indeed, the lush squalling violin threatened to level the audience completely.

"This is an old English Folk Song" Tim stated. Mark swapped his melodica for an accordion which is scientifically proven to be the octopus' favourite musical instrument. With great concentration he played a few slow chords, the audience appeared anxious wondering what the song was going to be, some of the audience started crossing themselves concerned that the band was about to play something by Foster and Allen. But no, Tim started to sing the opening lines to

'Sit Down' and some people around me were beginning to cry. It was a slowed down version, the audience struggled to sing along, it was delivered in an almost spoken manner but it sounded MAGNIFICENT! When the chorus kicked in the whole band piled into the song, Dave pounded the drums like his life depended on it and Tim didn't really need to do any singing at all, the audience were more than capable, except of course when it came to the verses. When the song ended cracks appeared in the walls of the venue due to the commotion caused by those attending the happening.

James quickly tore into an absolutely ferocious version of 'Next Lover'. The recorded version was a soft gentle lilting number; this version was its bastard offspring, a spurned lover, an angry plate smashing whirlwind of destruction. I was stunned along with half of the audience. I felt anger and rage that nobody I personally knew was sharing this experience with me. 'Johnny Yen' started up, the audience sang like they were at a football match, I no longer heard the shrieking little girls anymore, they were all hiding at the back of the room crying into their glasses of lemonade unable to face the pressure and force unleashed upon them by James, I was instead surrounded by an older crowd who knew EVERY word to EVERY single song. It was clear; crystal clear in fact that 'Johnny Yen' was a favourite amongst the hardcore James fans. 'Maria' was next, it had been played at Alton Towers but of course the acoustic version was again very different, gone was the big-beat version played on that rainy July evening to the deluged semi naked masses, the acoustic version punished the audience as the drums were beaten to a pulp by an extremely intense and wired Dave. The set dropped down a bit just to give everyone some breathing space as the band played a gentle version of 'Really Hard' from *Stutter*.

'Lose Control' followed, it was miles better in its stripped back acoustic form instead of that heavy handed big bass beat which featured on the recorded version, it sounded fantastic and the audience showed their appreciation. James had been on stage for over an hour, I knew it must have been near the end of their set. Tim thanked everyone for coming. The audience roared back their approval before the most wonderful version of 'Sound' I thought I'd ever hear began. It just built, and built and built until I was sure that the ceiling was going to come crashing down on top of us all, our heads smashed and our bodies squashed by the falling timbers. The still images that featured on the two screens started to spin furiously creating a blur; coupled with the strobe lights I worried for the safety of the audience. My head was spinning, my eyes closed, I felt the music swallowing me whole threatening to take me away to somewhere magical, destined never to return. After what felt like several eternities the song sadly ground to a halt, the band dropped their instruments, applauded the audience and then they were gone.

I was shocked at what I'd witnessed. I gurgled nonsensically and stumbled towards the very small merchandise booth with about 75% of the rest of the audience, it was difficult to see what was for sale but eventually the crowd dispersed and I could see what was on offer. It was all fairly familiar stuff except for one top which had a large cross on it made up from images taken from the Seven E.P. I didn't bother buying anything though, I couldn't really afford to. Outside the venue in the freezing cold were bootleggers selling imitation James t-shirts at half the price of the official stock but I wouldn't even consider buying anything unless it was the real deal. Instead I headed towards the train station along with many others and caught the train back to Harrogate, reflecting upon an evening that I knew had changed my life forever.

I was meant to be catching up with some friends after the show in town as it was someone's birthday, but I couldn't go. It would've spoilt the evening, an anti-climax. Instead I headed straight home and devoured the sandwiches and a large jug of orange that Mum had left out for me. I noticed the orange juice looked fairly cloudy but drank the lot due to the dehydration from the gig. The next day I woke up in some discomfort and then spent the rest of the morning being violently sick from the out of date orange juice that I'd drank the night before.

I caught up with Steve the following weekend.

"So, how was James then?" he asked with a smirk upon his face.

"Mate; it was one of the most thrilling experiences of my life. You should have been there; you'd have been blown away!" I replied.

"Really? I thought it was an acoustic show?"

"It was, but it wasn't all 'Ging Gang Goolie' and beards I can tell you!"

I explained the set up and the full on typhoon of noise that I'd experienced.

"Next time they're in town you'll have to come along!" I said to him and he agreed that he would.

In the New Year I went along to a record fair in town carrying out the usual desperate search though the millions of boxes trying to find *One Man Clapping* on cassette. I spoke to a number of the stall holders, none of them had come across the album in a very long time indeed. I was convinced that I'd eventually find it. But then a thought came in to my head, why didn't I just buy a copy on compact disc? At that point in my life I was really anti-compact disc due to the fact that I knew if I bought an album on compact disc and some of the tracks were not immediate then it would have been too easy to have been able to press skip thus spoiling the chance of learning to love an album in the way I'd done in the past with cassettes, it was generally too much bother having to fast forward and rewind cassettes all of the time. If I'd bought *Gold Mother* on compact disc then I'd probably have only listened to a few of the tracks and not developed the love for James that I had.

One Man Clapping was nowhere to be found though, feeling nervous and somewhat desperate I thought I'd try and find a version on any format possible. Before I left the record fair I managed to buy a bootleg copy of James on their acoustic tour which had been broadcast on Radio One. I returned to the shops in town and spoke to various people who worked behind the counters including Goth Girl, most of them had never heard of the album, the more specialist music shops, (Our Price) had stocked the album in the past but I was told the album had been deleted and they wouldn't be able to get it in stock any more! I cursed myself for not buying it when I had the opportunity. I knew I'd eventually find it though, or perhaps it would find me. The Radio One tape I'd bought from the record fair ended up being wedged inside my stereo for a long time. I'd sit for hours at a time staring out of my bedroom window watching the vapour trails of the overhead air traffic passing by whilst listening to it. Although I hadn't been present at that particular show (London) it brought back so many memories for me that I felt transported back to that cold and somewhat lonely December evening in Leeds.

Build 'em up, knock 'em down

1993

1993 started off fairly quietly regarding any news relating to James. The band appeared to have hibernated; well from me anyway. I didn't have a clue as to what they were up to and my focus shifted towards other bands and other albums. I became ever so slightly obsessed with *Are You Normal?* by Ned's Atomic Dustbin. I spent a month on work experience for the Canadian High Commission in London that April where I would listen to the album walking from Kings Cross (where I was staying with my Uncle Wally) to the High Commission adjacent to Nelsons Column and back to Kings Cross again. It was a walk I loved, street names I'd heard throughout my life, mad old people punching imaginary people, Mormons waving their Bibles at you and the general hustle and bustle of the commuters who'd pass you by without a glance. Posters advertising Blur's latest single 'For Tomorrow' were fly posted everywhere, I'd heard the song and it was rather gorgeous. Nine Inch Nails also came to my attention via the song 'Wish' which was featured on a compilation tape given away with Select magazine called *Island Select*. The tape featured other excellent racks including a fabulous Sabres Of Paradise remix of 'Everything' by the Stereo MC's and a song by the unusually named Sheep On Drugs.

Whilst in London I bought my first ever compact disc from HMV on Oxford Street. It was a two disc James package, disc one was an interview disc entitled *One Man Talking* just to persecute me in my fruitless quest to find *One Man Clapping*. The second disc was the single of 'Ring the Bells'. The main reason I bought it was the fact that it had a shiny gold sticker on the front that said *"500 copies only"*. I've seen the interview disc a number of times since the purchase but not the two disc version with the little gold sticker, I'm guessing its supposed rarity means it's worth at least £9000 now. It would be another eighteen months until I'd actually get to listen to the purchase though as I was still a bit of a Luddite when it came to compact disc players.

Before I returned back up north I left my copy of *Seven* at my Uncle Wally's chaotic dirty flat in London and wouldn't be able to retrieve it for another two years or so, an unintentional break from the album that would eventually reinforce its brilliance. The year continued to tick by, I developed a love for Blur and their warts and all film *Starshaped* made a massive impact upon me. *Modern Life is Rubbish* which featured 'For Tomorrow' was released in May of that year and it became my favourite album of all time. But what of James, had they dropped off the edge of the world? No.

It was early summer, I was on holiday in Bridlington (again) when I read in the NME that James would be releasing a new album in the autumn. I was flabbergasted! *Seven* had only been released the previous year, it seemed like such a short gap but I certainly wasn't moaning. The article stated a single called 'Sometimes' would be released at the end of August and that other album tracks included 'Raid' and 'Carousel'. It promised to be a more stripped backed affair too with none of the bombast of *Seven*. The article also mentioned that James were going to be supporting Neil Young on a few dates in July. I didn't consider attending though; Finsbury Park was quite a journey for me although I could have picked up my copy of *Seven* from Uncle Wally's flat whilst down there. Instead I made do with reading reviews for the performance which were extremely favourable towards James particularly in relation to the new material the band had played which included a song called 'Laid'. I realised that this was probably the song that had been called 'Raid' in the NME; the review mentioned that 'Laid' featured "*cheeky, naughty lyrics*".

It was early August when I first heard 'Sometimes' on the radio and I almost passed out at how different it was to the material from *Seven*. Tim's vocal delivery was more like a narrative. Once again James had come up with a song that sounded like no other. It was nominated as 'Single of the Month' in *Select* magazine, (I think it was *Select*) and the review stated it was *"easily the best thing they've come up with so far"*. I knew 'Sometimes' was going to be huge. The only fly in the ointment was the fact that on the day 'Sometimes' was going to be released the American band Nirvana was also going to release their eagerly anticipated new single 'Heart Shaped Box'. Hmmm, I was concerned the Nirvana song would possibly keep James from the number one spot and that 'Sometimes' would hit the number two position again just like 'Sit Down'. 'Heart Shaped Box' would be the new 'The One and Only', Nirvana, the new Chesney Hawkes.

On the Monday of release I caught the train and travelled across to Leeds to purchase 'Sometimes' from Virgin Records. As I entered the store 'Heart Shaped Box' was teasingly being belted out of the stereo to entice shoppers towards its dark charm. The James and Nirvana's singles were sat next to each other on the new release shelf and from what I could tell there appeared to be an equal amount of the singles on the shelf. I loitered for a while arousing the suspicions of the security staff as I tried to confirm what appeared to be the better selling single, at least on a macro level anyway and I winced each time somebody picked up the Nirvana single before glaring at them for not picking up the James vinyl. After thirty minutes I headed towards the counter with the 7" and 12" vinyl in hand and set off back home pleased that I was doing my bit for James.

Sunday, chart position day. I couldn't wait. I was actually working that afternoon as the picture framers had a large order to process for a customer based in Aylesbury. No bother though, the radio would be on and I'd bought some wine gums and pop to enjoy whilst I listened to the chart run down. The show started and the DJ immediately mentioned there would be a number of new entries that week including "big singles" by Nirvana and James. I was so excited that I thought I was going to wee myself and I almost did at one point as I'd drunk too much pop and when I needed to go John Dope was spending an eternity in the bathroom. He shouted angrily at me each time I knocked on the door to ask if he'd nearly finished and I eventually had to go outside and wee behind a wall. The chart run down had commenced....

And then......

Disaster.....

I almost missed the moment as I was busy making tea and coffee for my misfit colleagues, I never dreamt the song would enter the charts where it did.

"And it's a new entry for James who are this weeks number eighteen with their new release 'Sometimes'" announced the DJ, the familiar chords of the gorgeous song made a hasty entrance out of the speakers, my mouth was agape. I was gutted, absolutely gutted. What had gone so very badly wrong? There must have been a mistake? 'Sometimes' continued to play out whilst I chomped on half a pack of Wine Gums out of sheer despair and before I knew it we'd already moved on to the next chart position.

Nirvana crashed into the top five that particular week. I was happy for them, I really liked Nirvana and 'Heart Shaped Box' was a very good song but it was more of a feeling of betrayal from the record buying public that they hadn't gone out in droves and supported such a clearly magnificent song and band. James were going to perform on *Top of the Pops* on the following Thursday, because they were out of the country at the time on tour their performance was beamed into the studio by satellite. When Tim introduced the band and the song he appeared to look slightly down and disappointed, he obviously knew the chart position and like myself probably, definitely thought 'Sometimes' deserved a much higher chart position. Being a gentleman he was polite and professional (no swearing) and the band performed the beautiful song whilst a woman of unknown origin (I knew she was at least human) danced along next to the band. 'Sometimes' didn't climb any higher in the charts either and it proceeded to plummet out of the Top Forty like a stone dropped into a stream. Ah well, everybody was most likely waiting for the album release in September I thought to myself. And, I was right, kind of.

On the 20th September 1993 *Laid* the new album by James was released. The release date was celebrated on Radio 1 by hosting what they called 'James Day'. What this basically entailed was that James would be in a studio and they'd perform various album tracks live throughout the day. It was a great idea which got off to a very wobbly start as far as I was concerned. The first song was to be played pretty early in the day, something like 07:30. I can't remember who the DJ was but he blatantly didn't like James and he was a complete arse throughout. He sounded pretty disinterested but asked the questions that had been written out for him.

"So Timothy, tell us what you've been up to then prior to the release of your new album" he yawned.

Tim spoke and said something along the lines of,

"Blah blah, blah, *Laid*, blah blah blah, Brian Eno, blah, blah, blah, Neil Young etc.".

Obviously he didn't say "blah, blah, blah" at all, its just that as good a memory as I've got I can't actually remember what was said but Tim did reveal that as well as the album *Laid* they also had another album of alternative material they were hoping to release as well as a live album that they were probably going to put out at some point.

"Oh, so, you're not trying to rip off your fans then are you?" responded the DJ.

Tim sounded genuinely shocked and hurt at the response.

"Err, well, I hope not" he said in a fairly quiet voice bearing in mind that he was a man who liked a good swear or two.

I was as shocked as Tim was; I couldn't believe what a turd the DJ was. I was actually rather embarrassed and felt sorry for him, he obviously experienced a high level of self-loathing and probably personal hygiene issues too which meant that he had no friends and was despised and hated by his work colleagues. James then stormed into a song called 'Low, Low, Low', it sounded wonderful, just the kind of song to wake the country up with and the band sounded like they were having a right old laugh. It was the greatest song by The Pogues that never was. Once the song ended the DJ piped up again.

"Nice backing vocals" he said sarcastically. Tim politely responded and then James disappeared to make way for 2 Unlimited or something equally as turgid.

Before college I hopped, skipped and jumped towards town to buy *Laid* as well as the new De La Soul album *Buhloone Mindstate*. It had garnered some favourable reviews after the general backlash that their second album *De La Soul Is Dead* had received. In hindsight *De La Soul Is Dead* was a very good album, it just wasn't what everyone had anticipated following the astonishingly good *3 Feet High and Rising*. I called into Woolworths, headed towards the music section and quickly found the De La Soul album and grabbed a copy. I then had a scan for the new James album. I hadn't seen the artwork up till then, I scoured the shelves but I couldn't find it anywhere. Confused, I looked at the new release section and after a few moments I found the album. I hadn't noticed it due to the fact that the font on the album was so small that I'd initially overlooked it when I was searching. If I couldn't find it as a James fan then what would the casual record buyer do I thought to myself. Well, the album sleeve was a bit odd to say the least. The band members were all wearing dresses whilst casually eating bananas. Some of the band members actually looked quite hot, particularly Jim who looked like he had quite a nice set of legs on him for a man although I have to say that Saul looked like a drunk bag lady who'd probably be found staggering about Chapel Market in Islington shouting 'HERESY, HERESY!" I took the two cassettes to the counter, paid and headed towards college.

Richard was a lad in my college cohort who'd only just started to develop an interest in music. Keen to influence him I showed him my two purchases. Richard seemed genuinely interested in the James album; he knew the obvious hits/misses and he asked if he could borrow the album at some point. I told him he'd be best off buying a copy himself and he looked a bit taken back by my comment and my apparent tightness. James had announced a tour towards the back end of the year, I told Richard that I was going to the gig in York at the Barbican Centre where I'd seen Carter USM and I asked him if he was interested in going along with me. Indeed he was! Steve had also told me that he'd be up for it too. I spent the remainder of the day counting down the seconds until finishing time so that I could race back home and listen to the album. Come 15:30 I left college and ran the two miles home stumbling over my feet in desperation to get the stereo fired up for the first listen of *Laid*. The tape was briskly shoved into the player, the play button was pressed and I sat down in HUGE anticipation with a glass of pop next to me fizzing away.

'Out to get You' had been resurrected for the album, it was simply stunning. Soothing and extremely moving. I had tears in my eyes as the song picked up and the lightly played percussion announced itself with Tim repeating, *"what I need, what I need"* over like a prayer for forgiveness. It was a stunning start to an album I knew was going to utterly blow me away. 'Sometimes', also known in some quarters as 'Lester Piggott' was next, a song I was very familiar with after playing it at least 576 times since it had been released, the vinyl was actually starting to sound a tad iffy by that point. The song stampeded its way out of the speakers washing the room with florid colours and emotions before finally disappearing from view like water down a plug hole. And then, as ever with every James album I'd heard so far the next song made me go "oh". 'Dream Thrum' just never seemed to get going; it felt like a perpetual intro for what I felt could have been an amazing song.

'One of the Three' began, a quiet little number which ticked along minding its own business, it was very pleasant don't get me wrong but it left me a little bit cold. 'Say Something' I recognised from the Alton Towers gig but the version on *Laid* was much lighter and again like the rest of the songs I'd heard so far it was rather understated. There wasn't even the faintest trace of pomposity within the fibres of the song. The drumming was exceptional and really showed off Dave's talents. 'Five-O' ended the first side of the cassette, the song built up to the point where it felt like it was being rammed into my skull, there was a desperate feel to the song, the lyrics laced with pessimism and despair, *"if it lasts forever, hope I'm the first to die"* sang Tim, it was heart breaking stuff and to me it sounded like one of the bands finest songs to date.

61

An internal debrief took place. What did I think of the first side of the album? Hmm, well I was feeling *slightly* disappointed. The songs were fantastic, but as ever I guessed I was just expecting something different to what I'd heard so far. Oh well, side two then....

'P.S'.

Argghhhh!!! My goodness, what a bleak, sad desolate song! Of course I instantly thought it was absolutely wonderful although I was concerned about the emotional state the band must have been in during the writing and recording of the album. Lyrics such as *"my son says, dear father, what did you do when the world turned over?"'* I found particularly emotive. The song ebbed away and I composed myself as much as I possibly could. 'Everybody Knows' sounded like a huge snake slithering along the floor, I wasn't keen on it, Tim delivered a bizarre vocal melody which I wasn't comfortable with and it created an unsettling vibe. 'Knuckle Too Far' was another very quiet song that you'd hardly notice was there to be honest, and because of this it was simply wonderful. It sounded like it was being sung and played by exhausted musicians after an arduous journey into the wilderness and back. 'Low, Low, Low' was the kind of song that I'd been expecting and hoping from the album as a whole, it was chipper, silly, and up-beat, a sparkle of light and humour in an otherwise at times bleak affair. It was the sound of the band having a bloody good old time and it showed a side to the band which wasn't always portrayed, that of a goofy humorous bunch of youngish men who weren't as poker faced as they sometimes appeared to the casual observer.

And then, the title track......

"Oh my, what on Earth is this then?" I chuckled to myself. It sat comfortably next to the previous track; the two tracks were a brief period of respite from an album that had plenty of down beat numbers and moments. And as for those *"cheeky naughty lyrics"* which had been mentioned in the review for the Neil Young gig, well the lyric *"she only comes when she's on top"* would definitely affect its airplay I thought, but what the hell! 'Laid' was a great little number. 'Lullaby' brought the album crashing back into the world of the minor key. I was unaware at the time the song was regarding child abuse but I was still alert enough to realise the lyrics were touching and sensitive, the beautiful childlike keyboard melody complimented the song nicely, it was hauntingly beautiful. The album ended with 'Skindiving'. I listened to the song carefully, in some ways it didn't really fit in with the rest of the album but as per bloody usual with James for this very reason it meant it was the ideal way to end the album. Tim sang in a choir boy's falsetto throughout putting Aled Jones to shame, the song meandered through the underwater reed beds before spiralling down into the murkiness of the sand and mud. I exhaled and ejected the tape.

Later in the evening of 'James Day' I was excited to hear James were back on Radio One playing some more material. Tim announced they'd been practising some new songs during the day which hadn't been featured on their new album and the DJ instantly jumped to the conclusion the band had written some new material specifically for Radio One's 'James Day'. Tim tried to correct the DJ but he wasn't really listening to him and instead said,

"And here's James with their final offering of the day, a song they've written especially for Radio One".

I imagined the band raising their collective eyebrows in despair, Saul probably giving a rude hand gesture towards the direction of the DJ and then the band performed a song that wasn't featured on *Laid*, a powerhouse of a song called 'Tomorrow'.

And just in case you were wondering what I felt about *Laid*. Well, I liked the album as a whole although I was quite disappointed the album hadn't been filled with a number of tunes in a similar vein to 'Sometimes', 'Low, Low, Low' and 'Laid'. Again, if I'd bought the album on compact disc then I'd probably have skipped quite a few of the tracks and just listened to a select few. However, listen to *Laid* as a whole I did each day without fail and I quickly grew to love the album more so than I had done with the earlier James albums. Reviews for the album were once again quite mixed. The NME described it as "*boring*"; I'm guessing the reviewer probably listened to it in a busy noisy office therefore not appreciating the ambience and mood of the album. Some albums just don't work in certain situations and environments. *Laid* wasn't really a 'party album'. I'd once listened to *Seven* on the beach at Bridlington and it hadn't sounded quite right either with the seagulls squawking overhead spoiling the atmosphere.

I was looking forward to hearing the album chart run down the following Sunday, I was sure that *Laid* would definitely be a big hit, and this time I was right! Yes, straight in at number three in the charts which was one place less than *Seven* the previous year but it was still a fantastic chart position all the same. The DJ said they were going to play a song from the album but for some reason they decided to play 'Skindiving'. Now, as much as I liked the song I didn't really feel it was the best advert for the album, the title track would have been much better in my opinion instead of having that weird spooky song with the choir boy vocal being pumped out into radio land scaring the kids and adults alike. I felt paranoid that it was a campaign of some description to reduce album sales and interest in the band.

I was still absolutely stunned the following week though when the album had fallen from number three in the charts all the way down to number twenty five. This was pretty much unheard of as far as I was aware. Obviously all of the loyal James fans had rushed out and bought *Laid* the first week of release but once they'd made their purchases sales had dried up and the general public hadn't got in on the act. I was dismayed, heartbroken even. I blamed Radio One for playing bloody 'Skindiving' instead of 'Laid'. Or perhaps it was Nirvana's fault for diverting the public's gaze away from home grown talent to a band who sold records on the back of extreme self-loathing, bubble gum rock music.

There was some slight relief when I heard that the title track was going to be released as a single and in fairness 'Laid' started to get a bit of airplay but of course the commercial stations wouldn't go near it because of the risqué lyrics. Then an edited version started to be played where the lyrics were changed from, *"she only comes when she's on top"* to *"she only sings when she's on top"*. I was embarrassed.

The B-side for 'Laid' was a rather amazing track called 'Wah Wah Kits'. I simply couldn't get enough of the track; it was a squally mesmerising messy noise that entered my head and wouldn't shift one iota. I loved it. The CD single featured another song called 'The Lake'. It would be several years until I'd actually hear it though, until then it was nothing more than a phantom song to me.

'Laid' the single charted in October of that year, at a lowly 25, a complete failure. Why was this happening? Was there as I suspected a campaign to ruin the band? I knew the NME once had a t-shirt with the slogan "Build 'Em Up, Knock 'Em Down" as that's what the music industry likes to do, help a band build up a decent following and then when the band is at their commercial peak the music industry appears to take pot shots at the band as if they were participating in a cruel game of clay pigeon shooting, a game/sport that I think is pretty crap at the best of times. To me it felt like *Laid* had been a clay pigeon, it had reached a decent enough height before some knob took a well aimed pot shot at it and it came crashing back down to Earth as fast as it had risen. 'Laid' the single was another clay pigeon but one that hadn't sat in it's harness properly, when the release mechanism was pulled the clay pigeon skimmed low in the horizon before falling to the ground, it hadn't even warranted the effort of someone to take a shot at it, gravity did the dirty work instead.

I popped across to Leeds some point in November, I still wasn't buying Compact Discs but I thought I'd have a look at their '3 for £20' offer and with much sadness I found that *Laid* was already featured in its offer. There was a whole section devoted to the album, by the looks of it *Laid* was expected to be a big seller but the record stores were stuck with the challenge of trying to shift tons of unwanted James albums. It was a tragic sight to behold. Perhaps I should have bought one out of respect for the band. I didn't though. Oh the guilt.

Doc Marten

1993

Malaga, late November, 1993, I was on a week long college trip as part of my BTEC Travel and Tourism course and it was absolute carnage, gallons of alcohol was drunk each night by our rowdy motley crew as well as some behaviour that bordered on being illegal. However, there was one individual who wasn't partying hard, me. Looking back it was such a stupid reason but with a good enough intention at the core of it. On the 2nd December 1993 I was off to the York Barbican Centre to see James on the 'Laid' tour with Richard and Steve. The problem was we'd be flying back to the UK on the day of the gig, late in the afternoon. I knew the plane might possibly be delayed and we'd miss the gig. But I knew that after a week of "avin' it large" in Malaga the last thing I'd want to do was stand in a busy mosh pit being squashed to death by over eager James fans. I decided to take a vow to drink like a nun and I was in bed by 23:00 every night whilst everybody else, lecturers included were getting ratted on dirty cheap sangria and lager. Richard was going to the gig with me, his first ever gig, he didn't give a toss about going to bed early and he had a much more interesting and fun time than I did. I think he might have even got laid, not the album if you know what I mean.

On the day of the gig we arrived back to a damp and foggy Leeds/Bradford Airport in good time with no delays. The prearranged mini bus picked us up and dropped us off back at college, with suitcase in hand I dashed home as quickly as I possibly could with Richard in tow; he then went his own way home and told me that he'd meet me at the train station at 17:45. When I arrived outside my house, quite damp and sweaty I went to open the front door but realised with horror it was locked, no one was in and I had no key with me either. Mum was at work, the only problem was where she worked was a couple of miles away from where we lived, I knew she'd be there for a few more hours so I popped around to the back of the house, left my suitcase on the door step and set off running towards where she worked at a disabled home the other side of town. Thankfully my sober holiday meant that I wasn't too tired and I ran the entire journey without stopping and in good time too. Upon arriving at Mums work I found her pushing a vacuum cleaner around the floor, she hadn't switched it on which concerned and confused me somewhat, she was obviously quite surprised to see me and immediately asked me if I'd brought her any duty free cigarettes back from Spain, (I had, she was therefore very happy, Berkeley Red, her favourite brand). I told her that I needed to get changed and ready for the gig in York and asked for the house key from her which she gave me. She insisted I went home in a taxi but for some reason I argued that I didn't need one and as quickly as I'd arrived I was out of the door running the two miles back home. Exhausted, I fell through the front door and crawled towards the fridge. A bottle of Shaws Orangeade lay in wait and I downed the entire bottle before retrieving my very damp suitcase from the backdoor step. Everything was going to be alright after all.

Showered and washed I felt somewhat invigorated and extremely excited at the prospect of the gig, in fact I kept randomly shrieking from time to time. Then the phone rang, it was Steve with some terrible news.

"Listen mate, I can't make the gig tonight, I've really hurt my feet".

"Eh? What do you mean?"

"I've bought some Doc Martens and they've rubbed my feet red raw, I can't even walk on them let alone stand up at a gig".

I was gutted for him, I tried to cajole him into coming and suggested that we could possibly steal a wheelchair from the local A&E for him but his heart wasn't really in it (stealing a wheelchair) and he said he'd give the gig a miss. He sounded quite disappointed even if he still didn't really like James very much. I put the phone down, grabbed my coat and ran towards the station.

Well, after the chaos of the afternoon I somehow ended up arriving at the station early, I grabbed some crisps for my evening meal and a bottle of pop along with the latest edition of the NME. On the cover was Tim Booth looking unshaven and quite moody. The headline was *"Getting Laid on the Road"* and there was a decent enough interview with the band but I felt the band were a tad standoffish throughout, who could blame them really, they'd obviously had a bit of a crap time with journalists in the past and I'm guessing the albums commercial failure in the UK was largely responsible due to poor and mixed reviews.

Richard turned up on time and asked about Steve, he was disappointed for him but he also thought it was quite hilarious that Steve had bought probably the most comfortable shoes known to man and they'd somehow destroyed his feet. The train arrived; we bumbled on and yakked about the holiday. I was somewhat disappointed that I hadn't been part of all of the frivolous activities that everybody else had gotten up to but I managed to hide my disappointment through laughter. The train pulled into a rural station and by sheer coincidence Will and Jonathon, two lads I'd been to college with the year before sat down opposite Richard and I.

"Now then, where are you lads off to then?" asked Will.

"Yeah, where are you lads off to then?" repeated Jonathon with a crazed look upon his face, he looked wired and I guessed they'd been participating in the 'Touch the Electric Fence' game again, they'd mentioned this particular activity to me over a drink in the pub the year before. I explained that Richard and I were off to see James in York, interested in possibly attending they asked how much it was, were there any tickets left etc. The clickety clack of the train was like a metronome, we carried on with some general chit chat although my mind was a couple of hours ahead of everyone as I was thinking about the evening's entertainment that lay ahead, I simply couldn't wait.

York train station. It was imperative to get as near to the front of the stage as possible and I managed to coax Richard into running to the venue which he did, although I suspected it was somewhat begrudgingly as he kept swearing. It was cold and drizzly, the car headlights were blinding in the dark and wetness of the evening and the traffic was still fairly busy for the time of the day. As we were getting closer to venue I noticed a fair few people wearing James long sleeve tops, all walking in the opposite direction trying to find a decent pub I presumed. Then a lad stopped us, I almost slipped on the wet pavement and ended up underneath a bus.

"Alright fella's? Are you off to see James tonight?"

"Yes," I replied to him with some annoyance at being stopped.

"Sorry mate, it's been cancelled, the singers lost his voice".

I smiled at him.

"Ah, right, cheers mate" I replied whilst winking at Richard and before the lad had a chance to say anything further Richard and I were bounding along the pavement towards the direction of the venue.

"What an arse!" I shouted at Richard.

York Barbican Centre. There were a lot of people simply stood about; I noticed worryingly there was no queue of gig goers waiting to enter the venue. A small crowd was instead staring at something stuck to the entrances to the venue; we walked over towards the door to see what it was all about.

A note on A4 paper read,

"Unfortunately due to ill health the band is unable to perform tonight's show. The concert has been rescheduled for the 16th December. Refunds are available".

The 'arse' had been telling the truth. Except he wasn't an arse, just a decent caring music fan, that's all.

I, was, gutted.

And to think I'd been on holiday acting like a grandad too. All that running about only to end up damp, tired from running several miles and hungry from only eating a bag of crisps. Richard laughed out loud but I knew he was disappointed. The only silver lining was the fact the gig had been rescheduled and not cancelled which meant that Steve would hopefully be able to make it as long as his feet didn't become gangrenous and wither away. We made the slow downtrodden walk back to the station and caught the train home. We should have gone to a pub and gotten lashed but we went home instead and I ended up watching The Equalizer with Mum. I spoke to Steve the next day. He already knew that the gig had been cancelled as the kind staff at the York Barbican Centre had telephoned him to tell him not to bother turning up because Tim Booth apparently had a sore throat. Of course those were the days before every man and his dog owned a mobile phone so Steve and the Barbican staff couldn't telephone me to let me know. I advised him to bathe his feet in warm salt water. It would sting a bit but it would hopefully help them heal quicker.

The following two weeks flew by and the Three Musketeers were reunited, feet intact, Doc Martens shiny and new and we were back on the train again York bound. I was so relieved when I saw the large queue of people all lined up outside the doors of the venue and we gladly joined them. After what felt like several ice ages the doors opened and we were ushered into the venue, this time of course I wasn't suffering from the man flu that I'd had at the Carter USM gig the previous year. We milled about with the other James fans, everyone in their James uniform or so it seemed anyway and we headed across to the merchandise stall. The 'Get Laid' t-shirt that was designed in the style of a football top caught my eye but I'd have felt to self conscious wearing it although in retrospect my Neds Atomic Dustbin t-shirt which was emblazoned with 'Not Sleeping Around' was about as attention seeking as they come.

The doors to the auditorium opened and the three of us dashed across the floor to the left of the stage directly by the barrier. The place started to fill up rather quickly and I was chuffed that we'd made the effort to arrive when we had. The three of us made some small talk until the lights dimmed a bit and the support band walked on stage. Radiohead was a band I knew little about except that they'd had a sizeable hit with a song called 'Creep'. They started fairly promising, crashing chords and Thom Yorke's mop of hair being flung about right, left and centre. Steve was obviously very impressed, he told me between songs that I could buy him their album *Pablo Honey* as a Christmas present. There was little between song banter except when Thom thanked James for the support slot and before we knew it Radiohead ambled off to a sizeable applause from the audience.

I was extremely nervous. My hands were sweaty, my stomach lurched from time to time as we observed the roadies preparing the stage for James' appearance. Like the Leeds audience from the previous year there was quite a rowdy atmosphere, gone were the young female Smash Hits readers, there seemed to be quite a few couples there as well as a fair few beered up gangs of lads all chanting "Boothy, Boothy, Boothy". Finally the stage emptied, the roadies had performed their tasks and the house lights dimmed.

There was an almighty roar, the shrill screaming that had momentarily deafened me the previous year was no more and the three of us joined in the shouting and cheering. Fists pumped in the air as the members of the legendary James walked on stage and the band immediately launched straight into 'Heavens'. It really was a euphoric moment in time, it wasn't the song I'd have expected as a set opener but it worked so well and the fevered audience lapped it up like starving puppies. When 'Heavens' ended the place went completely berserk and then the distinctive rumblings of 'Sound' began, the black backdrop suddenly lit up by hundreds of fairy lights giving the impression of a clear starlit night, there was an audible gasp from all of those stood around me. I had tears in my eyes and I held onto the barrier as if on a White Knuckle ride.

I looked at Richard and Steve, they were both clearly "well into it" bearing in mind if you will that the previous year Steve had mocked me for going to see James and there we were twelve months later with him having the absolute night of his life. The set list went this way and that, songs I knew, songs I didn't, at one point somebody shouted out "PLAY CHAIN MAIL", Jim Glennie immediately started to play the bass line and the rest of the band picked up the song and played it in its entirety. Radio One's favourite James song 'Skindiving' started up with a light show that created an eerie ambience. Although I was mesmerised by what was taking place on stage I glanced towards Steve and was alarmed to see him slumped over the barrier, his hands hanging limply towards the floor, I realised with horror there was something very wrong. I immediately caught the attention of the security guys, they ran across and tried to gain Steve's attention but it was quite clear he was unconscious. More security rushed across and they man handled him out of the audience. I panicked; I was extremely concerned about my friend and I looked at Richard for support but he obviously found the whole thing to be hilarious as he was laughing hysterically as Steve was carted off by a couple of big burly security guys whilst James played on oblivious to what was happening a few meters away from them.

'Skindiving' ended but my mind was elsewhere. James continued the set with 'Say Something' but I couldn't stop worrying about my friend, was he hurt or injured I wondered? Was he being carted off to the hospital with paramedics pumping at his chest? A thousand thoughts went through my head. When 'Say Something' ended I caught the attention of the security and asked them to lift me out of the audience, the people next to me including Richard gave me a bunk up too. And then I did something that to this day I'm extremely embarrassed about.

First of all I wriggled around to face the audience and shouted out "WAHEY!" like an idiot, it caused a few people close by to laugh. Once I was on the floor I started jumping up and down waving at the band like an eejit whilst shouting,

"CHEERS TIM, YOU'RE THE BEST, WE LOVE YOU, YOU'RE THE BEST!"

Tim started to laugh, Martine the bands manager who was playing the guitar on a couple of songs that evening was also laughing. The rest of the band were either chuckling or staring in bemusement at the lunatic who was causing a bit of an embarrassing scene. The security guys escorted me to the right of the stage; I then saluted the audience and shouted out, "ALRIGHT CAPTAIN!"

I've no idea why I did this.

I'm cringing just thinking about it.

Somebody in the audience said "Who's that tit?"

I looked back at the band and saw that Tim was still laughing and shaking his head in bafflement.

I managed to find Steve straight away; he was stood casually watching the band. He looked absolutely fine and dandy. He then noticed me and looked as confused as the band and audience had been a few moments earlier.

"What are you doing here?"

"I came to see if you're alright? Is everything okay?"

"Yes, I'm fine. I just passed out from the crush. Probably didn't help that I've not eaten anything all day too" he said looking rather sheepish.

I was annoyed, very bloody annoyed! I'd lost my position by the barrier because my mate simply hadn't eaten his lunch. I wanted to punch him in the stomach but being a pacifist I couldn't bring myself to carry out such a violent activity, I simply told Steve to stay where he was and I was going to try and squirm my way back to the front again, but try as I might I just couldn't get back to the barrier. By the end of the final song I could just about see the back of Richards head, he was still stood in the same place I'd left him. The set ended and the band left to a massive round of applause, the house lights came on and I was left feeling silly and very hot and sticky from trying to battle my way to the front of the rowdy audience. Richard turned around and looked at me; he looked quite embarrassed after my foolish antics earlier in the set. I asked if he enjoyed the show and he replied that it had been amazing.

I was extremely jealous that I hadn't gotten to enjoy the show as much as he had. He asked about Steve and I told him that he'd fainted; I thought Richard was going to faint too from laughing so much! I wasn't laughing though, I was really cheesed off. We met up with Steve who also looked awkward and embarrassed. Richard instantly started making fun of him, laughing at him for being so soft however Steve said he'd have the last laugh in that he'd be receiving a card or letter from the band wishing him well?!?!?!? Where he got this idea from I've no idea at all.

(He never did of course).

When I woke up the next morning the first thing that came into my head was my stupid and embarrassing antics. My god I was such an idiot. I was paranoid as hell that I'd ruined the show for everyone in attendance. I was quite sure that Richard would hate me and not want to be my friend anymore; I knew that James would probably ban me from attending future gigs too. I immediately grabbed some paper and a pen and wrote an apology letter addressed to Tim Booth and posted it to their fan club address in Manchester. I said how sorry I was for being such a fool and I explained that I'd been concerned about the well being of my friend in the hope that I'd appease his wrath. I sealed the envelope, popped into town and posted the letter at the main post office before heading to Our Price to buy a copy of Radiohead's *Pablo Honey* for Steve's Christmas present. Over the next few weeks I waited patiently for my personal reply from Tim Booth that I knew I was sure to receive, because musicians always reply to fan mail don't they?

Booth bashes Britain

1994

I'd bought a new item of James clothing, well; it was second hand if you want to be specific. Steve had purchased a lovely black long sleeved top at the York gig and for some reason or other, possibly due to the fact that he was skint he asked me if I wanted to buy it off him, so I did for a fiver. It was a nice, simple classy design; it simply stated 'James' on the front of it. It probably wasn't the best fitting item in the world as it was a size too big for me but I carried it off quite well, I think I did anyway. I also bought myself another James top although looking back it was rather rubbish. It was a red t-shirt although the colour looked washed out so it was more pinkish, perhaps the shirt had been left in direct sunlight for a long time. The front design of the shirt had numbers 1-6 on it and on the back was a large number 7. I only bought it because it was in the bargain section in HMV in Leeds, (along with several million copies of *Laid*), it was almost like donating to a charity as far as supporting James was concerned.

I also finally got my backside into gear and joined the James *Chain Mail* fan club. Now, I believe U2 fans sometimes receive limited edition remix albums as a thank you for being in their fan club, what I received as a *Chain Mail* member and for what at the time was quite a lot of money was a green metal 'Chain Mail' badge, a signed photograph of the band and a rather thin magazine which had a feature in it regarding toxic shock syndrome in relation to not changing your tampons regularly enough. And then, just to rub a smidge more salt into the wounds no sooner had I received my first instalment from the fan club another package turned up with a blue metal 'Chain Mail' badge and a couple of other issues of the magazine. An accompanying letter stated it was no longer viable to run the fan club so they were knocking it on the head hence the extra bits and pieces that they'd sent in the accompanying envelope. A bit of a disappointment, but there you go, life's full of them.

The second hand record shop Traffic Records that I used to frequent had closed down, a lad I knew from around the corner had struck up a deal of sorts and bought the entire stock for a rock bottom price and he opened up his own record shop up the road from where I lived. The shop was above a butchers shop, was poorly advertised, it was probably the worst possible location for a music shop of any description. Being a supporter of small local businesses and being an avid music fan I visited the shop on a snowy Tuesday morning. Music by the Manic Street Preachers was blasting out of the stereo at too loud a volume, the room was a fug of cigarette smoke, the lads mum was minding the shop for him and she was clearly a chain smoker as was evidenced by the overflowing ashtray. My James radar switched on, unsurprisingly *One Man Clapping* wasn't present but a vinyl copy of *Strip Mine* was for sale along with some James material I'd not seen before. For two pounds I bought a copy of the *Village Fire EP*. "*Five offerings from James*" it promised. I also bought a vinyl copy of *Some Friendly* by The Charlatans which was encased in a white rubber sleeve. *The Village Fire EP* was something else, the tracks 'What's the World', 'Folklore', Fire So Close', 'If Things Were Perfect' and' Hymn from a Village' were a rattly bare boned affair, a million miles away from their later material but they were extremely enjoyable nonetheless, the vinyl rarely left my turntable except perhaps for when I wanted to listen to some of Public Enemy's early material.

It was my final year at college and in early 1994 we were advised to seek out somewhere to go to for work experience that related to the travel industry. As previously mentioned the year before I'd gone to London, this time I wanted to try and do something even more exciting. I'm not sure where the idea came from but the thought of going to a kibbutz in Israel sounded like it could be a lot of fun. So in February 1994 I flew to Israel and secured work on a kibbutz. Initially it was a bit depressing, it rained most of the time plus I didn't really get along with my room-mate Marcus although after a bit of a heated argument one night we cleared the air and got along famously. Marcus didn't like James; he was into bands like Carter USM and Kingmaker although I seem to remember him being a big fan of Joy Division too. I knew nothing about Joy Division apart for what people had said to me about them, "they're really depressing".

I'd only brought a small selection of music with me to Israel which was a bit silly considering that I'd be there for a couple of months. I'd brought *Laid* and a double live album by The Orb called *Orb, Live 93* which went on for about nine days from start to end and it only featured eight songs on it. A few weeks into my stay an envelope arrived from Steve. Inside was a letter and some various bits of paper. I read the letter first of all, standard affair "hope you are having a good time etc." but what really caught my eye was *"I've included an article on James for you, don't think you'll like it though"*. My heart skipped a beat and I scoured for the article, and this was what I found….

The article was entitled *"Booth Bashes Britain"*. It was an interview with Tim where he described the bands massive disappointment in the fact that *Laid* had done so poorly and had been ignored in the previous year's end of year round ups in the music press. He said that the band felt like they had been *"taken for granted"* and the British public were more bothered about fashion and trends than material that truly meant something. Tim mentioned the band Suede at this point. Tim said James was going to release a new double 'A' side single entitled 'Jam J/Say Something'. 'Jam J' was a new song that was going to feature on an alternative collection of songs that the band was hoping to release later in the year whilst 'Say Something' was to be the final single released from *Laid*.

I was intrigued at the thought of new material being released so soon. The article went on to explain more. It stated that the track 'Jam-J' was from a collection of 'jams' that the band had recorded; some of them were seventeen seconds long whilst some of them were seventeen minutes long. As they were spontaneous pieces of music they were all titled 'Jam A', 'Jam B', 'Jam C' etc. as a way of keeping a log of them. Tim stated if the band had its own way then they wouldn't release any more music in the UK and that they'd produced a video to accompany 'Say Something' but that it was a pointless exercise really as the video wouldn't be shown on television because it featured him in it naked with electrodes attached to his and the rest of the band members heads. I could see why that one might possibly escape being shown on *Top of the Pops!*

Tim mentioned that DJ, producer and remix wizard Andy Weatherall who'd worked with the band in the past remixing 'Come Home' had remixed 'Jam-J' and his mix would be released as a 33 minute long track as part of his *Sabres of Paradise* project. Interestingly enough Tim mentioned that Mr Weatherall incorrectly thought James hadn't liked previous remixes he'd done for them and Tim wondered if somebody in the music industry had possibly been stirring up ill feelings with those connected with the band. Both Andy Weatherall and the band had wanted to do a full album together as *James Vs The Sabres of Paradise*, but the record company had rejected the idea. The band had by all accounts been playing a lot of dates in the USA and had been using the jams, which Tim described as "monsters" to warm the audience up before hand. It was a fairly damming article, justifiably so you might say but it seemed like such a strange thing to read at the same time, there was a definite feeling of crankiness to it. I'd never heard of a band before who publically became so annoyed with such a lack of success relating to their latest offering. Steve said in his letter that he'd buy the remix single on vinyl for my return and that he'd buy the compact disc of the single 'Jam-J/Say Something' for himself. I couldn't wait to get back to the UK.

During a moment of boredom after work I became a tad over excited when I noticed that a woman by the name of Gaynor Lukes who'd signed my official fan club membership card had been given a 'thank you' credit on the inlay card of the album *Laid*. It felt like I'd received an autograph from someone close to the band and I felt like I'd joined The Masons without the weird handshakes. I even used this extremely sad and tenuous link with the band to try and impress a very attractive girl one evening whilst drunk. She was a fan of James so I gabbled on at ten to the dozen about how amazing they were etc. I became slightly over animated in the process before trying to encourage her to come back to my room so that I could show her the membership card and the *Laid* inlay card to prove to her how close I was to the band. Naturally she thought I was a bit of a weirdo so she declined and instead went off and had five vodka jellies which had solidified inside some condoms, (it was apparently all the rage with students in those day but I have to say it wasn't really my cup of tea). Well, I didn't mind the jelly, or the vodka, but the condoms I could live without, unless of course you needed one for an emergency situation. Am I waffling? I think so too. Let's move on. Or perhaps not, no, let's definitely move on.

Another girl called Charlotte who I'd made friends with on the kibbutz ended up with my red/pink James t-shirt and I'd never see that James t-shirt ever again although weirdly enough the red /pink t-shirt would rear its head again some 16 years later, I'll return to that later on. Similarly a grey short sleeved 'Come Home' t-shirt that I'd also bought ended up going missing whilst on the kibbutz, I think that one was stolen mind you! However I did manage to return home with at least one James item of clothing, a grey long sleeve shirt with a large daisy on the front of it, a copyright symbol and "1993" which sat comfortably underneath the daisy. A very nice top and I've still got it too.

I almost got into a James related fight one evening in the kibbutz bar whilst I was persistently and drunkenly trying to persuade the barman to let me play 'Low, Low, Low' on the stereo. Some lad kept taking the piss out of me when I slurred that the song would make an ideal "football anthem".

"What, like 'Here we go, here we go, here we go?'" he sarcastically said to me with a sneer.

I looked at him with a certain amount of contempt, he looked at me like I was an idiot before somebody intervened and separated the two of us. The barman then gave in and gave me access to the stereo but the stereo's rewind and fast forward buttons didn't work which sadly meant the future football anthem mega hit wasn't played that evening, instead I slipped in my cassette single of Blur's new song 'Girls & Boys' that my sister had posted to me. I then pogoed around the bar in a frantic state along with some Israeli soldiers who had guns slung around their backs which kept clobbering me from time to time.

One day a South African lad came up to me and told me that Kurt Cobain was dead after blowing his brains out of the back, side and top of his head with a rather dangerous gun. I was as shocked as anybody and arranged that evening to have a 'Nirvana Tribute Night' in the pub which basically comprised of me playing *Nevermind* on repeat until I managed to cunningly slide *Laid* into the stereo which of course really got the party going. As a thank you to the South African lad I then ended up trying to kiss his girlfriend although thankfully someone pulled me away seconds before he walked into the pub otherwise somebody else might have died too. He was a big strapping fella, and I definitely wasn't. I looked a bit like the character described in 'So Macho' by pop Goddess Sinitta, you know, the *"seven stone weakling"*.

After my two months abroad I returned home from Israel and caught up with Steve a few days later. He played me the single 'Jam-J', it was a very odd song with Jim Glennie's scratchy scraping bass playing appearing to be all over the place intermingled with hand claps, Larry Gott's aggressive guitar playing and Tim's odd lyrics about *"satellite dishes"*, *"coffins"* and *"funny books"*. I loved it, it was a massive departure from the mood and feel of *Laid* and I asked Steve where it had gotten to in the charts. He said that it had reached 24 which weirdly enough was a higher entry than the lead single from the album. The other tracks on the single were 'Say Something' and 'Assassin' which featured Mark the keyboard player on guitar. There was also a new version of 'Say Something' which was basically a more polished version of the original track.

However, the big surprise was the Andy Weatherall mix. To be honest it sounded like it was playing at the wrong speed; we experimented with the turntable flipping the track between 33rpm and 45rpm to see which sounded like the right speed. The 45rpm version initially sounded a lot better but of course a 33 minute song would have ended up a lot shorter, (I can't be bothered to do the maths to work out exactly how much shorter it would have been). Resigned to the fact that the slowed down version was in fact the correct one I sat back and listened to it in confused wonderment. I'd come to expect remixed songs as basically the original song with a dance beat slapped on top of it, but this was something else. Weird, trippy space music, you'd never guess it was James, Tim was barely audible, the original instruments appeared to be mashed up or missing completely and I couldn't really hear the actual song 'Jam J' at all in the mix. But it was fantastic and I'd loved to have heard a full album featuring James and The Sabres of Paradise. Steve was equally impressed although he appeared to take more delight in playing the new Nine Inch Nails album, *The Downward Spiral*. Now, THAT's a *really* uplifting album, full of warm humour and love.

In June of that year James were playing Glastonbury and although I never went to the festival that year I managed to catch some of their performance on TV as Channel Four were broadcasting and showing the festival for the first time. Rather annoyingly James' performance was at the very end of the show close to midnight which meant a lot of viewers would have probably already gone to bed as it was a Sunday evening. I was extremely cross; again, it all felt like part of the 'let's bury James' conspiracy that appeared to be in full flow. However, their performance was amazing. 'Out To Get You' aired first and it was a terrific and powerful version of the song and the crowd seemed well into it. After the song finished Tim spoke and said,

"Here are a couple of new ones for you from our alternative thing that's coming out soon".

The band then proceeded to play a fantastic version of 'Jam J' which must have confused the majority of the crowd who knew James from the obvious, ahem 'hit' singles. When the song finished to a decent enough round of applause the band slipped straight into a new song called 'Honest Joe'. To say that I was gobsmacked would have been an understatement. Tim barked through a megaphone throughout the song, Saul looked rather splendid in a rather nice fetching white shirt and he joined in on a megaphone too, Larry's leg kept lifting off the ground as if he had a nasty bit of cramp whilst he played what I can only describe as dirty sounding guitar lines. Dave played the drums like a sea monster, Jim's side parting bobbed about here there and everywhere and as for Mark, the synth lines he played throughout the song were just something else, particularly the full wig out synth attack at the tail end of the song with Tim spinning around for what seemed like forever, his megaphone threatening to destroy the bands equipment or kill somebody should it have accidently slipped out of his hand. Even the strobe lighting was mesmerising bare in mind if you will that it was a mid afternoon slot and was naturally not very dark at all. The crowd from what I could tell appeared to enjoy the material.

The following week in one of the weekly music magazines I read a review for James at Glastonbury. Apparently when the band started to play 'P.S.' the audience started cheering, Tim said,

"Don't lie, you didn't fucking buy it".

The review made me laugh by describing Tim Booth as *"a narky bastard who sulks when the kids don't buy his records"*. But if he had been acting like "a narky bastard" then you couldn't really blame him. Whilst the UK had largely ignored the album other territories such as the USA were lapping it up particularly at a time when James was as ever quite a couple of steps out of the zeitgeist. We should have been proud and supported the fact that a British band was having some well deserved success overseas, but no, as ever we knocked them down instead. In fact, it was worse than that, they were simply and sadly ignored.

As mentioned, James never really felt like part of the scene, any scene to be honest, even when 'Madchester' was in full swing they didn't seem to fit in with the other bands glutinous drug taking, maraca shaking, indie dance crossover image. But there was another musical scene starting to emerge, could James really stand head and shoulders next to the likes of Blur and another Manchester band called Oasis? I didn't think so. Even before the summer was really upon us and well before the last notes of 'Honest Joe' was played on that big old stage at Glastonbury I was already heading in another musical direction known commonly as 'Britpop' headed by one of my other favourite bands Blur, and for a while at least they'd try to wrestle the crown of "My Favourite Band" from James.

By the way, my reply from Tim Booth still hadn't arrived; I guessed it had most probably been lost in the post.

Footnote time: I was informed that Marcus my room-mate from Israel died in 2011. I've no idea how and I only found out a few months after he'd died. We'd kept in touch on and off over the years and he'd even given me some advice and help regarding my first book too. We'd talked about meeting up for a beer so many times over the years but it was something we never got around to arranging. He was a smashing bloke and was clearly much loved by those who knew him. Wherever you are mate, take care.

Frequency Dip

1994

Another record fair, another attempt in my miniature quest to find *One Man Clapping*, it was a quest even Indiana Jones would have found frustrating. Naturally it proved to be another futile exercise; there was plenty of James' back catalogue for sale except for their elusive live album. As despairing as it was I knew I couldn't or at least shouldn't leave the record fair empty handed. I'd read in a number of articles that Tim had been hugely affected by an album called *Horses* by the American Punk poet Patti Smith and I was naturally curious to see what was so special about it. After a rummage through the stalls a copy of the album was found and swiftly purchased. I'd never heard anything by Patti Smith, the album turned out to be an emotional listening experience particularly the nine minute plus 'Birdland'. I was aware that 'Birdland' had a profound impact upon a young Tim Booth during a difficult time in his life, having lost my father at an early age the song touched me like no other, in fact it's haunted me since the first time I ever heard it. The album is a wonderful collection of scenes, moods, feelings and emotions, an essential album for anyone interested in the schizophrenic medium that is music and it would have been an album I'd probably never have bothered to explore if it hadn't been for James.

One of the monthly magazines that July announced James were going to be releasing a new album of "*alternative music*" they'd recorded during the sessions for *Laid*, it included material premiered at Glastonbury the month before. The album was to be called *Frequency Dip*; I thought it was an absolutely fantastic album title! Once again I was starting to feel rather excited at the prospect of owning new material by my favourite band. Well, James was still my favourite band even if Blur had moved me in ways that a lot of music hadn't for long time. *Modern Life is Rubbish* had completely blown me away and although I didn't think *Parklife* was quite as good an album I'd grown rather fond of it. The first single 'Girls & Boys' naturally reminded me of my time in Israel, it brought back a lot of happy memories for me from my time spent on the kibbutz, whilst James on the other hand would forever remind me of being given the cold shoulder by attractive females and almost being pummelled in the pub by an idiot with a bad attitude and a lack of respect for songs that would have sounded ace bellowed out on the terraces.

It may amuse you to know that James actually ended up re-recording 'Low, Low, Low' as 'Goal, Goal, Goal' as an official World Cup song for England during the 1994 World Cup, however England had embarrassingly failed to make the finals and instead a large proportion of the country started banging on about their supposed Irish roots and ancestry and supported Ireland instead. As for the re-recorded song itself, well, it's funny in a goofy kind of way! Hilariously bad lyrics! *"He was, never, ever, ever offside"* being my particular favourite however if a song has the power to be able put a smile upon your face then it can't be all that bad can it? Except perhaps for something like that 'Mr Blobby' song, I mean, that was just disturbing.

During August 1994 whilst I was in the middle of my ever growing obsession with *Parklife* I'd bought a copy of *Select* magazine due to the fact that there was a cassette of new 'free' music attached to the cover which included The Prodigy and James. Naturally I couldn't wait to hear the new James track particularly when I discovered it was the 'Folk Testosterone' remix of 'Honest Joe' but I ended up feeling rather disappointed with the song. It just sounded so lumpy and tuneless. I found some solace in the other tracks on the tape which included a fantastic live version of 'Impact: The Earth is Burning' by Orbital and 'Johnny L' by Johnny L.

Over the August bank holiday weekend Steve, Richard and I headed down south and experienced the cultural phenomenon that is the

Reading Festival. It was the first time any of us had been to a music festival and we were fairly naive in what to expect, I wasn't feeling very well as I'd been living at my sisters for a while and had only gone and caught chicken pox from her kids. Still, it was a good weekend which had initially got off to a bit of a ropey start when a Big Issue seller started a proper fist fight with the three of us during our journey from Reading train station to the event. It was simply because we refused to buy a copy of the magazine from him whilst we carried a case of lager that we'd just purchased from the off licence. We were saved from a proper pasting from the scruffy homeless bloke when his friend ran to our aid and pulled him away from us; it was actually quite a scary yet hilarious situation to end up in.

The headlining acts on the main stage that weekend were Cypress Hill, Primal Scream and the Red Hot Chilli Peppers. Nothing special to be honest, the best bands that played there over the weekend were Gravediggaz, Fun-da-mental and Radiohead who played an exceptional set of new material from their (unreleased at the time) album *The Bends*. I was accosted at the festival by a crazy Danish girl who kept following me and commenting upon my new James t-shirt which was light blue in colour and had half a daisy on the front and the words "Laid Back" emblazoned on the reverse. I was never overly keen on the shirt to be honest, there was no real shape to it and it hung on my skinny frame like a sheet on a clothes horse. The Danish girl just wouldn't bugger off though and she followed me for absolutely ages in a stalker like manner even when I ignored her every word which in retrospect was quite rude of me, she obviously just wanted to be friends with me, I think she did anyway, there was lots of staring going on. If truth be told I just felt very self conscious as my face was covered in large pus monsters from the pox that I was really suffering with. (They were everywhere, and I really do mean everywhere.)

Plastered around the arena were a number of posters advertising bands and their new albums, and there, just to confuse me was one for the new James album which had been rechristened as *Wah Wah* instead of *Frequency Dip*. I was annoyed at the name change, it seemed to lack a certain something; I didn't even know what the title meant. It just sounded silly. The rest of the festival passed by in a bit of a blur and on the return journey home we watched *Hercules in New York* on the coach, what a film. On the 29th August I ran into town and headed towards Mix Music and picked up a cassette version of the new James album. From what I could tell it was a joint album between the band and Brian Eno and it promised "23 *compositions*" for my listening delight. I headed back home, well I actually headed back to my sisters house as that's where I was still living after moving out of home for the tenth time in as many months. I inserted the tape into my stereo that was housed in my loft room, I hit the play button very hard indeed and quickly grabbed a glass of pop and took an almighty slurp from it.

A few moments of tape hiss passed by before the first track 'Hammer Strings' wound its way out of the speakers like a ghostly snake with what appeared to be something like a choir boys vocal warm up, synths and percussion moaned and ticked along drawing me in before a trembling, tiny little guitar line made its presence known to me. It was an astonishing start to the album. 'Pressures On' sounded like a proper song, beautiful, haunting yet uplifting in every aspect. 'Jam J' then kicked in, the song was now as familiar to me as the rest of James' back catalogue that I'd come to know and love. The next song 'Frequency Dip' sounded like a bit of a mess though, I just had the feeling that it could have been something much more worthwhile if the band had worked it some more but the very essence of *Wah Wah* was to capture a free spirit with minimal tinkering regarding the production and mixing. 'Lay the Law Down' came and went in less than a minute. Had the song been entirely instrumental then I'm sure it would have been used on as many TV programmes just like the gorgeous 'Hoppipolla' by the Icelandic band Sigur Ros. I knew that 'Burn the Cat' wouldn't offend too many animal lovers, It was just a rather brilliant organic piece of music that meandered this way and that, initially subtle and understated before the shipping forecast bizarrely made itself known. 'Maria' was a song that I'd initially heard on the Alton Towers broadcast a couple of years prior as well as on the acoustic tour in Leeds but the *Wah Wah* version just sounded plain evil, I wasn't sure whether I liked it or not. 'Low Clouds' sounded like you were stood on the peak of Cader Idris in Snowdonia with the clouds scraping the top of your head. 'Building a Fire' was another mood piece, acoustic guitars gently being plucked, Marks keyboard swirled overhead whilst Tim kept the lyrics to a minimum before 'Gospel Oak' launched itself forward with much gusto, Mark again took the lead throughout the songs 2:48 lifespan. 'DVV' was a minutes worth of filler, it didn't really go anywhere in particular but maybe that was the point as it ended the first side of the cassette version of the album.

I ejected the tape and for the first time since I'd been a fan of the band I'd not felt either let down or disappointed by what I'd listened to. I turned the tape over and hit the play button again in a rather aggressive manner. The confusingly titled 'Say Say Something' initially made the hairs stand up on the back of my neck, its joyful trajectory kept on travelling onwards and upwards, Saul's violin sounded like the most life affirming piece of string playing that I'd ever heard before the song disappeared over the horizon and out of my sight and hearing, if such a thing is actually possible. The gorgeous 'Rhythmic Dreams' had a country feel to it and the percussion throughout was simply sublime. 'Dead Man' was not a song. I'm not sure what it was to be honest. It's possibly the sound that accompanies something drifting down a Pacific abyss, bumping and scraping against the sharp sides until it reached the end of its long, black, cold lonely journey.

'Rain Whistling' rattled along; again it sounded like a non-song, beautiful, melodic and rather soothing in its entirety. 'Basic Brian' had a bubbling electronic rhythm throughout; again I had the feeling that if the song had been held back like 'Pressures On' for a 'proper album' then it could have been a centre piece for the said album in question. Another version of 'Low Clouds' aired although it was shorter than the first version and then it was the simply delightful 'Bottom of the Well'. Oh the joy it must have been to have been stood in the studio whilst the band jammed away and came up with this unearthly piece of music. The Glastonbury monster 'Honest Joe' blasted its way out the stereo, except it was nowhere near as good as the version that was performed on stage in June but it still managed to sound a thousand times better than all of the songs in that week's Top Forty put together.

'Arabic Agony' was another unsettling piece of music that must have scared the musicians who were spontaneously playing it, Tim sounded tired and resigned as if he'd been hung, drawn and quartered but had lived to tell the tale before a familiar song began called 'Tomorrow', I recognised it as the "especially written for Radio One" song from the 'James Day' the September before. It's wonderful, frantic pace brought tears to my eyes for some reason or other, it sounded like James were saying goodbye to me, I wasn't sure why but that was how I felt upon listening to it. The penultimate track was called 'Laughter'; it was simply a recording of Tim laughing hysterically for some unknown reason. Its simplicity and lightness made me smile bearing in mind how serious the album has sounded up to that point and then the final song 'Sayonara' played out the album proper. It really was James saying goodbye to something which I'll return to later.

Two words sprang to mind regarding the album. One of them was 'Industrial' although not as full on as Nine Inch Nails ever were but it's there draped over the instruments and machinery throughout. The other word was 'ambient', of course Mr Eno was involved in the project so what did I really expect? It was the first James album that I genuinely loved upon its first listen and it spent an awful long time hibernating inside the warmth of my stereo slowly losing its recorded quality due to being overplayed. I lent the tape to Steve, he was really getting into ambient music at the time although I wouldn't say he was a connoisseur of the genre, for him it was stuff like The KLF and The Orb but he really dug the album and described it as an "ambient pop masterpiece". I couldn't have agreed more. *Wah Wah* influenced Steve into buying an album which featured collaborations from Robert Fripp and Alex Paterson called *FFWD* and I ended up buying a copy of the album myself. It really was a world away from *Parklife*.

Wah Wah received positive if somewhat baffled reviews across the board. I mean, the NME gave it a good review so something was definitely amiss. Another review on Ceefax mentioned that Tim had said that he wanted to experiment with dance music; I shuddered to the very core of my soul at the thought of such lunacy! I dreaded to think what a dance version of James would have sounded like? Could you imagine what a dance version of 'Sit Down' would have sounded like I thought to myself! Ha, but of course, such a thing was unimaginable back in 1994 and I knew that James would never, ever commit a mortal sin like that. Then something rather amazing happened. Well, it wasn't that amazing; I'd simply given in and decided that I was going to buy a new stereo which meant that I'd finally own a Compact Disc Player. At long last I'd be able to listen to the James interview disc I had bought nearly eighteen months earlier in London. I popped into town on a cold October morning with Gavin who I'd reconnected with to find a half decent stereo, he was a bit more clued up than I was regarding the spec of electrical products and I ended up buying a fairly basic but practical midi system for £180.00.

I'd been given the 'Jam J/Say Something' single by Steve and that was the first thing that that was played on the stereo, it sounded amazing, the clarity of the song took my breath away. To think that I'd been a pro-cassette anti-Compact Disc Luddite for so long and there I was listening to a version of 'Jam J' that sounded clearer than it had ever done on my cassette version of *Wah Wah*. The James interview disc was rubbish though, well it wasn't rubbish, it just wasn't very exciting and it sounded like it had been recorded in the middle of a building site. I went back into town the following day and bought my first compact disc proper in the form of Nirvana's unplugged performance from the previous year and it was a wonderful piece of music that annoyingly hinted at what might have been if Kurt hadn't committed his final desperate act.

And that would be that, for a while at least. It was the end of a chapter in the James story in more ways than one. The next time I'd hear any new James material some major changes would have taken place, gone would be guitarist Larry Gott who could only ever be described as a key member of the band and instead Adrian Oxall would take his place, although not in a spiritual sense of course. Larry would leave during a difficult time in the James story and he'd end up becoming a furniture maker for a while. However, Larry doesn't disappear from the James story completely.....

And as for me, strange times were definitely ahead.

Escapism

1995

Steve and I were both working in ultra crappy jobs after finishing college and there was nothing of any interest at all going on in the town where we lived, we used to call the people that we'd gone to school with 'The No Hopers', they used to frequent the same bars and clubs week in week out, they all dressed the same, drank the same lager and smoked the same brand of cigarettes as each other. No ambition at all. I really felt like a fish out of water, I knew I had to escape my home town and see a bit of the world to broaden my horizons otherwise I'd have been totally and utterly doomed. The live music scene in our town was dire to say the least; the only ray of sunshine was when Jason Feddy played his regular slot on a Sunday night at Jimmy's night club. A nice enough guy Jason, he always performed a spurned lover's song called 'Bitch' as his encore. I therefore decided upon a return to Israel and I managed to persuade Steve that it would be an exceptionally good idea if he went along with me; I thought the heat would also toughen up his feet for future live events.

I was working as an untrained chef in a well-respected and extremely posh restaurant which was often filled with celebs lining their gluttonous stomachs with the food I was making, burning and undercooking. Seriously, I could burn the water upon request, not that this was requested very often of course, that would have been too weird. My unwashed greenfly coated salad that was angrily returned to the kitchen by my raging boss is probably still talked about at the establishment some fifteen years or so later. The salad had been for a Leeds United football player who immediately got up and walked out of the restaurant in absolute disgust. The best thing about working in the kitchen was the grease coated stereo and I'd often create searing compilation tapes at home to create a good vibe in the busy kitchen. More often than not my music was either turned off or lowered in volume by my colleagues including the guy who ran the place who had lots of personal issues relating to the fact that he was a bit of a toad. My colleagues' just didn't get or like Nine Inch Nails, Black Sheep or Blur, the philistines. I'd played *Stutter* and *Strip Mine* a number of times and the albums had gone down like torpedoed cargo ships.

Thankfully one of the lads Nigel who I worked with liked my taste in music. Nigel was only four and a half foot tall, he was a bit of an old school punk, you know, proper punk music not like that Good Charlotte cack that the kids listen to these days, or is it me who's out of touch with what the kids are listening to? His height or rather the lack of it presented a few issues in the kitchen, he struggled to reach the cupboards to acquire ingredients and any food he was cooking on the back hobs often ended up being burnt. Well, I managed to tune Nigel into James as like the majority of Joe Public he only knew 'the hits'. (I've used a plural on purpose just to remind you that it wasn't all about 'Sit Down'). I offered to compile him a compilation tape, a 'Best Of James' which he became rather excited about and he started drooling at the prospect, it was quite an unsettling sight that remains with me to this day. I can't remember the actual running of the compilation that I lovingly crafted at home using a top quality TDK cassette but I do remember that it started with 'Heavens', 'Laid' and 'Sit Down'. I know that 'Born of Frustration' was definitely buried on it somewhere and the gap on the end of side one was filled up with 'Laughter' which repeated itself a few times over.

Nigel loved it. And best of all it was on repeat on the kitchen stereo. The rest of the chefs, waiters and waitresses were all forced into listening to James and plenty of my other colleagues ended up copying the compilation tape I'd created by using the stereos double cassette deck. It seemed as if every time I was working somebody would approach me and say, "Can I copy that James tape of yours?" I was of course only too happy to oblige.

Steve and I saved up enough cash to pay for return flights to Israel with a bit of spare dosh left over for the acquisition of ale and other treats. A few days before I was due to leave the country I asked Nigel if I could borrow the tape to copy it for myself. I didn't really have time to sift through my cassettes and start compiling a version for myself. I was a bit lazy though and I never actually got around to copying it, so I took Nigel's tape with me on my second trip to Israel in April 1995 which looking back was a bit of a mean thing to do. Sorry Nigel.

Like my first trip to Israel I'd foolishly only brought a few albums which consisted of *Niggamortis* by Gravediggaz, *Maxinquaye* by Tricky and a couple of other compilation tapes that I'd dug out from my cupboard back home. Steve had been much cannier than myself and had brought at least a dozen compilation tapes of I have to say varying quality. There was way too much dodgy stuff from the '80's' in my opinion. We settled down into the Kibbutz lifestyle fairly quickly and made friends with pretty much everyone there; we were the only two from the UK as the kibbutz had officially banned any Brits after a bunch of them had trashed the place the year before. Arson had been included in their drunken frivolous activities. Steve and I had managed to sneak on due to a clerical error in the kibbutz office in Tel Aviv. Now, I'm not sure if you know how life is for a volunteer on a kibbutz but it was pretty much like this. Up for work in the early hours, finish in the early afternoon and then chill out for the rest of the day. We'd do this for 6 days of the week with Saturday being our one day off. There was way too much alcohol being drunk, I'm sure my liver had aged ten years by the time I'd returned to the UK in October 1995.

As there was a good deal of time spent relaxing in the sunshine the volunteers including myself ended up listening to a lot of music. Now, as I'd been to a kibbutz before I knew it was imperative to bring a cheap, light stereo so that Steve and I could monopolise the kibbutz playlist without being forced into listening to someone else's god awful music. It was a little bit selfish really, but there you go and I have to say that people really benefited from it, our taste in music would ultimately make them better citizens of Planet Earth. Steve and I were sat having a few beers, actually a lot of beers as well as jugs of vodka and coke with a few Irish lads, good lads they were too, not really interested in U2 either as I incorrectly presumed ALL Irish people only ever listened to U2 or Daniel O'Donnell. These lads were instead besotted with The Pogues and Christy Moore.

Some of the other kibbutz volunteers of varying nationalities were also present and conversing in English, I have to say that I'm always very impressed with other nationalities mastery of speaking in my own language; it makes conversation a tad easier whilst at the same time it makes me feel rather ignorant and silly. I once asked a French person,

"Parlez Vous Francais?"

"Yes, I speak very good French thank you, I'm French".

I casually popped the slightly greasy and sticky from the kitchen James compilation tape into the player and pressed play. 'Heavens' started up; no one commented upon the song, the merry volunteers carried on as they had been moments before. The song finished and then 'Laid' began. The good humoured song bopped along, familiar to Steve and me of course but not to anybody else. It was then that I noticed that Michael, a lad from Cork was silently staring at the stereo.

"Jesus Christ, who's this?" he said.

"Er, it's 'James'" I replied nervously.

"Jeeessuuss, its feckin' amazin'!" exclaimed Michael and because of his reaction the other volunteer's attention was caught.

"Who the feck is James?" asked Tony, another one of the lad's from Cork.

I explained to the captivated audience that 'James' was a band from Manchester that had been knocking about for ages, of course none of the kibbutz volunteers had ever heard of them.

"Ah, he's got a grand voice that James fella hasn't he!" another Irish voice piped up.

I tried to explain that James was not a person but a band, but it really was a case of "lost in translation" when it came to explaining this to some of the other volunteers, particularly the Swiss and the Venezuelan volunteers for some reason or other. The song finished. Michael spoke.

"Jesus, seriously, that's one of the best songs I've heard in my entire life! Can I put it on again?"

"Course you can mate" I replied enjoying the moment.

Michael then began the rather annoying task of trying to find the exact start of the song, not rewinding enough, fast forwarding too much and rewinding again until the familiar opening bars of 'Laid' stirred up once more. Michael stood up; the expression on his face gave the appearance that he was trying to stare the stereo out. I'm quite sure he could actually see the music pouring out of the speakers; he stood with one hand covering his mouth and the other one on his hip, gently swaying to the music. I was rather touched yet at the same time I found the scene to be highly amusing. The song finished and Michael walked away from the rest of the group, both hands on the top of his head before returning a minute or so later just as 'Sit Down' was finishing. He was more composed but he looked fidgety and rather clammy.

"Tell me, is there more like this?" he asked me with the look of a desperate crack addict in his eyes.

"Oh yes Michael, there's more, lots more".

"Good, good" he replied rubbing his mouth with the back of his hand whilst he appeared to be staring at something distant and unobservable to the rest of the group. The rest of the volunteers listened intently and asked me various questions relating to the magnificently compiled masterpiece (that I'd lovingly put together some time back for Nigel and then stole back from him).

The tape soon became the talk of the kibbutz, volunteers asked me if they could listen to it and I was only too happy to oblige. Of course other music was also listened to on the kibbutz otherwise it would have started to have gotten a bit weird, a bit like a cult, our very own 'Waco' of James obsessed international party goers and banana pickers. On the kibbutz there was a building known as 'The Pub', it was actually a fairly dilapidated building that housed a make shift bar constructed out of a load of old crates and a broken door, in the room adjacent was a rather knackered pool table. Playing a game of pool was akin to Crown Green Bowling. One of the Venezuelan volunteers used to DJ in the pub every Friday night, I'm being rather generous when I used the term DJ because all he ever did was play ABBA, Boney M and Scat Man Joe.

However, the majority of the kibbutz volunteers were well into the second rate disco and they lapped up the same set of songs week after bloody week. I'd had enough. One day I spoke to one of the Israelis who used to chaperone the volunteers and I asked if it would be okay if I had a go at sorting out the music that night. He agreed and I spent the remainder of the afternoon gathering as much "good music" as I possibly could from various sources. That night changed everyone for ever, well; I like to think it did. Gone was the 70s disco and instead the place rocked with the finest indie, dance, rock, rap and metal that had ever been heard south of The Golan Heights (a mountainous range in the north of the country).

Of course, a number of James songs were played, just the hits mind you but when 'Laid' was played I honestly thought the pub was in danger of collapsing! It was a mêlée, rougher than when I'd played Nirvana's 'Teen Spirit'. I thought Michael was literally going to punch someone out from sheer over excitement and jubilation. He just kept shouting "YES, YES, YES" over and over. Later on I thought I'd try and play a James song that wouldn't be considered as a typical dance number so I dropped in 'Born of Frustration' and although it never received quite the same reaction as 'Laid' it went down a storm, the Israeli kibbutz chaperone entered the bar and he immediately started banging his head aggressively to the song before grabbing a beer and coming across to the DJ booth.

"Hey! Great music!! I love this song by 'The James', (he also called Blur 'The Blur') I've got a tape in my apartment that a British girl gave me last year, it's got this this song on it" he shouted at me whilst pointing his finger into my face although not in an unfriendly manner of course. We shook hands, mutual respect shared between the two nationalities. The final icing on the cake was when I played 'Sit Down' later that night and everybody sat down, holding hands whilst swaying to the song, beer and cigarette ash was spilt and dropped whilst I just stood behind the DJ booth, my hands raised towards the ceiling, I knew that I was doing my bit for The Peace Movement, bringing people together from all walks of life, countries and territories all though the power of a song by my favourite band.

The rest of the summer was spent picking bananas, up at 04:00 in the morning and finishing before the midday sun burnt us to a crisp. It was hard graft but great fun all the same. Like the other volunteers I waited patiently for mail to arrive from back home, the odd letter would arrive informing me what was happening, the temperature in the UK had been hotter than in Israel, I'd annoyingly decided to travel to the Middle East in the one year that the weather back home had been raging hot like the summer of 1976. A British kibbutz volunteer who'd returned to the UK posted an album by Shaun Ryder's new band Black Grape to me. *It's Great When Your Straight ... Yeah!* featured a couple of good tunes on it but overall it wasn't really that great or straight. The sample of Adolf Hitler featured on the lead single 'Reverend Black Grape' caused some of the German volunteers including a German girlfriend of mine to become very upset indeed.

Other people back home sometimes posted compilation tapes out to us including Richard who was at university; his tape included the wonderful 'Common People' by Pulp as well as some other second division indie schmindie rubbish. Steve's brother sent him a copy of the debut album by Supergrass and a newspaper article on the battle between Blur and Oasis. He also included a compilation tape with their two latest singles on it. The first time I heard 'Country House' I thought it was easily one of the worst songs I'd ever heard. I was pretty disgusted and as for the Oasis track, well it wasn't much better. Included on the cassette were a few live tracks including tracks by The Prodigy and Pulp who were beginning to really hit it off big time, the tracks were live recordings from Glastonbury 1995 and they sounded pretty amazing.

"Ah, there's something here for you!" Steve said to me.

He handed me a rather small cut out article from a music magazine, the title of the article had me momentarily at least holding my breath.

"James Deny Split Rumours".

My bottom lip wobbled and my forehead developed beads of sweat, an unholy stench made its presence known from the lower part of my body. I read and reread the article a number of times. To paraphrase the article it stated that James denied that they were about to split due to a number of personal and financial circumstances that had apparently arisen, details regarding the tribulations the band had been experiencing was lacking. The end of the article mentioned James would return with a new album in 1996 which promised to feature *"Industrial Jungle".*

Now this was good if slightly surprising news. I wasn't aware that there had been some issues going on behind closed doors, but again, it was 1995, the internet wasn't in full flow and sources of information were hard to come by, obviously I was overseas picking bananas and being shouted at and bullied by the Israelis but the mention of *"Industrial Jungle"* really confused me and I assumed that it was obviously a tongue in cheek gesture only. I'd eventually be proven wrong though.

I know for a fact that a large number of kibbutz volunteers copied my James compilation tape during the six months I was there, people from all around the world including South Africa, Canada, South Korea, Australia, Venezuela and various European countries. When it was finally time to leave and return home I gave the Irish lads the original tape as a goodbye present.

I arrived back home in October 1995, it was a massive culture shock to end up back at my mums house, with no job and little in the way of any future plans. I felt quite fed up and depressed not helped by the fact that when I did acquire a job it was at an army base. I spent the majority of the time wearing hideous blue overalls that were two sizes too big for me whilst I continuously mopped the floor which remained dirty no matter how much I pushed that mop around. I sent the Irish lads another James compilation tape that I'd complied for them which included The Sabres of Paradise remix of Jam J. From their written response they apparently liked it, but probably not quite as much as the 'hits and misses' compilation that had been the soundtrack to the best summer of our lives up until then. 1995 had been a rather quiet year on the James front for me at least and I was curious to see what the following year would bring. A new James album was apparently on the way and as Elvis Presley might have said "I was a bit suspicious".

Footnote: I was in an electrical store during the latter stage of 1995 when I bumped into John Dope and his wife. They were buying a new kettle. It looked rather nice. Jut thought I'd share that with you.

Jealousy and mind games

1995/1996

Vicky was a rather attractive and at times quite a funny girl I'd met on New Years Eve 1995. Steve and I had gone out that evening to celebrate the New Year and of course to try and "get lucky with the ladies" even if 99% of the time this never happened and we had to make do with leaving the night club empty handed and making a detour via a filthy kebab shop. I was living out 'How Soon Is Now' by The Smiths except I didn't want die prematurely. The nightclub was pretty shady with over priced beer and a terrible DJ, it really was a dive, full of attitude. 'The No Hopers' frequented the place, it really made me feel like a bit of a failure for returning to my home town. On one occasion a bespectacled lad threatened to smash my face in when I apparently had the gall to compliment him for wearing an Oasis t-shirt. Rather predictably the DJ would play 'Sit Down' and 'It's Raining Men' by The Weather Girls, the latter of which is easily my most detested song of all time.

After several pints of tasteless lager Steve and I somehow managed to strike up conversation with Vicky and her attractive friend Anna who was originally from Bermuda, we hit it off straight away to be honest, Vicky was loud, had a dirty laugh and smoked Marlboro Lights cigarettes and she could neck pints of lager pretty well too. One of the first things she said to me was,

"Do you like music?"

My eyes lit up.

I told her that yes; I quite liked music.

"So, who do you prefer then, Blur or Oasis?" she asked in an over excited manner before taking an almighty gulp of lager which was so large it drained the full glass by half. I paused ... I knew that my response could have a consequential bearing on the rest of the evening.

"Er, Blur" I said rather cagily.

I knew the country had been split in half by the over hyped events of the previous summer, whilst I'd been stomping about the Middle East fist fights had taken place between Blur and Oasis fans, it was like football hooliganism had spilled out onto the indie dance floor. Not that I thought that Vicky and I would end up wrestling each other to the floor or anything, but if I gave her what she perceived as the wrong answer I could end up with a pint of lager over my head.

"ARRGGGH!!!! I ABSOLUTELY LOVE BLUR!!!!!" she shrieked almost falling off her stool in excitement.

I breathed a huge sigh of relief and untensed when I realised I wasn't going to end up being pushed off my stool by her or having beer chucked over me. We gabbed on for ages about how brilliant Blur were, what their best B-sides were etc.

"Hey, do you remember (name removed for legal protection)?" she asked me in a rather excited manner.

Indeed I did remember (name removed for legal protection). He'd been quite a successful recording artist in the 1980's and my sister had quite a few of his records.

"Well, he's my uncle!" she said to me smugly before downing the rest of her pint in a mighty single slurp.

I was very impressed; she then continued to yak on about him for ages regarding what he was doing musically whilst I tried to retain the information for any prospective pub quizzes that I might possibly partake in in the near future.

It was now my turn for questions.

"Er, do you like James?" I asked her. Her brow furrowed. Even before she replied I knew exactly what she was going to say.

"Who's he?"

"It's not a 'he', it's a band, yer know, 'Sit Down', 'Born of Frustration'?" I said to her with some annoyance although I hoped she didn't pick up on it too much (despite my furrowed brow and disheartened expression).

"Oh, yes, them. Err, I can't stand them to be honest" she said looking quite embarrassed whilst lighting up a cigarette.

Well, that could or really should have been it! I was tempted to go swiftly to the toilet and then sneak out of the pub and go home but I liked her and I thought that you know, well we can't all like the same bands or stuff otherwise the world would be a rather boring place, right? Subconsciously I knew that I had to help this young lady in a similar way to how I'd helped and cured the kibbutz volunteers. I needed to show her what she was missing, ENLIGHTENMENT and I would be the one to help her experience it. I internally heard myself go "Mwoah-ha-ha-ha-ha-ha" in a big booming Biblical voice at the very thought of me changing her distorted way of thinking. I then proceeded to use the world's worst chat up line on her.

"Err, I've just bought a great new stereo. Do you fancy coming around at some point and having a look at it?"

Vicky just laughed.

Vicky and I ended up going out together, by that I mean as girlfriend and boyfriend and we struggled for nearly two years together. It was great fun as well as being extremely stressful due to her volatile temper and moodiness. She was pretty hot headed and cantankerous and we bickered with each most of the time. She was also extremely possessive and very jealous regarding me having any kind of life that didn't directly involve her. I started to lose touch with friends such as Charles, Steve and Richard. However, our love for music kept things on an even enough keel; we both had quite similar interests and taste in music, except of course when it came to James. I introduced her to some of James' back catalogue. She was polite enough about it but I knew that it wasn't really doing anything for her. Apart from being in love with Blur Vicky was into other bands such as Marion, Elastica, Echobelly, Mantaray, Sleeper and Smudge. Her comments regarding James' early material was,

"It just sounds so tinny and thin".

I knew what she meant. When your favourite album is Elastica's debut *Elastica* then 'Skullduggery' and 'What For?' aren't really going to float your boat. Remember this, I found most of James' back catalogue to be really hard work and not entirely immediate so trying to influence a hot headed eighteen year old 'indie chick' into the delights of *Stutter* and *Strip Mine* was going to be very hard work indeed. She quite liked 'Don't Wait That Long' though which I'd rather predictably included on a compilation tape for her, and she didn't mind 'Lose Control' either but sadly that was about it.

As for James, well, I initially didn't have any real inkling into what was going on with them but that changed later on in the year when I read that Tim Booth would be releasing an album with Bernard Butler the ex-guitarist from Suede and Angelo Badalamenti famed for his work on the *Twin Peaks* and *Blue Velvet* soundtracks. A single was going to be released called 'I Believe'. Well, I was fairly excited, okay, so it wasn't new James material per se but it was better than nothing. But then I heard the single on Radio One and I was seriously underwhelmed by it. It was pleasant enough, just not very exciting, at least it wasn't for me. I managed to see Tim perform 'I Believe' on the ITV programme *This Morning*. I was shocked to see that his lovely long curly locks of hair had been aggressively sheared off. Gone was the manic dancing I'd come to know and love and instead this skinny looking man simply swayed in time to the music which was a perfectly appropriate dance as the song was an unexcited mid tempo number. I decided to pop into Mix Music in town and buy the compact disc single anyway and listened to it a fair bit in the bedsit I was living in at the time. The song certainly grew on me but that was about it really. Still, I looked forward to the release of the album entitled *Booth and the Bad Angel*, I was sure I would buy it on the day of release. I didn't though, I found the album for sale in Mix Music; picked it up and examined the cover of the album. A semi-nude Tim Booth cheerily gazed from behind the back of a chair where a Boris Karloff lookalike sat looking rather regal and grand; I came to the logical conclusion that the older man was 'The Bad Angel' aka Angelo. I've no idea why I didn't buy it, maybe I just didn't have the money at the time but I returned it to the shelf and left the shop with a reduced in price Supergrass single instead.

Booth and the Bad Angel received some good reviews with the odd exception here and there, particularly in the 'cool magazines' such as the weeklies. A couple of months later I bought a compilation album from Mix Music called *Wired* which consisted of a number of varying in quality 'electronica' tracks. 'Electronica' the genre was doing big business on both sides of the Atlantic due to the critical and commercial success of artists such as The Chemical Brothers, The Prodigy, Oribital and err, Fluke. The second disc had a *Booth and the Bad Angel* track on it called 'Dance of the Bad Angel'. I was intrigued, was the 'Bad Angel' material wildly different from the 'I Believe' single then? I suddenly had a vision, yes, a vision of Tim yodelling over big slamming beats, screaming synths and squelching 303's. But no, disappointingly upon listening to the song for the first time I was even more underwhelmed than I'd been with 'I Believe'.

The remainder of the year was spent listening to some turgid mid-period 'Brit Pop'. I was still at a loss as to why everybody thought that the second Oasis album *(What's The Story) Morning Glory?* was so brilliant. It clearly wasn't a patch on *Definitely Maybe* yet people had bought it in droves. Blur had released their fourth album *The Great Escape* whilst I'd been in Israel and their star didn't appear to be shining as brightly as it had around the *Parklife* period, however, I thought *The Great Escape* was a fine album although it sounded much better on shuffle mode on the stereo because the sequencing on the album was pretty poor as far as I was concerned. Bands that I was really starting to get into included the Eels and the Manic Street Preachers. Vicky and I went to see The Manics at the Town and Country Club in Leeds where I'd seen James perform for the first time, it brought back a lot of very happy memories of that cold December evening back in 1992 and I annoyed Vicky by wittering on about it for the majority of the evening. And as for the Eels, we used to listen to them in a theatre bar in town where the guy behind the bar had their debut album *Beautiful Freak* on heavy rotation, a truly wonderful album featuring one of the greatest singles of all time in the form of 'Novocaine for the Soul'.

So, due to a lack of new material, being wrapped up in a rather intense relationship and being flooded with constant new musical material

James had started to slip away from my consciousness. I didn't always get or fully understand James but I knew that they certainly reflected a lot in the way I thought and my outlook on life in general. I really wasn't an obsessive fan of James although to the untrained eye I may have come across a bit like one that but I wasn't really, I just loved the band very much indeed. As mentioned much earlier, I felt the opening lyrics to 'Sound' could have been written especially for me. Vicky naturally groaned one day when I said to her,

"I feel I can really relate to the band".

"God, I hate it when people make comments like that!" she snapped making me feel small and insecure in the process. I tried to make my point clearer by saying,

"What I mean is that James are capable of moments of pure brilliance but they're always out of time with everything and everyone else around them, just like me".

She just rolled her eyes.

During the summer of 1996 I headed back to the Reading Festival this time with Vicky in tow. It was a weekend spent mainly arguing with one another and waiting patiently for The Stone Roses appearance on the Sunday evening. Of course, I won't go into too much detail about The Stone Roses performance here, it's been documented to death already but I'll say something that may cause some people to think I'm quite mad. I actually really, really enjoyed their performance on that cold Sunday night! Okay, so my eyes were filled with tears through sheer embarrassment as they lumbered through 'I am the Resurrection' especially when Ian Brown struggled to hit a couple of the right notes. However, I still think that they blew the rest of the bands off stage that played there that weekend though. The other marvellous thing about the weekend was that I wasn't attacked by any Big Issue sellers either.

Autumn came along and visited us. I was working in a cash and carry and I would say for my sins, but actually it was a great laugh if somewhat poorly paid, but at least there was no chance that I was going to poison anybody with a dodgy green salad or end up being sliced and diced by a stray Stanley Knife blade. Towards the tail end of 1996 I finally discovered some movement on the James front. I'd bought a copy of the NME that November during a lunch break from work and I almost wet myself when I found an article about the band. The article stated that James were going to release a new single entitled 'She's A Star' in early February of 1997 as well as a brand new album entitled *Whiplash* and to top it all off a tour. Tim stated the band had made a conscious break from one another to concentrate on other projects such as the Bad Angel album and erecting conservatories. Tim then continued to voice his disappointment and hurt regarding the reaction the two previous James albums had been met with.

I couldn't wait to tell Vicky! She was bound to be just as excited as I was at the prospect of hearing the new album and going to see the band live, right? Of course I was utterly wrong. Vicky, being Vicky just acted indifferent and gave a rather bored sounding "Oh" at the news. I really felt quite hurt, had it have been the other way around regarding one of her favourite bands then I would have been over the moon for her. Looking back now I think that she held a weird kind of jealousy regarding my passion for something that didn't revolve around her. On a cold and blustery Saturday afternoon we both travelled by train together to Leeds so that we could buy tickets for the gig direct from the venue. All was fine until we arrived at the box office, then she started to act strange.

"Actually, you go, I'm really not too fussed about seeing them, don't worry about me!" she said with a big smile upon her face, her usual act of playing mind games with me had begun.

"But, you said you'd go with me! I'm not going by myself! Please, come on, don't do this to me" I stammered.

"No, no, you go. I'm not too bothered really".

"Look, I'm either going with you or not at all" I said to her quite sternly.

"Oh, okay, well let's go home then" Vicky said and then she quickly walked away from the box office and headed back down the street in the direction of the train station.

I couldn't believe it. I was shocked, shell shocked even, I couldn't understand why she was acting the way she was. I really couldn't figure out her agenda. She knew how much James meant to me and there she was acting quite frankly like a complete and utter bitch to me. Sadly I acted like a pathetic little lap dog and I started to follow her down the road before I eventually caught up with her and we walked along in silence. I was in no mood for any kind of conversation; I was seething, raging in fact and she knew it but she was obviously starting to get off on the fact that she held some kind of control over me as she then started yapping away to me in a bouncy chirpy manner, talking about this and that and ignoring the fact that we'd travelled to Leeds to purposely buy tickets to see my favourite band and now there we were heading home without them. I was seething and a thousand thoughts went through my mind. I should have just bought a ticket for myself like any sensible person would have done and told her to sling her hook, but I was too weak and under her spell. We approached the station doors. She stopped dead in her tracks and turned to face me.

"You know what, I think I'll go to that concert after all" she said to me with a big smile upon her face.

I knew then that it was simply a control issue for her. Things had to be on her terms only; she didn't like the thought of someone else taking the lead, now she'd turned something I loved and was extremely passionate about into something totally focused upon her. I smiled at her pathetically and said "thank you". We turned around and headed back to the venue and bought two tickets to see James, live at the Town and Country Club in Leeds, dated the 12th March 1997. The date sounded so bleak and ominous, I had a bad feeling about that date.

Whiplashed

1997

I was at my sister's house on a rather damp and pathetic January afternoon in 1997 the first time I heard the new James single 'She's a Star'. My sister was in a bit of a foul mood as I'd just broken her door yet again, it was probably about the seventy fifth time. I just couldn't help it; it was like a need, it just didn't feel like a proper visit if the door hadn't incurred some minor or major damage. Like a futuristic robot from the Vega Star System she glided across to the kitchen work top and made us a cup of tea. The kitchen radio was rattling away in the background whilst my two young nieces danced around my feet trying to persuade me to play with their dolls. I hadn't purposefully been listening to the radio and the song was half way through being played by the time that I realised it was James.

From what I'd initially heard I thought it sounded alright, hardly a galactic leap forward but if James had returned with their jested 'Industrial Jungle' new direction then god only knows what the record buying public would have thought. I was pleasantly surprised and pleased with the song and it ended up being on heavy rotation on the radio, it was a big comeback, the first big comeback of the year and interest in the band finally appeared to be at an all-time high. Vicky had also heard the single and commented that it was "okay", which was a huge compliment on her terms but typically non-committal as per usual. This really annoyed the hell out of me and I was sure she was just saying it on purpose to wind me up, paranoia once again gripping me like a vice.

On the 10th February 1997 I walked into town during my lunch break in pursuit of music, forgoing the act of eating any lunch and heading straight towards Mix Music. I pushed open the glass doors as if entering a Wild West Saloon Bar, the shop stereo stopped abruptly, the staff and other shoppers stared at me wondering who the stranger in the red trousers, white shirt, red tie and red jacket was (I was wearing my cash and carry uniform so looked a bit out of place and rather ridiculous). I coolly nodded at them and slowly made my way towards the new release section. I soon found the single; it was hard to miss as there were three different versions of it on sale for £1.99 each. I was obviously going to buy all three versions as they all featured different tracks on them but using a bit of mental arithmetic I figured that the album would only be a few pounds more than buying the entire 'She's a Star' single collection! Some might have considered it to be a bit of a rip off. Still, I was happy to do anything that would help the band achieve a decent chart placing (within reason, I mean I wouldn't re-mortgage a house or undertake a hoax wedding for them no matter how many great songs they've written). I handed over my money and left the shop with the staff and other shoppers still staring at me. I headed home to have a listen during the remainder of my sacrificed lunch break; the excitement was akin to a journey through the Star Gate that featured in *2001: A Space Odyssey*. Terrifying, startling, I was fearful at what I was about to experience.

I entered my cosy little bedsit with its mismatching furniture and dead plants, turned on the stereo and popped in disc one of three. I skipped past the lead song and went straight for the live material which comprised of two live tracks from the Alton Towers gig from five years earlier. 'Johnny Yen' and 'Stutter' still sounded fantastic, big and very loud, it was certainly a reminder for the purchasers of the CD's what a mighty force James were live. The second disc gave me a hell of a shock. 'Chunney Chops' spilled out of the speakers and I almost fell over in surprise. It sounded utterly, utterly fantastic! It wasn't a song as such, it was more of a groove with a cool little keyboard riff throughout and Tim's vocals were distorted by technology. I'm not exaggerating when I tell you that I actually started to run around my bedsit with my arms held out like a child pretending to be an aeroplane whilst shouting loudly in exultation. The noise resulted in the downstairs neighbour complaining and yelling at me to "SHUT UP!!!"

I hoped and prayed that this was the true new direction that the band was heading in and I wondered if this is what they had referred to when they'd mentioned "Industrial Jungle". 'Fishknives' was the next song and bloody hell, James had suddenly gone all Hip-Hop! I liked it, it sounded rather peculiar with quite an odd vocal delivery alongside a phat slammin' beat. The last song was 'Van Gogh's Dog' and once again it was another odd little number. It had some bizarre squeaking sounds throughout that sounded like an alien mouse had invaded the studio during the recording process along with other bizarre sounding machinery noise. I absolutely just loved the warm shimmering guitar towards the back end of the song. After such a high the third disc was definitely a disappointment though, it comprised of a couple of iffy remixes of the title track and another remix of 'Come Home' which had featured on at least nineteen different formats by that point. Ho hum, you can't win them all. When it finished I quickly put 'Chunney Chops' back on and squealed with delight as if I was a little piglet stuck underneath a gate. My back was damp with excitement, breathing was difficult and my right elbow throbbed. To say that I was on a massive high would have been the understatement of the century. That evening Vicky came around to my bedsit, I simply couldn't wait for her to hear the new material, particularly 'Chunney Chops'.

"Seriously, you've got to hear this new James song! It's the greatest thing I've heard in years!" I blurted out to her. She started to laugh at me whilst rolling her eyes as per usual and I nervously pressed play on the stereo. The song came to life and I stood there as proud as a peacock with my sweaty hands placed upon my hips and a huge smile upon my face. Her reaction was,

"Oh. Isn't Eastenders on now?"

I was totally and utterly crestfallen. From the look on my face she knew she'd hurt me and she started to make positive comments about the track but it was too late and she'd dampened my enthusiasm. When

111

the song finished I sadly turned off the stereo and put the television on for her.

The single ended up sneaking into the top ten the following Sunday of release. I was overjoyed; it was a vindication of sorts. Okay, so having three different versions of the same song obviously helped it's position (I think?), but because the single had done so well and had reached the masses the band ended up performing on *Top of the Pops* with Saul playing a silver star shaped guitar. James was suddenly like a musical plague; they appeared to be everywhere and ended up making numerous other television appearances. Vicky watched one of their performances with me on the Saturday night; the band performed a couple of numbers on a TV programme that I can't for the life of me remember the name of which included a slowed down stripped back version of 'Sit Down' with their new guitarist Adrian Oxall playing a cello part. The band wanted to do something a bit different with their best known song and I thought it was great. Vicky's almost predicatable by now response was,

"Well, it's one of those songs isn't it? You can't really do much with it can you?"

It was easily one of the most stupid and nonsensical comments I think I'd ever heard up until that point, why on earth was this girl still trying to piss me off with her attitude towards the band that I loved? Was she that insecure that she actually felt jealous of my affection and interest in the band? It was baffling and kind of unsettling at the same time. And, why was I still going out with her? Was it I who was the insecure one?

A few weeks later I cantered back to Mix Music once again forgoing lunch in pursuit of music, but on this occasion I was at least wearing civilian attire and I hadn't been subjected to having French Fries thrown at me by the mischievous kids outside McDonalds. On this particular occasion I was going to purchase a copy of the new James album *Whiplash*. The album cover like the lead single was a tad freaky as it featured a person; I couldn't really tell if it was a man or a woman with a spooky mask upon their face. I suppose it was kind of sexy if you were into fetish which I wasn't, honestly. I paid my £12.99 and headed back to my bedsit and slammed the compact disc into the stereo. Shaking like a wilting leaf I sat down upon my bed with my chin resting on my hands and I eagerly awaited the results of James' latest harvest.

'Tomorrow', the album opener burst into life, I recognised it immediately as the same song, yes, the very same song from *Wah Wah*. It was a confusing move in my opinion, I started to feel a tad short changed and I'd only listened to the first fifteen seconds of the album. Thankfully the version on *Whiplash* was quite different, it sounded better produced and less rushed, it made the original version feel more like a demo but if I was to say which version I preferred then I'd probably say the version on *Wah Wah*. 'Tomorrow' raced along at breath neck speed until it abruptly and dramatically ended. I was really quite impressed. The next song 'Lost a Friend' on the other hand didn't really get me too excited, it reminded me of 'Baby Face' by U2 and I felt it sounded half-finished.

'Waltzing Along' was a pleasant bluesy sounding number which ambled along in a happy and jaunty manner, it was rather lovely and my face lit up with a huge smile. The lyric, *"be opened by the wonderful"* which repeated throughout the song was simply gorgeous. The lead single 'She's a Star' followed and I skipped past it hungry for what was next. And what was next you may ask? Well, err, you know that I've mentioned *"Industrial Jungle"* a few times? Well the next track 'Greenpeace' was what the band had obviously been referring to when they'd promised *"Industrial Jungle"* nearly two years earlier. The song started off quiet enough, quite haunting in fact until the song raged into life and brutalised my ears. 'Greenpeace' was quite simply a punishing drum and bass track. Tim sang in his often used choir boy's falsetto during the chilling chorus whilst at the same time man and machine battled it out for ultimate supremacy, the song abruptly stopped and collapsed into a haunting and brooding ambience. Tim menacingly dropped in his favourite curse word before the evil sounding rattle built up once more and shook my bedsit to its very foundations. Somewhat surprisingly the guy downstairs didn't shout at me though, he'd apparently left the building thinking that World War Three had just kicked off and I watched him out of the window as he ran down the street holding his backside with his hand. The song sounded as far away from any incarnation of James that I could have ever imagined. I absolutely love it and I knew from its first listen that it would become one of my favourite ever songs. If I'd thought that things couldn't get much better then the next song 'Go to the Bank' shocked me just as much as the previous track had done. It featured a big old stomping beat; samples, loops and of course guitars battled it out whilst Tim deadpanned his way though the song sounding a little bit flat on occasion about the perils and evils of consumerism. In my opinion it was bloody amazing.

'Play Dead' began with a sample of an unknown male declaring that "music depresses me". The track then started up proper, drum machines and synths clattered along until a ferocious albeit brief angry sounding guitar revved into action and then the most beautiful song simply blossomed into life, a swooning yearning number with the most wonderful backbeat and strings throughout, Tim sang his heart out, it sounded incredibly sad, desperate and sincere and my heart was ablaze with absolute joy. 'Avalanche' again sounded nothing like the band I'd come to know and love, it's warm yet bittersweet lyrics leapt out at me, I was totally convinced it would definitely be a single, and in fact it was the song on the album that was going to make them all multi-millionaires. 'Homeboy', was born, lived and died in the blink of an eye. This I have to say is not a criticism, it was a playful up-tempo little number and I was humming along before I even realised it. 'Watering Hole' followed and we were once again back in the land of the strange, its brooding atmosphere consumed me whole, it frightened me, the song sounded threatening particularly when the bass line plummeted from time to time. The final track on the album 'Blue Pastures' was minimalist at its very best and it gave Tim plenty of space to sing with literally nothing more than a bass guitar for company. It was a fine end to what had been the most immediate James album I'd experienced so far.

Finally, apart from Wah Wah I'd heard a James album that I'd genuinely loved upon its first listen and the weird stuff such as 'Greenpeace', 'Go to the Bank' and 'Watering Hole' were the songs that

I'd end up listening to the most. I called around to see Vicky later in the evening with the album in hand of course. She could see how excited I was and she turned on her dad's rather grand stereo and told me that I could put the album on. I was trembling with excitement, she obviously picked up on this and told me to chill out somewhat. The album began to play and I almost passed out from holding my breath in expectation to what she thought of it. And, guess what? She loved it! Genuinely, she really loved it, particularly the weird songs! "Oooh, I'm liking this!" she said as 'Go to the Bank' stomped out of the speakers and she played it three times in a row until her mum knocked on the door and told her off as the thudding bass was clearly scaring the dog and making it whimper. In fact, she pretty much liked the entire album and she even said she'd probably buy a copy of her own.

Whiplash received what could only be described as 'mixed reviews', anything else would have surprised me, James were always receiving 'mixed reviews'. Several reviews commented on the albums lack of coherence and flow, one commented that it should have been called *Mishmash*. To me, the album was nothing but a resounding success, everything I'd have hoped for from James. Okay, it did feel a little bit raggedy in parts and it didn't flow fantastically well either and I was quite sure that the majority of the hardcore James fans were going to hate the awkward stuff too. However, I knew that when James ended up playing any of the *Whiplash* material live then it was going to sound nothing less than incredible. *Whiplash* crashed into the top ten at a respectable number nine position, obviously not as good as their last few releases but the passage of time had flowed since then and an awful lot of water had passed under the bridge both musically and culturally.

12th March 1997. Vicky and I set off to Leeds to see James; it was going to be the third time that I'd seen them and her first. I asked Steve and Richard if they were interested in attending, Steve declined, and Richard had pulled a face and said,

"Well, if I was to go then I'd probably just stand at the back and get stoned". I finished work extra early that day and Vicky did the same. I really wanted to make sure that we were stood by the barrier directly in front of Tim's microphone. The doors were due to open at 19:00 but we arrived a bit earlier at 17:00, first in the queue. I was surprised, I thought we'd be somewhere down a long line of people who'd already be waiting there. I became paranoid as hell, I considered the possibility that the gig hadn't sold out and the bands popularity had diminished. It wasn't until about an hour into our wait that people started to turn up, all polite smiles and nods of the head but nobody really engaged in any conversation with us apart from a guy who sold me a copy of the James fanzine called *A Change of Scenery*. An expectant atmosphere brewed up, ticket touts repeatedly asked if anyone had tickets to sell or need and a few people bought tickets at over inflated prices from them. At 19:00 the venue doors opened, we handed our tickets over to the security bods and entered the building. I felt honoured to be the first person through the door on the first night of the first James tour in a number of years. We walked in; I remember looking at some of the posters for up and coming shows at the Town and Country Club before casually sauntering over towards the barrier and securing the places where I'd wanted us to, right in front of Tim's microphone.

We stood and waited patiently, my heart pounded the whole time, conversation between the two of us was kept to a minimum although now and again I'd pipe up with another fact about the band. Vicky replied with,

"Yes, I know, you've told me a hundred times already", or "really?" which she said in a polite but bored manner. There were two support acts that night, Hard Body, (rubbish) and Silver Sun (ditto). I wanted the bands to bugger off and for the Mancunian legends to take to the stage and save us from mediocrity and from the sound of the braying audience I wasn't alone. It was becoming a bit of a squash, the audience lurched forward from time to time crushing my ribs in the process and this was before the band had even taken to the stage. Silver Sun finished their dull set and the warm up music seeped out of the venues PA system.

An ice age passed by until the houselights dropped and the audience roared like the venue was a Roman coliseum cheering on bloody and bruised gladiators. I was shouting, screaming and raising my fists along with everybody else all except Vicky who's just stood there with an odd smirk upon her face. Her reaction confused the hell out of me but I quickly diverted my attention back to the stage. A piece of music that I recognised from the *Wired* compilation album I'd bought the year before played out of the PA system, it was 'One Night Stand' by The Aloof, it sounded grand and epic, the perfect intro music. It became apparent that there was some kind of a problem on stage though, one of the roadies ran on and started to frantically fiddle with equipment for a while delaying the bands entry, I hoped it wasn't an omen for the night ahead but after thirty seconds or so the roadie ran back off stage and the band marched on, Tim's face initially hidden behind an expressionless mask that I recognised from the album cover. I was transfixed by the scene, the band was all smiles and waves, the audience was extremely loud with a definite masculine tone.

"Boothy, Boothy, Boothy" the blokes all chanted, Tim smiled. He was clearly lapping up the attention.

The band opened the set with 'Come Home' and the building started to shake, the audience surged forward pushing this way and that squashing me to the point where it was difficult to breathe. It was like being molested by a ravenous pack of wild beasts. I looked towards Vicky and was absolutely horrified to see that she was simply stood there lifeless against the railings staring at the floor. I was transported back to York to the evening where Steve had fainted and I feared that history was about to repeat itself but at least he'd managed to survive half of the gig, Vicky looked like she was about to pass out within the first twenty seconds! I stared at her for a moment or two, it was then that I noticed she was smirking and just staring at the floor, blinking quite normally in fact and I realised with horror that she was just being an ignorant, self centred manipulative, rude, first class bitch towards not only me but the band as well. I knew that I had to put a stop to her behaviour, I caught the attention of one of the security guys and I pointed towards Vicky indicating that there was something wrong with her. Security immediately ran to her aid and grabbed her arms. I laughed to myself when I saw the panicked look on her face as she was grabbed, she quickly made it quite clear that there was nothing wrong with her and the guys eventually backed away from her. Her eyes never left the stage for the remainder of the show.

James ploughed through their back catalogue as well as dropping in a number of new tracks from *Whiplash*; the audience appeared to lap them up myself included. As they played the opening bars of 'Greenpeace' I simply just stood still with my mouth wide open, there was a fair bit of chatting from a number of people who were stood near me which was made ever more obvious due to the initial quietness of the song but of course that soon changed once the strobe lights and the drum and bass line kicked in. I pumped the air with both of my fists shouting myself hoarse; I looked over at Vicky as I knew that she loved the song. She was crying. Tears were rolling down her face whilst she had a smile on her face that would have made a dolphin jealous. My eyes closed tight and the throbbing bass line and Tim's falsetto cascaded over me.

The song finished and the venue erupted, James then brought a calm to the proceedings with 'Out To Get You', it was just too perfect to comprehend, Tim sang the tender song to the rowdy yet mesmerised audience, he then made his way across to where Vicky and I were stood and he stared down directly into my eyes and locked onto them. We held the gaze for a while until I couldn't help but burst into laughter, Vicky shook my arm smiling her dolphin smile once more as she knew that for a brief moment the song was being sung solely to me before Tim broke eye contact and walked away from us.

During the gig I noticed that there was another musician on stage right during the show who I wasn't familiar with who kept switching from playing the guitar to singing backing vocals, his voice was very different to Tim's but it complimented the songs extremely well, his name was Michael Kulas, a Canadian who somehow ended up playing guitar with this ragtag collection of musicians. He made the band look quite hip with his chiselled good looks and posturing. Adrian Oxall, Larry's replacement was quite a distinctive looking fellow too and Adrian did a great job but it felt like a very different band to the band that I'd seen back in York.

James continued with their set before the inevitable walk off where for some reason the majority of bands pretend they've finished their set, drop all of their instruments and applaud the audience (sometimes) before returning to the stage to perform another three songs that they had already agreed to play beforehand. These days it's often a bands opportunity to pop outside for a quick cigarette and I've actually been to a gig, (The Brian Jonestown Massacre) where the band started to jam for a while as a couple of band members at a time popped outside for a smoke because they couldn't wait until the encore.

James wandered back on stage to a riotous reception and 'Honest Joe' was played to a half bemused half blown away audience, I was in the latter of course. The song finished before an unfamiliar at first song started up, at first I was totally convinced it was 'Chunney Chops' and I shouted it into Vicky's ear, she hissed at me to "SHUT UP" as I was now obviously distracting and spoiling the gig for her. She returned her gaze back to the stage. The song actually turned out to be 'Homeboy', it just had a longer intro than the recorded version, its fast pace caused the audience to pogo and surge forward and a stage diver rolled overhead and was nimbly caught by the burly security guards who gave him a clip around the ear for his naughtiness. The set ground to a halt and the band, all smiles and arms held aloft walked off stage again, but the rowdy Leeds audience were not quite finished with their Lancastrian friends just yet, every pair of feet stomped the floor, every pair of hands clapped and every set of vocal chords bellowed out until the band walked back onstage once more with massive grins on their faces.

"We weren't going to play this tonight but you deserve it" said a beaming Tim to the audience and the band played 'Sit Down'.

It was the song that the majority of the audience had been waiting for all night but I personally felt that they didn't really need to play it, in some ways the inevitability that it would be played as the final song was the only sour point of the evening, but in the grand scheme of things it wasn't really that sour if truth be told. For probably 95% of the audience it was the perfect ending to the evening and if they hadn't played it then that same 95% would have left the building saying,

"They didn't' bloody play 'Sit Down'!"

One of the most famous songs never to grace the top of the charts ground to a halt and the venue exploded with delight, (not literally of course) and James finally made their way off stage all except for Tim who stood there for a minute or so applauding the audience, it was quite a touching sight to behold and it made Vicky cry once again. And then he was gone, the house lights were turned back on and we started to shuffle towards the exit and the coldness of the March night outside. Vicky told me through tears that it was the best gig she'd ever been to. We both returned to the train station along with hoards of other excited and chattering fans and caught the train home discussing in some detail Jim Glennie's bass playing.

The next morning I received a phone call from Vicky, I expected the conversation to be regarding the previous nights events but it wasn't. Through tears she told me that as we'd been heading across to Leeds for the gig four of her friends had been killed in a horrifying car crash, the worst accident the fire services had attended in a number of years. If we hadn't set off early she would have probably heard of the terrible news which would have resulted in us not attending the gig. She was obviously totally distraught and we arranged to meet up later in the day. We didn't talk about the gig for a long time and she didn't really want to listen to James either as it reminded her of the day of the crash, understandable I guess but I selfishly felt really annoyed with her and the awful situation.

The return of the Bad Angel

1997

The 'Whiplash Tour' continued its journey across these fair isles visiting exotic and romantic places such as Middlesbrough, Newport, Southampton and of course James' hometown Manchester. I'd never considered going to more than one date on the tour, the prospect of this had only been brought to my attention when Vicky and I had been leaving the Leeds Town and Country Club and another young couple had asked us how many other dates we were going to attend. Wow, so people actually went to more than one date on a bands tour then? It seemed such a strange idea to me even though I knew that the band was renowned for playing completely different sets each night often without the use of a set list. You could probably go to each date on the tour and discover a completely different mood and experience.

I'd read a review in the NME for the gig that Vicky and I had attended in Leeds, sadly it was fairly damming and it slammed the band for playing 'Sit Down', this was the first comment that was mentioned in the article. Alongside the review of the gig was a photograph of Tim Booth and not the most flattering photo either as it appeared to over empathise his apparent loss of hair! Now my role model of sorts was losing his hair too, this was surely against the rules set in the tablets of stone that all rock legends must have a fine head of hair. Coincidentally my own hair was starting to thin on top making me feel even more insecure with myself. Well, if I was going to lose my hair then it was nice that somebody else who I respected was going through the same despairing situation I thought, mind you though, Tim had a fair few years on me so for him it was kind of acceptable, yet there I was, twenty two years old with an unwanted thinning head of hair. I'm waffling, a thousand pardons and apologies to you.

Then another magazine article alarmed me even more. In fact, for a brief period of time it left me feeling extremely upset. During a lunchtime break I'd bought a music magazine for the sole purpose that I knew it featured an interview with James. I quickly turned to the page and was faced with a picture of Tim Booth dressed like a Cowboy for some reason or other. Now, it was a strange look in my opinion, I'd only ever associated Cowboys with grainy coloured films that were shown on television on a Sunday afternoon whilst my dad slept in the armchair wildly drunk after consuming far too much ale. Plus, wasn't there a Cowboy in the Village People? (All of this was of course many years before *Brokeback Mountain* had been released). I quickly decided to give Tim the benefit of the doubt and realised that he was probably just six months ahead of everybody else in the fashion stakes. James were as previously mentioned always out of synch with everybody else anyway so surely my thinking was right. I had a gut feeling that the country would resemble the Wild West before the end of the year but without the horseshit.

So, back to the article, well I was reading away, enjoying hearing about this and that, what the band had been up to, how invigorated they'd been from having a break from one another and how excited they were being back in the arena of pop that they'd returned to. But then it was all ruined. Tim casually commented upon the fact that he'd dabbled in "recreational drugs" of some sort or other; his comments went something along the lines of,

"I'd hate to get to fifty and to have always wondered what it must have been like to have been a rock and roll star".

I had to reread the comment at least three times before it actually sank in. It came across as such a terrible cliché. I had nightmare images that Tim would soon be throwing televisions out of hotel windows, trashing hotel suites, driving cars into swimming pools, having his teeth knocked out by German body guards, learning how to fly, recording an album of acoustic material with the London Philharmonic Orchestra, purchasing an orphaned African baby, opening a fast food chain that would fold within its first six months and having his own portaloo at a music festival. Part of me wondered if Tim's comment was solely to make him appear to be a little bit closer to the publics perception of what musicians and front men should be like, a bit like Gary Barlow's comments about taking Ecstasy when he was clearly trying to keep up with Robbie Williams during a period when Gary's own career was wobbling a tad. I'd been very proud that my favourite band hardly drank any alcohol and never took any drugs; of course looking back I was just being extremely naive to have had this kind of mindset but when I read Tim's words my heart sank and I felt a sense of betrayal from him and the band.

I guess Tim's comments may possibly have just been a reaction to the fact that the band had always been perceived as "vegan Buddhist weirdoes" who wore fisherman's jumpers and had big old beards whilst singing bizarre songs that resembled sea shanties. In reality the band were actually a big bunch of bruisers who once ended up being chucked out of the Brit Awards due to their rowdy behaviour. Whenever I'd read about James in the past the articles often stank of lazy journalism regarding their descriptions of the band, but when I'd seen some photographs and read a few articles and interviews from the bands much earlier days there did appear to be some truth in the matter of the bands non-band image. Does that make any sense? Well, I know what I mean anyway. Then again, maybe Tim was just being Tim, honest and not afraid of what others thought about him or what he said. Honesty in the music industry is such a rare and noble thing although sometimes the truth can also be very boring. Paul Heaton's Crisp packet fascination doesn't over excite or impress me.

Tim's comments stung so much because as I've already mentioned I'd known quite a few individuals on a personal level that'd succumbed to substance misuse of some sort or other, I'd hated the way it had changed them so much and that friendships and trust had been lost and now the front man of my favourite band was making casual comments about drug use. It reminded me of a horrible dream that I'd had as a young boy. In the dream I was in my classroom along with my peers, one by one they started to eat a black and red charcoal type material that the teacher brought into the classroom on a wooden tray. Each of them nervously tried the substance under the direction of the teacher which made all of them immediately boisterous, edgy and hostile. I was scared throughout the dream and I didn't want to succumb to this poisonous substance. I was crying, pleading with my friends not to fall prey to the substance but the more who took it the more persuadable others were until everybody except me had taken it. Everyone was surrounding me, evil eyes telling me that I had to have it; the more I resisted the more intimidating towards me they became whilst I cried in fear, distraught at how everybody had changed so quickly never to truly return to how they once were. I awoke with a start and was very upset indeed. The dream has stayed with me since. In a freaky way the song 'Riders' from *Strip Mine* had a number of parallels with my dream, I really could have been the character in that song. In retrospect becoming so upset regarding the articles comments probably said an awful lot more about me than it did about anybody else, particularly Tim Booth.

In April 1997 the second single 'Tomorrow' was released, again it was available to buy on three different versions of the compact disc which I once again bought from Mix Music, I was still trying to do my bit for the independent record stores although I guess the main reason I was buying from this particular shop was that Our Price had closed down a few years earlier and ASDA had a rubbish multi-media department. Disc one was eagerly inserted into the stereo and like the first single I skipped past the title track and headed for the other material. Again, live performances were the order of the day. 'Lost a Friend', 'Come Home' and 'Greenpeace' were from a radio session that the band had participated in, I wasn't very keen on them though, 'Greenpeace' sounded particularly bad, tinny and reedy with Tim sounding like he was singing over a recording of the song that was being played on a stereo two rooms away.

The second disc though was a head turner. The first song 'Gone Too Far' was another frantic drum and bass track, something the band appeared to be rather good at. 'Honest Pleasure' was a fairly standard but pleasant enough stomp along tune, definitely a 'B-side' and the last track 'All One to Me' was fairly forgettable. Overall the material wasn't a patch on the second disc of the 'She's a Star' single. The third disc featured three exceptionally bad remixes of 'Tomorrow'. Hmmm, well, I was disappointed but 'Chunney Chops' had previously set the bar to high regarding my expectations. Vicky loved the drum and bass track as much as 'Greenpeace' and she'd insist on playing it whenever she was around at my bedsit.

James performed on the Channel Four programme *TFI Friday* hosted by the over excitable but not in an annoying Timmy Mallet kind of way Chris Evans. Chris appeared to be a big fan of James and Texas, the band not the place although perhaps he liked the place too. If I ever meet him I'll ask and amend any future editions of this book. As for the television performance, well I was in for a shock. Tim had shaved his hair off and was as bald as a coot! He was also wearing a rather distinctive t-shirt which had an image of the Earth on it, I was quite sure that I'd seen the very same shirt on sale on a market stall in Bridlington at some point the summer before. The rest of the band looked ultra-cool and slick looking appropriately enough like a mid to late nineties British rock band and Tim was shaking his hips like a sexy electrocuted penguin. Even Dave the drummer was wearing shades whilst Michael Kulas shook the maracas like a distraught blind man. Due to a decent amount of promotion and the multiple purchases of the single by fans the song 'Tomorrow' crashed into the top twenty the following weekend at a respectable number twelve position. I cheered and held my hands aloft for a few hours.

Interviews and articles regarding the band continued to pepper the media, I tried to keep up with them as much as I possibly could and I became aware that the band were heading overseas again to promote the new album and obviously follow on from the success that they had enjoyed in the States during the *Laid* era. I was sure they'd continue their good fortune and become a big selling band in the States, but then again I had my doubts as the Americans are a funny lot when it comes to British music aren't they? It's not a racist comment, it just feels that anything that's big in the UK is often overlooked or distrusted and then they'll surprise you by buying enough copies of an album by Radiohead so that it ends up at the top of their Billboard chart. And *Whiplash* was a very odd British sounding album and it also lacked the cohesion of *Laid*. 'Greenpeace' was a world away from 'Laid', actually, it was at least a universe or two away. I'm pretty sure you'd need to travel by a worm hole to reach it.

I was overjoyed and I have to say that Vicky was too when it was announced that the band would be playing at a music festival in Leeds. 'V97' was to be held at Temple Newsam in North Leeds. James would be sharing a bill with Blur, The Prodigy, Beck, Foo Fighters, The Chemical Brothers and of course the mighty Radish, (no, I've never heard of them either.) We bought tickets pretty much straight away, Blur as previously mentioned was one of my favourite bands and their latest self-titled album *Blur* had been released earlier in the year, overall it was rather excellent featuring the number one hit single 'Beetlebum' and the number two mega smash 'Song 2'. When I'd heard that the band was releasing 'Song 2' as a single I mistakenly thought of it as commercial suicide. Bare in mind here that I would definitely have been the person who turned down the opportunity in signing The Beatles plus I'd also once commented that The Spice Girls wouldn't amount to anything much either.

James were also due to play a number of other festivals that summer including Glastonbury; however disaster would strike the band on their overseas jaunt. In a nutshell, Tim badly injured his neck to the point where the majority of the tour had to be cancelled. He ended up having to hang upside down attached to a metal bar by his ankles like a bat for long periods of time to try and strengthen his neck. Now, this really wasn't very nice to hear and Vicky and I wished Tim a full and speedy recovery, we even considered sending him a box of chocolates and a card to cheer him up a bit until I heard that the band would probably be cancelling some of their festival appearances that summer. Needless to say I became rather concerned I wouldn't get to see them. Having bought tickets for V97 it was then horribly confirmed that they'd definitely be cancelling all live performances bar the Reading Festival and I was very upset indeed. A spokesperson for the band apologised to those who'd bought tickets on the back of them appearing on the bill. Vicky consoled me a tad and reminded me that there were plenty of other good bands playing at V97 including Silversun and Radish.

There was a fair amount of sympathy for the band in the States due to the crisis and a pleasant young man offered the band a slot on the American touring festival Lollapallooza which featured bands very similar to James such as Korn, Snoop Dog, and Tool. Naturally the band was going to win over a whole new legion of fans. I'd find out at a later date that the tour had been total carnage for the band, substances were consumed by the band members at an alarming rate as a form of escapism from the excruciating experience that playing to legions of Korn fans was. The band really camped it up in a big way by wearing spangled dresses and shirts which offended the homophobic redneck sports obsessed frat boys. Tim often descended into the crowds and sang to individual audience members causing them to cry and come out as being secretly gay, and then they were probably beaten up by their big butch Budweiser drinking friends in the car park after the show.

Vicky told me that she'd heard 'Waltzing Along' on the radio whilst she'd been browsing in an independent record store in the pretty market town of Knaresborough. She said that it sounded "different", in that it was faster and a bit rockier than the sweet lilting album version. Within the same week I'd heard it, she was right, it sounded a lot more "radio friendly" and it was released in June just in time for the bands non-appearance at Glastonbury. I once again made the pilgrimage to Mix Music to purchase the three different formats of the single. Disc one once again consisted of live tracks. 'Greenpeace' (again), 'How Was It For You?' (I'd forgotten what a great song it was) and 'Homeboy' which in fact was a riveting version with the extended intro that the band had played earlier in the year at the Leeds gig Vicky and I had attended. The second disc featured 'Your Story' which was just pure smut and filth, an instrumental entitled 'Where You Gonna Run?' which was alright and

'Long To Be Right' which was pleasant enough. I braced myself for the third disc of remixes which included a 'Disco Socks Mix' and a 'Flytronix Mix', they really weren't that terrible either. The single entered the charts at number twenty three that week which was pretty good for a third single from the album plus the band was overseas so there was minimal promotion on television with no *TFI Friday* appearance either. Chris Evans wept like a child who'd fallen off his bicycle and he had to book Cast instead.

In the early summer Vicky and I travelled to Leeds to do some shopping, I bought a rather nice yellow Nike t-shirt from Top Man and whilst we were in the city centre we visited a second hand record shop called Polar Bear Records. It was a lovely little shop down an arcade and we spent ages in there browsing through the racks of records and compact discs. We'd both grabbed a handful of compact discs ready for payment when I stumbled across the *Booth and the Bad Angel* album which had been released some twelve months earlier. I'd pretty much forgotten all about it. Although it was second hand I still ended up paying £9 for it which meant I would have to put the Earl Brutus 'Life's Too Long' single back on the shelf. Vicky however bought it instead so everyone was a winner including the shop keeper.

When we returned to my bedsit later that day we gave the *Booth And The Bad Angel* album a listen. The single 'I Believe' was up first, it had grown on me since I'd bought it the year before and I'd even included it on a compilation tape that I'd compiled the previous Christmas entitled *Hits of 96*. The next track was that awful 'Dance of the Bad Angel' song, I was about to skip past it but Vicky insisted on letting it play as she'd grown to really like it after hearing it on my *Wired* album. It still really grated on me for some reason or other. The third song 'Hit Parade' I loved upon its first listen, Tim's vocal soaring skywards throughout the tracks up tempo charge which had an underlying desperation bubbling just underneath the surface. Vicky exclaimed it was "The best James song I've ever heard that isn't actually a James song!" I knew exactly what she meant.

The third song knocked me for six. 'Fall In Love With Me' was simply gorgeous, gorgeous, GORGEOUS! Its simple electronic beat paddled along gently supporting what I can only describe as some of Tim's most beautiful lyrics ever. It was a pure and simple love song through and through and I was blown away by it. 'Old Ways' was another amazing song! I was seriously starting to wonder why these songs hadn't been on any of James' albums, had Tim been holding them back purposefully? Had the songs been written in the period when the band weren't knocking about together so much? I didn't really care! 'Old Ways' made me jig and dance about my bedsit happy in the fact that life is sometimes rather wonderful.

'Life Gets Better' sounded like it should have been the soundtrack to a moody American movie; Tim shared vocals throughout with Angelo, the song was edgy and ever so slightly menacing. 'Heart' was I felt the strongest song on this excellent album featuring some absolutely fantastic guitar playing from Bernard Butler, (the kind of guitar playing that made the pit of my stomach lurch forward and made my eyes well up). The song ended up being played five times in a row before we moved onto the next sad sounding song 'Rising', such a tender little number, I just wanted to cradle and cuddle it throughout its brief two minutes and fifty seconds lifetime. 'Butterfly's Dream' was probably the sexiest sounding song I'd ever heard, even sexier than the entire *Blue Lines* album by Massive Attack. Bernard's guitar playing in perfect symbiosis with Tim's sultry yet menacing undertone, it was eight minutes of groovy dirty sexiness and I loved it.

'Stranger' followed. Again, the only word that sprang to mind was "wonderful". I was in shock at how amazing the album was. How had I missed it the first time around? The single 'I Believe' was a terrible choice when compared to some of the other songs I'd heard, once again the best songs being held back for those brave or curious enough to part with their cash. I felt annoyed with myself that I had almost forgotten about the album; maybe it was fate or just meant to be, perhaps I wasn't supposed to hear it until then for some reason. 'Hands in the Rain' the final track closed an exceptional album. Vicky loved it even more than *Whiplash*. We discussed the album in some depth over a bottle of cheap fizz.

"I wonder how the album would have sounded if it had been James who'd recorded it?" she said, I thought it was an interesting enough idea. Tim certainly appeared to be unshackled from the past and James but at the same time and as much as I absolutely loved the album you could tell that a lot of the music was performed by session musicians, the invisible bond that appeared to exist between each of the members of James was definitely missing, however in my opinion *Booth and the Bad Angel* was a triumph. Another lost classic album.

I managed to find a rather fetching new James t-shirt from HMV during another shopping trip to Leeds. It was navy blue with 'James' printed in the same font that had been used throughout the *Whiplash* campaign with a bright yellow daisy on the front of it. It looked rather fetching; I was proudly wearing it one day when some old man approached me in the local supermarket.

"Hey, I'm called James too!" he shouted at me before bursting into maniacal laughter causing everybody in the vicinity to stare at the two of us. We were both immediately carted off to the local mental hospital together until I somehow eventually managed to persuade them to let me go.

Even without James V97 was a blast. The highlight was when Dave Grohl from the Foo Fighters was chased by a wasp on stage mid-way through a song. We initially thought the microphone was simply cutting out but it was Dave Grohl running away from the microphone mid-sentence, it happened a few times during one number and after the song finished Dave explained what had been happening causing one and all to belly laugh to the point where we all ended up vomiting over each other. Blur appeared narky and surly throughout their set which was a big disappointment. The crowd kept chanting "SONG 2, SONG 2", Damon Albarn replied by saying "Yeah, yeah, you know we're going to play it last". I felt let down that a musician I really respected appeared to have developed such an attitude.

As the summer ended I found myself listening less and less to James' back catalogue; I was instead listening to other music and buying singles and albums on a regular basis faithfully from Mix Music, regularly putting money back into the local economy. I managed to find a copy of *Laid* on compact disc for only £5 in my local supermarket and I bought it replacing my well worn cassette version which was starting to sound a little bit muddy and muffled from being overplayed. A further story of note to mention regarding *Laid* was that on one occasion Vicky and I ended up having a blazing row in town and I'd stormed off home by myself back to my bedsit, let myself in, opened a can of pop and put *Laid* on. I was feeling rather sorry for myself and very angry with Vicky and then there was a knock on the door, it was Vicky of course. I let her in to my room, the bad atmosphere continued; the soundtrack playing in the background was *Laid*. We shouted, and bitched at one another for quite some time.

"Please turn this music off will you! It's really not helping matters" Vicky said through tears. 'P.S.' was playing at that moment in time, its sad desperation fitted the mood perfectly. I did as she asked and turned off the stereo, it seemed like the decent thing to do. After a while we made up and I put on *The Great Escape* by Blur and there was much rejoicing.

A week or so later I managed to hear some of James' Reading Festival performance when I was round at my sister's house. James ended up playing a festival friendly greatest hits set, Saul Davies actually stated at one point "My God it's just hit after hit" even if they did chuck in 'Jam J' and 'Honest Joe' to test the crowd out. Vicky and I had been preparing to go overseas to go backpacking around Australia. We'd decided it was best if we just travelled as friends though, a relationship would complicate things and although we never officially broke up we started to wind down our relationship somewhat which sounds like such a strange and cold thing to say but it pleased her parents somewhat as they'd never been overly keen on me, in fact they actually thought that I was a bad influence! I knew travelling meant that I was going to be out of the musical loop for quite some time and I wondered what kind of a sonic landscape I'd be returning too. I needed to take some of James' back catalogue with me so I transferred *Strip Mine* and *Whiplash* onto a C90 along with a live recording of James' Shepherds Bush Empire gig I'd recorded a few months earlier. I also made up a couple of compilation tapes which featured the odd James track or two. I managed to convince myself that James would probably take a sabbatical in 1998 and therefore I wouldn't miss too much action from them. I was right of course.

Actually, I couldn't have been more wrong.

The loneliness of the long distance backpacker

1997/1998

October 1997, it seems like such a long time ago, actually it is. By the time this book is published it will be almost fifteen years ago and that's a long time in anyone's life, however I remember it like it was only yesterday. Everyone has certain key events and times in their lives that shape and change them beyond all recognition including their outlook on the world. Well this was mine and the period of 1997 and 1998 certainly changed me forever. I look back now at photographs of that time remembering how it felt so futuristic and I may as well be watching television footage from the early 1980's, it all looks so grainy and fuzzy, the fashion already looks dated beyond belief. As for the music, well, it was the arsehole end of Brit Pop; a movement that at one time felt all conquering and powerful had folded in on itself under a blizzard of cocaine, champagne, ego and some questionable music. The smart bands had tried to side step Brit Pop (Radiohead) in the hope of achieving some longevity, some bands had been wholly consumed by it (Pulp) and some bands just couldn't fit in with it even if they had wanted to (James).

As previously mentioned Vicky and I were going overseas for a year or so to spread our wings and escape the doldrums of our lives back in our middle class predominantly white ambitionless town. To paint a picture of this town I still saw 'The No Hopers' from time to time, still drinking too much, still going to the same pubs and clubs that they'd been going to for years. I rarely saw any of my friends, Charles and Steve were getting on with their own lives, Richard had changed to the point where I really didn't like him very much anymore and apart from bumping into him in a pub in early autumn I never saw him again. I knew that leaving the country for such a long time would mean that when I returned; indeed if I returned then things would never be the same again. It felt in a weird kind of way that I was experiencing bereavement and rebirth all at the same time. I was frightened and enthralled at the prospect of having to survive in such an unfamiliar environment. I was about to launch myself into the abyss of the unknown, the unfamiliar. I left the house on a Sunday night (in October 1997). I placed my headphones on my head, pressed play on my personal stereo and the opening synthetic rumbling of Ride's 'Leave Them All Behind' stirred up just as I had planned and I marched up the street where I'd spent the majority of my life to that point and headed towards the train station.

Vicky and I arrived in Sydney Australia via a stopover in Bangkok and we set some brief roots down in the Coogee Beach area of the city, backpackers swarmed and buzzed around like flies over a rather attractive piece of animal dung but I have to say that it was then one of the most amazing places I'd ever visited, well it was on par with Bridlington which in my world is as high an accolade as you can get. I'd brought just one James t-shirt with me, the navy blue *Whiplash* shirt and when I wore it British backpackers would often stop me upon the realisation that they were most likely going to be conversing with another Brit. The backpackers were more often than not from down south and they struggled with my northern accent, in fact it was a rarity to hear a northern accent which made me think that most northerners were probably working in some industrial quagmire whilst the southerners were instead spending daddies hard earned cash which upon running out would be replaced via a phone call home and a visit to Western Union. Am I being cynical? Maybe. Bitter? Perhaps.

One of the first things Vicky and I did in Sydney was purchase tickets to see Blur play at the Hordern Pavilion near the Sydney Cricket Ground, the gig had pretty much sold out but we managed to acquire some returned tickets from a booking booth on Martin Place in downtown Sydney. Blur were playing three nights in the city, the other two dates were at the Metro Theatre but as it was a much smaller venue the only way to acquire a ticket would be through a tout and as Blur were riding on the back of the success of 'Song 2' and their self titled album then this would have been very costly indeed.

The gig itself was fantastic, extremely hot and physically quite rough. I think the capacity was something like six thousand but from the crush I expect that there were many more there, probably another few hundred at least. The band piled through a ragged set of harsh guitar pop deliberately ignoring the "Chimney Sweep" music that had made them such darlings back in the UK. During a break from the madness and heat we left the auditorium for some fresh air. Vicky recognised some bloke stood by the bar who apparently "acted" in the woeful soap opera *Home and Away*.

We approached the sweaty yet overly handsome individual who'd just purchased a plastic schooner of VB. (VB is a tasty alcoholic beverage)

"Hey, are you whatshisname?" she said to the person who I still didn't recognise.

"Yeah! Alright?" he said to her in a warm Aussie accent.

She smiled her toothy grin at him.

"You're shit!" she said and before he could reply she quick marched it away leaving me stood there looking rather embarrassed although not quite as embarrassed as he was as everyone in the vicinity started laughing. I offered up a mumbled apology and made my exit.

After a couple of weeks of knocking around the city we settled down into the Balmain district, it was once a rough old place but when we arrived it had experienced a bit of a renaissance and was full of attractive looking young professionals with a mere ten minute bus journey to the city centre. There was a veritable smorgasbord of trendy bars and shops including an excellent music shop called Fish Records located opposite Australia's version of Woolworths.

The first time I popped into the aquatically named music shop I almost fell over in surprise after I found a James album that I'd never seen before! On the cover was a white daisy on a navy blue background, the album was simply entitled *James*. I excitedly turned over the case but was rather disappointed when I realised that it was simply *Gold Mother* with the running order jiggled about a little bit. I placed the album back on the rack and had a nosey around the record store; it was a mixture of familiar material, (Blur, Oasis, and The Verve) and unfamiliar band names such as Regurgitator, Tism, and The Mavis's. I decided to have a listen to Regurgitator's latest album which was called *Unit*; it was rather good in a retro, funky, quirky electro guitar pop kind of way although I fear that this description may be slightly over egging it particularly when you consider that one of the songs had the rather attractive title of 'I will lick your arsehole'. Probably not one of Gran's favourite songs me thinks. And to think I thought that Australian music would simply comprise of Midnight Oil and Rolf Harris!

During my time in Balmain I was working on Pitt Street in a mailroom for backpackers sorting out mail that was posted out to them from their various homelands. The other employees were also on working holiday visas and they were mainly Dutch although there was another British girl who I have to say was easily one of the most unpleasant people I've ever had the misfortune to come across in my entire life, but that my friends is once again another story. The work was badly paid and rather mundane but it was made a bit more bearable because of a girl called Esther.

Esther was a Dutch girl who was music mad or should I say music mental, perhaps even slightly music psychotic. She was the first person that I'd ever come across who actually believed that the Foo Fighters were superior to Nirvana. She also had some connections with the Dutch music media in some capacity or other; I think it was a music magazine and she was therefore pretty clued up when it came to music of most types, apart from Brazilian Hardcore Poetry. Jesting aside, she was a great person to work with; she brought in new music each day which we'd listen to on the mailroom stereo to help pass away the laborious work. Unsurprisingly she'd never heard of James. "Aha, another victim, someone else for me to influence" (I frantically and desperately thought to myself.) First on the list was the Shepherds Bush gig that was blasted out to the utter confusion of Esther and the rest of our colleagues.

"What the hell is zis?" asked another Dutch girl in a rather bad tempered manner.

"Er, it's James, a British band, my favourite band" I replied.

"Ah, well, I don't like it" she replied nonplussed, I promptly made a mental note to exact some kind mailroom related revenge on her. And indeed I did. Later that day I zipped her up in a mailroom sack and posted her off to Tasmania. She was never to be seen again.

Esther on the other hand was rather polite about James.

"Well, it sounds very British to me. I'm not sure if we'd hear much of it in The Netherlands, but you know, it's kind of okay".

Like I said, she was polite enough, however when 'Greenpeace' began screeching away in the background of the mailroom she spoke again.

"Is zis the same James?"

"Yes" I said with some trepidation.

She raised her eyebrows.

"Oh wow, now zis sounds very good. We'd listen to zis at the Pinkpop Festival you know."

She nodded along to the frantic beat which must have given her a bit of a headache then when the song finished and without asking she marched straight across to the stereo and rewound the tape to have a second listen. She missed the start of the song before asking me for some assistance so she could play it again. I lost count of how many times it got replayed but I'm sure by the end of the day that particular section of the tape had been worn out. She wasn't too keen on *Strip Mine* though but you can't win them all can you?

Vicky and I remained in Sydney until the end of February 1998; she headed off to Melbourne whilst I spent another week in Sydney with some friends we'd made during our stay. I was very sad to say goodbye to Esther, she'd become a very good friend and I hoped we'd see each other again at some point, although sadly we never did. On my last day in Sydney I returned to Fish Records and bought the James album that I'd seen some time before, the blue covered one with the white daisy.

Whilst paying for it I asked the young girl who served me if the album was a good seller.

"Erm, I'm not a fan so I can't really say" she foolishly replied. I told her that she should check the band out because "they're going to blow your mind away".

"Right, gee, thanks for that" she said in a rather unconvincing manner before dropping the plastic package into a brown paper bag for me and sending me on my way out into the warm Australian evening air.

Whilst travelling between Sydney and Melbourne on the famous 'Oz Experience' backpacker bus I had the opportunity to play the album on the rickety transportations stereo. The bus driver and co-driver were a couple of idiots who wore sunglasses during the evening and they kept trying it on with the females on the bus at any given opportunity. I passed the album over to the Canadian co-driver.

"James? Who the hell is James?" he said with a smirk on his face whilst the bald headed driver sniggered a response similar to that of Beavis and Butthead.

I tried to explain as per usual that James was a *band* and *not a person*, neither of them appeared convinced or the least bit interested, however the disc was inserted into the player and the opening bars of 'Sit Down' struck up.

An attractive Swedish girl who was sat next to me gave out a big groan, although not in a sexual manner.

"What's this?" she asked me rather patronisingly.

I chose to simply ignore her.

Victory was mine though because there was a few drunken Brits on the bus and the album went down a storm, it became the soundtrack to our journey right through the Snowy Mountains and beyond, it felt like a further sweet vindication when I noticed the Swedish girl tapping her hand along to 'Gold Mother'.

I arrived in Melbourne a week after Vicky had and after a few days in Melbourne we caught the Sea Cat Hydro Ferry across Bass Straight heading towards Tasmania. The sea appeared to be relatively calm yet there was a definite roll to the boat and within ten minutes people were vomiting everywhere and lying on the decks with blankets on top of them. It was marginally amusing until the smell hit you. My only distraction was staring out of the window at the horizon listening to the Shepherds Bush concert on repeat for pretty much the entire six hour journey. The batteries were certainly well worn on my personal stereo by the time we arrived in Tasmania but I thankfully never developed any seasickness. We arrived in a small town called Greymouth before heading off to Launceston where we made our base for the week in a hostel that used to be an old psychiatric hospital. I felt quite at home there for some reason I could never quite fathom out. Each day we'd set off on journeys exploring the island and each and everyday I'd search the music stores to see if by some miracle of God I could manage to find a copy of *One Man Clapping*. I never did though, I never found anything by James apart from when we were in a pub one evening and I discovered 'Laid' on the Juke Box and played it on repeat for about twenty minutes or so until a local shouted at me and told me to put some Hunters and Collectors on instead.

After a fantastic week on the wonderful island we headed back to the mainland to Melbourne where we ended up staying in a hostel that used to be a university building. Hotel Backpack was hardly The Ritz, we ended up sharing a room with a girl who only had one and a half arms, a lovely girl she was and I helped her where and when I could. Vicky and I worked for two hours a day in the hotel keeping it clean and tidy discovering to our horror that some people were proud to live in deplorable filth but it resulted in a night's free accommodation so it was well worth it, used condoms, syringes and takeaway boxes aside.

One sunny yet cool afternoon Vicky and I popped into HMV to have a browse because that's all we could really afford to do. I found a newish copy of the NME and had a sneaky read through it but I certainly wasn't prepared for what I found. There in the live section was an advert for James! It advertised a few live dates which knocked the wind out of me for a start but there at the bottom of the advert in teeny weeny writing was this,

"New Single: 'Destiny Calling' out now, James the Best Of coming soon".

New single?????? a best Of???? It was a complete disaster!!!! James were going to split up! That's pretty much the only reason that a band releases a best of I thought.

These terrifying thoughts happened in nanoseconds and when I finished reading the last bit of text I let out a guttural,

"NO!!!!!!!!!!!!!!!!! which caused a lot of people to jump in alarm.

Vicky dropped a compact disc she'd been examining and ran across to me asking me what the hell was wrong. I just pointed at the advert, my mouth wide open whilst making an "unnngg" sound. A security guard came across to the two of us.

"Hey, are you okay buddy?"

I couldn't speak.

"He's just had a bit of a shock, he'll be fine in a moment or two" Vicky said smiling at the security guard who'd embarrassingly referred to me as buddy.

I somehow managed to return the copy of the NME back to the shelf and with some support from Vicky I staggered out of the shop whilst Jeff Buckley mournfully howled away in the background.

We found somewhere to sit down so that I could compose myself. The more I thought about it the more likely it seemed to me that perhaps James wasn't about to split up, maybe it was a genuine "Best Of" and not a swansong, maybe the band had new material under their belt ready to unleash upon the northern hemisphere. I knew that I was potentially going to be missing a fair bit of action back home as I wouldn't be back in the UK until the end of the year. Unless of course the *Best Of* wasn't a success.…

My mind remained on overdrive for the next few days, I was constantly thinking about James, my thoughts repeatedly drifting back to the UK, when I really should have been concentrating on my time in Australia.

Then Vicky had a great idea.

"Why don't you use the internet and try and find out some more information about what's going on with them?"

Now, I'd never used the internet before but I'd obviously heard of it and how it was going to change the world as we knew it. She suggested we called into the Melbourne Library and book some time on one of their computers. My eyes lit up and I licked my lips in a way that could only ever be described as being a bit creepy and we set off towards the large stone building, harassing the librarian into letting us use one of the computers.

"You can use computer number five, the person who's on it at the moment is nearly finished" the bespectacled lady said to us in an overly nasally manner.

We hovered nearby and waited, and waited and waited. An elderly man was still using the computer. I coughed an inpatient cough trying to get the message across to him that his time was up and I peered over his shoulder and was aghast at the fact that he was looking at some dodgy porn site that featured hamsters. He turned around, panicked and quickly closed the internet browser and made his getaway. I checked the seat, thankfully it was as clean as a whistle and I made myself comfortable whilst trying to fathom out how to actually use this internet thingy.

With some assistance from Vicky I eventually worked out how to find websites and I popped onto the NME website, it featured a chat room and I asked if anybody had heard the new James song.

"It sounds a bit like David Devant and his Spirit Wife" replied 'Big Fist'. This didn't make a right lot of sense to me; I'd heard of David Devant and his Spirit Wife but I didn't quite grasp the connection between him, his spirit wife and James.

"It's crap, they're crap, listen to The Verve maaaan!" replied 'Nocturnal 178'.

On another visit to the library I managed to find a website specifically related to James called Stutter. I excitedly browsed the website and left a message on its message board stating that I was in Australia and I was kind of limited to the amount of information relating to James and wanted any information on what was happening with them so very far away. I said that if anyone could enlighten me it would be very much appreciated. I returned to the library the following day and plenty of messages had been left for me from the UK regarding the band. A couple of girls mentioned that they lived in a village just outside of Wetherby and that they were in fact Tim Booth's cousins. Now, this excited me greatly, I was actually in contact with possible blood relations to the great man himself! The general consensus from the message board was that the two new songs to be featured on the *Best Of* were "*absolutely fantastic*". Of course I didn't think that anybody would say that they were toilet or anything but I was pleased to hear positive feedback nonetheless. As I was making daily, sometimes twice daily visits to the library Vicky started to give me a bit of a hard time and complained that not only was I becoming overly obsessed with the band but also the usage of the internet. I ignored her and remembered her apparent jealousy from the gig at the Town and Country Club in Leeds.

"You might as well face it you're addicted to James" she kept singing in tune to 'Addicted to Love' by Robert Palmer, a song I despised.

Back at the wonderful yet chaotic Hotel Back Pack we continued to cover accommodation costs with two hours of daily chores. One day I was mindlessly vacuuming a twin room when I noticed a copy of a music magazine called *Vox* on the floor, I had a sneaky peek and my heart almost leapt out of my chest when it mentioned on the cover that it included a feature on James. I really wanted to open and read it but I knew that this was wrong and that if the rooms occupiers returned then I'd be in big trouble so I left a note and it read as follows......

"Hello there! I'm from England and I'm the guy who cleans your room for you! I hope that this doesn't come across as being too weird or rude but I noticed you have a copy of 'Vox' magazine and I was wondering if I could possibly have a quick read of it when you have finished with it as there is a feature on the band James in it that I'd love to read if possible. I'm in room 314, sorry for being cheeky!! Thank you!"

Later that day there was a knock on my door and two British lads introduced themselves as the room occupiers and of course the magazine owners. They were both smiling and had the magazine with them which they gracefully handed over to me. I was ecstatic and shook their hands wildly like a mad man during a full moon. They then spoke to Vicky and I for a while, one of them explained that he was in Australia for a golf tournament, the other lad was his caddy. They were both very friendly and we wished them luck with the tournament and bid them farewell and then I frantically tore open the magazine, found the article and read with furious might. I was a tad confused with Saul's new image; he'd shaved all of his lovely hair off and was now sporting nail varnish whilst wearing a pair of sunglasses and drinking what appeared to be a radioactive cocktail of some description. He looked quite rock and roll in a Martian kind of way.

A couple of days later I was midway through my cleaning round when I opened a door to a double room, I immediately recognised the pair of golf clubs strewn on the floor. I flicked on the vacuum cleaner and was getting on with the job when the occupants of the room entered; it was the lads who'd given me their magazine. Upon recognising who was cleaning their room they both stood there looking awkward and embarrassed.

"Er, alright lads!" I said in a chipper manner.

"Yeah, err, hi", one of them softly spoke without making any eye contact with me.

"Cheers again for the magazine" I piped up trying to diffuse the awkward situation, well, it wasn't awkward for me at all. I kind of felt sorry for them as I'd obviously uncovered something they'd been keeping quiet from others. I finished the vacuuming and left them to their privacy.

I was directed to a second hand record store by an Aussie who was staying in the hostel. The name of the shop was Au Go-Go and I knew it was probably my best chance at finding a copy of *One Man Clapping*. After an age I found the store which was situated on the first floor of a building tucked away from the main strip. I didn't find the album but I did find a selection of seven inch early vinyl James singles. I asked the guy behind the counter if he'd give me a discount if I bought all of the records off him. He stated that he didn't own the store but he guessed that the owner might knock "a couple of dollars" off the price. Aghast I put the records back into their rack and left the store in protest. I had a change of heart though and returned a few days later but the singles had all gone. I left the store feeling even more aghast than I'd been on my previous visit.

After a few weeks Vicky and I left Melbourne and headed towards Adelaide, a lovely city that's often overlooked by backpackers or is simply used as an overnight stop before heading north towards the centre of the country or west towards Perth. During the latter stages of the journey via another Oz Experience bus I was dismayed and rather devastated to find out that somebody had stolen my copy of *Whiplash* that I'd thoughtfully given to 'Bones' the driver. He'd added it to the pile of tapes that he'd pooled from the other travellers and it had obviously caught somebody's eye, or ear. Nobody owned up to having it or even seeing it and I was very upset. Bones felt sorry for me and he gave me an original copy of The Stone Roses *Second Coming* tape instead, it was a consolation of sorts as I loved the controversial album more than most people but now I only had a copy of *Strip Mine* plus the live Shepherd Bush to last me until I returned home.

We made Adelaide our home for a number of months and I managed to secure a job at Norwood Football Club, not playing the game, just washing up in the hospitality area. We stayed at a place called New World Hostel, its owner an old expat called Bill was as camp as a week at Butlins, a lovely fella very welcoming and very laid back. He had great plans for the hostel; he wanted a large crystal chandelier in the reception and plush red carpets throughout. Sadly the hostel would close by the time we'd leave Adelaide due to Bill suddenly becoming very poorly with angina and ending up in hospital. As we didn't have too much disposable income Vicky and I would often spend the time we had wandering around the parks and shops which of course included all the music shops. I almost exploded when I discovered a copy of the new James *Best Of* album and I spent some time examining the artwork which featured the distinctive James Daisy in multiple colours. I noticed that the shop had a listening booth and I ran across to the girl behind the counter to eagerly ask if I could have a listen.

"Sure you can" she said in a friendly and helpful manner, she slipped the disc into the stereo and passed me the headphones. I skipped past the tracks I knew until I reached 'Destiny Calling' and listened to it a couple of times realising that it was really rather wonderful with lyrics that appeared to reference The Spice Girls of all things.

"He likes the black one, she likes the posh one, cute ones are usually gay". I wondered if this lyric would give them any earache back in the UK. The other new track was called 'Runaground'. I didn't like it as much as 'Destiny Calling' but it was fairly pleasant all the same and appeared to be indicative that the band had settled down comfortably as far as song writing was concerned after the upheavals and uncertainty of the previous years.

The girl in the shop stopped her smiling though after I'd called into the shop for the fifth time that week and asked if I could to listen to the album.

"Are you actually going to buy this?" she asked me in a rather curt manner.

I explained that I was backpacking for the year and couldn't really afford to buy it, plus I only had a cassette player as far as a personal stereo was concerned.

"Right, well this is the last time that you're listening to it" she said to me before slamming the disc into the stereo. If I'd been a dog my tail would definitely have been between my legs as a direct result of the scolding I'd received from her.

Naturally I'd already located the library and was making heavy use of its internet access and I excitedly read about James' busy schedule playing gigs here and there and how they appeared to be enjoying their resurgence in popularity. I also discovered that the library stocked both the NME and Melody Maker and I managed to find recent articles in both magazines relating to the band including interviews and reviews for the Best Of, the press begrudgingly showed their respect for the band and gave the album positive reviews in both publications, this was a major surprise due to the rather shaky and fractious relationship that the band had developed with the press over the years. On the cover of one of the magazines was Tim Booth surrounded by what appeared to be The Spice Girls with him naked from the midriff up, his white pasty skin covered in melted chocolate.

"How on Earth have they managed to coerce The Spice Girls into getting involved with them?" Vicky snorted in absolute disgust.

I didn't bother to tell her that they were actually Spice Girl impersonators and I left her wondering if it was her who'd gotten James and their popularity so very wrong. I was resigned to the fact that I was potentially missing James' biggest and most successful year to date due to being on the other side of the planet. It didn't really matter though, I was proud that the band was finally getting their dues of sorts and I kept abreast as much as I possibly could via the internet. *Strip Mine* quickly became my most played James album ever (up till that point) and it was the soundtrack to my journey through the centre of the country to Darwin, the long bus journey from Darwin to Cairns and the lonely depressing nights spent wandering the streets of Brisbane when I couldn't sleep. The insomnia was due to worry and stress as I couldn't find even the most basic of work to supplement my travels. Steve had been in touch with me and had kindly posted me a compilation tape including a James song from the 'Laid' CD single that I'd never heard before called 'The Lake'. I have some very fond memories of lying on a boat listening to the beautiful song on repeat whilst sailing around The Whitsunday Islands. It was moments like that that really made me think life couldn't get much better.

It was the last few months of my year in Australia and after having such a crap time in Brisbane I decided to take the Greyhound bus southbound towards Sydney. Vicky and I would part forever as she flew back home to go to university in order to make something of herself, it was the end of a significant chapter in my life but I was glad really. She'd stripped me of a lot of confidence and my self-esteem had been ravaged by her cranky attitude and jealousy. After being unable to secure any work in Brisbane for two long weeks I'd managed to acquire two jobs within a day of being back in Sydney meaning that I wouldn't have to return home early. I was up for work at five in the morning and back home by ten at night. During the day I sold bunches of flowers in the city centre and in the afternoon and evening I worked in an office, cold calling and conning people into attending a seminar where they could invest their hard earned life's savings into some dodgy timeshare up on the Gold Coast. The weekends were spent pottering around the city and the beaches, often popping into Red Eye Records on Pitt Street or checking out other branches of Fish Records in my eternal search for *One Man Clapping* as well as any other James rarities of course.

In a discount bookstore which once upon a time had been a bank situated on George Street I managed to find a copy of *Booth and the Bad Angel* sat all forlorn, unloved and lost. It looked completely out of place next to Rolf Harris and The Triffids, (or so I thought at the time, those in the know will know what I'm hinting at). I did the decent thing and bought the dusty copy with the intention of posting it off to Vicky. The guy behind the counter was a Brit and he commented upon my *Whiplash* t-shirt I was wearing. I told him the compact disc I was buying was by none other than Tim Booth. He appeared quite shocked and stated he'd have a look in the back store room to see if he could find a copy for himself. Whether he ever did or not I'll never know.

I left Australia in October 1998 and headed towards New Zealand. During those three weeks the Shepherds Bush gig would become even more worn from repeated plays on the backpackers 'Magic Bus' bus. The tape managed to win over new fans from various countries around the world who voiced their love and amazement at the music pouring out of the tinny speakers on the bus. Of course in each and every town and city visited I scoured the record shops for a copy of *One Man Clapping* sadly to no avail, but every time I found a James album or an imported single I'd flush with pride that my favourite band had reached so far from home to some of the most obscure places around the world. I never found any James material in Fiji, Raratonga, Tahiti or Moorea but the west coast of America was quite the opposite, sadly I *still* never found a copy of *One Man Clapping*. The day that I returned to the UK was the same day James were playing at the NYNEX Arena in Manchester celebrating their most successful year to date, had I returned home a few days beforehand I'd have bought a ticket but of course I was too late and instead had to make do with watching *Blind Date* or something equally mundane before I fell asleep on my mums battered old sofa.

Footnote time. During the latter stages of putting the book together I managed to contact Esther via a certain social networking site. She no longer works in the music industry; she told me she still had the CD single that we'd given to her on her birthday back in 1998, I can't for the life of me remember what it was though!

The Golden Mile

1999

Nineteen hundred and ninety nine, it felt like Mankind was on the cusp of greatness as well as total disaster. I was convinced the world was going to be blown to smithereens before the end of the year and I felt I'd achieved relatively little in my short time on the planet. I reflected upon 1998, it had been a great year for me but sadly I'd missed the enjoyment and involvement of my favourite band finishing off their year of excellence with a number one album, top ten singles and them playing at every blummin' festival and venue throughout the land including Glastonbury! James had apparently upset the landowner Michael Eavis when they arsed about with their stage times so that it didn't clash with England's performance during the World Cup. Now that's called sorting your priorities out! James had prepared two different set lists that they could play, a low key set list if England lost the game and an up-tempo greatest hits set if they won. Win they did so James had played the hits, the audience danced and Michael Eavis nodded his head in approval in time to the music whilst making a vow never to book the band for the festival ever again.

James' 1998 success had hung over me like a raincloud throughout my entire trip in Australia. There had to be something wrong with me as James had remained constantly at the forefront of my mind when I should've instead been experiencing a sensory overload from all of the wonderful and magical places I'd visited and been privileged enough to experience. It was probably like making love to the most beautiful woman in the world whilst at the same time you're thinking about tidying out the garage and wondering what you should take to the tip. Maybe

Vicky had been right and I was actually addicted to James? I'd turned into a James junkie, I needed a regular hit otherwise I'd go cold turkey, sweating profusely and having terrible nightmares about saluting the audience in York and shouting "ALRIGHT CAPTAIN" at them. I was feeling quite fed up. I was back home and once again working at the cash and carry where I'd worked prior to my trip. Sometimes whilst unpacking pallets from the warehouse I wondered if my trip abroad had been nothing more than a dream because that was exactly how it felt. I had no one to really share my experiences with; and it seemed nobody really wanted to talk about my trip for some reason or other. This was my mums reaction upon arriving back home.

"Did you have a nice time then?"

"Oh yes, it was brilliant, absolutely brilliant".

"Lovely, do you want a cup of tea?"

I felt like the character from the song 'The First Man in Space' by Sheffield's The All Seeing I; the song features vocals by Steve Oakey from the Human League. It's a fantastic song, definitely worth checking out. Am I voicing self pity? Sorry! It was however a good time to catch up with some lost friends. This included Charles and Steve, I'd felt some pangs of guilt in that I'd let my relationship with them slip so badly due to my relationship with Vicky but being true friends they welcomed me back into the fold, their voices sounded heavily northern after being away for so long and it took me a while to acclimatise to them and what they were saying. I threw myself back into my music in a big way making several visits to Mix Music each week purchasing singles ten to the dozen. Of course this included a copy of the *Best Of* which came with a second disc of live acoustic tracks. Although the recordings were of a very high quality it wasn't a patch on the battered old cassette I still owned of the 1992 Acoustic Tour, a much more atmospheric ensemble because of the intense audience noise compared to the new recording where the audience appeared to be comprised of music industry types who politely clapped between each song, except for 'Laid' where they went slightly hysterical, but only slightly. It should have been recorded in front of true James fans, but maybe the band had been trying to repair burnt journalistic bridges. If so then I guess it was a sensible move.

I purchased a copy of 'Sit Down 98', it was a remix of the original song and it had crept into the top ten late in 1998. It had an amazing sleeve which featured some old dears sat amongst various bits of chintz and hideous furniture, a bit like a Shakletons Chair advert, (they've been making furniture for over fifty years you know!) The song was in my opinion unintentionally funny; I'm not suggesting that it was crap or anything it's just that it was such a bizarre version of the song and it sounded to me like it had been made in a bit of a rush. It did have a fantastic intro though and some rather amusing whinnying guitars mixed into the track. The first time that I actually heard it was when I was out having a few welcome back beers up town with Charles.

"Hey, this is that 'Sit Down' remix, you've probably not heard it yet have you?" Charles said to me between mid slurps of his watery lager as the song started playing on the juke box. I burst out laughing upon hearing it as it sounded quite camp but everyone in the pub started hollering along to it, the pretty girls who were dressed up in their best attires for their Christmas parties shook their booties whilst the blokes stood near them gave them the glad eye, Charles and I included.

Christmas crept upon us, I bought a copy of the *Best Of* for Charles at his request and he bought me a copy of Madonna's *Ray of Light* album which was the first material I'd ever liked by the so called 'Queen Of Pop'. It's probably a bit of controversial thing to say but I find her a bit over rated I'm guessing that these are the words of either a fool or someone who thought that The Spice Girls would be a flop. *Ray of Light* is a very good album mind you probably due to the fact that the legendary William Orbit produced it. The new year began and I knew that I had to think smart regarding what I was going to do with myself longer term otherwise I'd have ended up like the majority of the people who I'd grown up with in the town where I lived and end up doing nothing with my life. I knew that the cash and carry work would eventually destroy me. I needed an exit strategy, but what and how?

Music continued to be my solace as it had been for countless years. The NME was my main source of information although I intermittently bought some of the monthly magazines too. I'd managed to catch up on as much James news as I could from these various sources including the internet which I'd grown to love and loathe at the same time. However it was invaluable regarding keeping abreast with what was hot and what was not in the world of pop music. I was very excited to hear that James would be releasing a new album proper later in the year and there was the prospect of live dates to attend as well. In April I left the cash and carry job for good and started a new job working in Leeds, the job was as a customer service representative for a 'local world bank' which was sure to lead to a fantastic career in finance for me, it didn't really matter that I'd flunked my maths exams a few times, I was living in the world of super computers that did all of the donkey work for you.

The best thing about working in Leeds was that adjacent to the call centre was a new shopping complex which housed a HMV store. I must have visited the store each and every day mainly just to browse but I ended up making several purchases a week the majority of which were impulse buys! Why I bought the crappy Gay Dad *Leisure Noise* album is a mystery to me to this day although the first two singles from it were pretty okay. I felt like a teenager again who'd just discovered music for the first time as I bagged umpteen singles a week, no wonder I was into my overdraft each and every month. As for my new job, well, for some reason I kept myself to myself somewhat and I'd often sit in my car at lunch time eating my sandwiches and listening to the radio. I must have looked like a bit of a weirdo to those who walked past the car but I ended up catching some great bands because of it.

The first time I ever heard the wonderful 'Sea Song' by Doves was on one of those lunch breaks and I leapt out of the car and ran across to HMV and bought a copy of the single for five pounds, yes FIVE POUNDS!!!!! Another gem that caught my attention was 'Jumbo' by Underworld and I ended up buying the album *Beaucoup Fish* on the day of release, it's a brilliant album and 'Jumbo' is both astonishing and very, very beautiful. I won a HMV voucher at work one day for achieving a target or some other patronising achievement and I excitedly headed across to HMV after work. I couldn't find anything that really leapt out at me so I did the decent thing and used it to purchase a copy of *Strip Mine* on compact disc. The guy behind the till raised his eyebrows with an impressed look upon his bearded face when I handed him the album and voucher for payment.

"Top band mate" he said.

"Top band indeed, mate" I replied before skipping out of the store like a prancing pony on roller skates.

I was spending nearly every Sunday driving across to Bridlington; I've briefly mentioned my car a few lines back, I'd purchased it from Charles's father, a C registration sky blue Vauxhall Astra (the car not his father). There was a fair amount of rust included which I felt gave the car a certain amount of panache. Anyway, the drive across to Bridlington helped blow all of the rubbish out of the engine and it helped me brush up on my hardly ever used driving licence that I'd managed to fool the DVLA into giving to me in 1993. I loved Bridlington, I still do, its shabbiness compensated by beautiful beaches and a true working harbour. Nice fish and chips too at the Dolphin restaurant. Sunday was market day, the usual tat of course but some guy had a CD stall of new and second-hand albums with a few bootleg CD's chucked in for good measure. And I finally found *One Man Clapping*! (I didn't of course) No, what I found was....

Blur: *Death of a Popscene* (an excellent 'Secret Gig' performance that included the wonderful 'Inertia').

The Stone Roses: *Reading 1996* (apparently a Japanese radio recording, it so wasn't, it had blatantly been recorded using a Dictaphone by some chancer, appalling sound quality but it featured two excellent Stone Roses songs that never were. 'Ice Cold Cube' was later recorded by Ian Brown for his debut solo album and 'High Times' that although it never was, would have been a fantastic single for the band).

James: *An Evening of Our Past* (Manchester Apollo performance for the 'Best Of' tour).

My car didn't have a CD player; in fact it didn't even have a tape deck so it was a case of listening to them when I got home. The Blur album was probably the best of the bunch though, The Stone Roses second and James propped up the rear end due to the fact that although it was

153

obviously very good it didn't really contain much in the way of surprises. Nice though.

In May I was overcome with excitement to the point of virtual collapse when an article in the NME mentioned that James would be releasing a new single in July called 'I Know What I'm Here For', as well as mentioning that the band would be playing a few festivals over the summer too. The all too brief article stated that the new album *Millionaires* would be released in the autumn along with another single called 'Fred Astaire'. Now, that was the kind of news that made my already very boring job seem worthwhile. Okay, *Millionaires* wasn't a great album title in my humble opinion but the album could have been called *Aardvark Dances with the Tulip Fairies* and I would have been equally as happy if not even more intrigued than I already was.

In June further news leaked out that the great man and long time friend of the band Brian Eno had once again been involving himself in all sorts of trickery regarding the new album. Sinead O'Connor was also to feature on the new album which worried me slightly as I was convinced bad karma followed her which may trip the new album up somewhat. She'd featured on an amazing song by Marxman some years earlier called 'Ship Ahoy', the song was sure to be a hit of some description yet the song peaked at a miserable number ninety nine in the charts. Surely the same thing couldn't happen to James I thought. It was promised to one and all that *Millionaires* would be *"the bands best work to date"*. I couldn't wait.

Now, I can't actually remember the first time that I heard 'I Know What I'm Here For' which is a bit of a surprise as I can generally remember the first time and the events surrounding the release of pretty much every other piece of music James had released since I've been a fan. It's even more unusual due to the oddness, the strangeness and the downright groovy weirdness that the song is. It was a confusing move to say the least and as ever it really didn't sound like anything the band had done up until then, in fact, I'd never heard a song like it and to this day I still haven't! The keyboard line sounded very tongue in cheek to me and appeared to be a world away from the sombreness of *Laid*. An unkind comment was voiced by one of the darlings in the music press, they said that the song sounded like Jesus Jones and although I can kind of see where the critic was coming from it is of course complete hogwash, the comment of course not the song.

Charles however stated that it was easily the worst James song he'd ever heard and he was in fact quite venomous about it. He thought it was a complete joke, the kind of joke that only a successful band could ever release and get away with, a bit like *Be Here Now* by Oasis. However BBC Radio DJ Chris Moyles made some positive comments about the song when he was doing his afternoon slot which I listened to on a return trip from Bridlington.

"Hey, this new James song's alright eh?" he stated in his broad Leeds accent and the cheesy keyboard riff was used as linkage music between songs throughout his show. The song was definitely going to be a big hit, possibly even trumping 'Sit Down'. It had to after the success of their previous year.

Even more good news was announced. James were going to play at the famous and historic Blackpool Tower Ballroom on the Friday night of the week the single would be released. I was due to travel to France the following Sunday but I decided that I simply had to attend the show in Blackpool. I bought two tickets, the other ticket was for a female acquaintance, she was a few years younger than me, well, only about five years but it felt like a cultural chasm as far as music was concerned and I was keen to show her a good time, musically of course. Lucy was a very pretty girl who I'd met after getting to know her mother from an evening computer class I enrolled on. During the last evening of the course her mum gave me a piece of paper with her telephone number on it.

"Here, give Lucy a call at some point if you can, she'd really like it if you did".

I was a bit embarrassed yet intrigued.

"Err, does she know about you giving me her number?" I asked, my voice trembling somewhat.

"Oh yes, she knows" Lucy's mum said to me, and then she gave me an odd wink.

To this day I'm unclear as to what exactly was going on, I wondered if I was being set up by her mum on a bizarre blind date, or was it simply that Lucy was finishing Sixth Form and she needed somebody to knock about with over the summer before she commenced university the following October. I went for the latter option and never tried to make a move or even question the unannounced friendship which had suddenly developed out of nowhere.

On the day before it's official release I went to my local supermarket where Steve worked and I managed to obtain 'I Know What I'm Here For' because he opened up the delivery box for me which looking back was probably a naughty thing to do, I wasn't too concerned though as I knew that my early purchase wouldn't really affect record sales at all. The single was released on two compact discs and both of them featured new material, the highlight was the wonderful 'Imagine Ourselves' which was simply stunning. Haunting and melancholic with Tim's vocal wavering as if on the edge of tears during the verses. I loved it more than the lead track and pretty much ignored the other songs that were spread across the discs. I listened to the song obsessively throughout the week, excited at the prospect of finally seeing James again, the first time since the Leeds show back in 1997.

Lucy met me on the Friday evening of the Blackpool gig. She'd caught the train to Leeds and then travelled by bus to where I worked. Being a proper gentleman I should have offered to have picked her up from home but it would have meant a round trip of about fifty miles so I soon knocked that idea on the head. I'd been feeling very giddy throughout the day almost to the point of being sick. We both piled into my knackered old Vauxhall Astra which coughed out a ton of filth from its exhaust and headed westbound across the M62 motorway before heading up the M61 towards the dilapidated yet beautiful in its somewhat fallen grace seaside that was the host of the show. I persecuted Lucy during the entire whole journey by rabbiting on about the band which firmly ruined any chances of anything more than a passing friendship as I presented myself as a ranting madman swerving dangerously and desperately past the already speeding too fast tons of metal, rubber, bone and sinew that was heading in the same direction as us.

We made Blackpool in ultra quick time, so quick that we were actually quite a bit early. I parked the car up and we went to find somewhere to eat that didn't guarantee food poisoning and eventually we stumbled across an Italian chain restaurant where I ended up paying for EVERYTHING, she didn't dip her hand into her pocket once! Conversation carried on, and on, and on about James and I'm sure she'd switched off somewhat midway through the meal. After our faux Italian meal we headed to the venue. I was of course wearing a James shirt, the light blue 'Laid Back' shirt that I still didn't really like too much and I was given thumbs up and waves by other James fans as we wandered through the seaside town. Lucy appeared to love the attention that we were receiving and I felt pretty good about myself too. We joined the throngs of people all kitted out in various faded James items of clothing and headed towards the venue, it was a pilgrimage of sorts.

Had I have gone to the gig by myself then I'd have arrived some hours earlier and made sure that I was as near to the front as possible if not indeed by the barrier itself but due to time constraints and the fact that I was with the lovely Lucy I played it cool and mingled towards the back of the auditorium instead. The white noise of a few thousand people talking over one another mixed in with the warm up music created an expectant vibe, it was quite a beery boozy atmosphere with quite a fair few drunken lads arsing about, drinks were being slopped about and cigarette smoke got into our eyes. We kept ourselves to ourselves and conversation was kept to a minimum mainly due to the fact that you had to shout yourself hoarse to keep conversation audible. The support band was Exit 52 which featured Jim Glennie's brother. The band didn't do much for me really and I was glad when they trooped off stage and the roadies started fiddling about with the equipment as they do in preparation for the arrival of James.

I was extremely curious as to what the new material would sound like and how much they'd play that evening. Eventually the lights dimmed and the audience roared into life, the usual chant of "Boothy, Boothy" rose up and I joined in as well carried away with the audience's excitement. Suddenly, there was movement on the stage but it wasn't the usual act of the band walking on stage one by one picking up their instruments with beaming nervous grins on their faces. Instead a familiar keyboard line started to play although it had a 'Sound of Yesteryear' quality to it. It became apparent that the sound was emitting from the venues old fashioned organ which rose from underneath the stage with Mark Hunter playing 'Laid' on it.

The audience went wild and the air was filled with much laughter, it was almost like a Monty Python sketch and I half expected Mark to turn, look over his shoulder and smile a cheesy smile at the audience whilst a twinkling light gleamed from his teeth. Suddenly the rest of the band made themselves known and the band crashed into 'Laid' proper. Lucy was smiling and clapped along politely like she was at a Labour Party Conference. I copied her and hollered along to Tim's yodelling. The song finished to a roar from the audience and the band immediately ripped into 'Destiny Calling', I was immediately whisked back to that record shop in Adelaide with the headphones on my head and I closed my eyes throughout. 'She's A Star' followed and as Saul had said back at the Reading Festival it really was just "hit after hit!"

Then they played the first of the new songs. 'Crash' began with Canadian new boy; well, newish, Michael Kulas making a nonsensical "Whooing" sound which somehow made perfect sense. The song picked up and it sounded groovy and catchy as hell, I realised that if the song was to be released as a single then it would be Number One for months. Bizarre lyrics aside such as "Cut the Herman free from the Hesse" it was a major triumph and appeared to herald a massive boost in confidence and self belief from the band. The song finished, the audience went wild, as much as they did for the opening salvo of songs which is a rare thing for any band when premiering new material. 'Sometimes' followed, its familiarity particularly following the Best Of was embraced by everyone in attendance. Tim chatted for a moment between songs and commented that the next song was called 'Fred

Astaire' but that they might have to change the title due to issues with the Fred Astaire Estate who were being difficult relating the usage of what had become a trademark of sorts. The song sounded beautiful, contemporary and a league ahead of most of their back catalogue, the audience again showed their appreciation fully. I was a whirlwind of emotions; it was like my birthday had come early or something.

'Johnny Yen' started up, the 'football crowd' making themselves heard well above Tim. It was the first time all evening that I really let myself go and I started to dance a frenzied Tim style dance whilst Lucy stood as still as a statue. I initially felt really self conscious, I hadn't drunk any alcohol as I was driving but I decided that I couldn't care less; this was going to be my time, my show, and of course my band! If I wanted to dance like a fruitcake then that was exactly what I was going to do and by the end of the song even Lucy was tapping her foot along. 'Out To Get You' followed and gave me a chance to catch my breath for a few minutes.

"Are you enjoying it?" I asked Lucy.

"Yes, they're brilliant!" she squeaked back at me.

The band played another new song, 'Someone's Got It In For Me' which for some reason reminded me of 'The Power of Love' by Frankie Goes To Hollywood, very dramatic and slightly over the top. The audience paid attention but there was a lot of chattering going on around us which spoilt the ambience somewhat. Another couple of familiar songs were played before another new song was unleashed. 'We're Going to Miss You' sounded odd and quite foreboding, almost like a warning or a threat to anyone who had ever dared to cross the band. The new single was then played and during the song a troupe of dancing girls all dressed in red leather walked on stage and started gyrating like it was a Christina Aguilera gig, writhing and squirming as if there was no tomorrow. Blokes nearby were cheering, Lucy asked me if this was usual for a James gig.

"Oh yes, it happens all of the time" I said to her.

"Did you know that they're good mates with the Spice Girls?" I shouted into her ear hole.

"Really?" she said in surprise.

"Yes, Jim has recently shacked up with Sporty Spice" I told her.

"Who's Jim?"

"The bass player, left hand side of the stage!"

She just gawped at the fop haired bass player coolly playing with his musical tool. By the end of the song I thought the floor had the potential to cave in from the bouncing stomping throng of the audience myself included and then the band finished the evening with a selection of greatest hits interspersed with an encore, and concluded with that song, again.

(Well, they had to really, didn't they?)

We left the venue with the hordes of sweaty drunken fans and quick marched it towards my parked car which thankfully remained intact even though I'd left it in a bit of a dodgy sand blasted car park that was plastered with chips and seagull poo.

"Well, what did you think then?"

"Really good, thanks so much for sorting the tickets out" replied Lucy with a beaming smile on her face and then she proceeded to sing 'Sit Down' in a rather sweet voice. Lucy insisted on having the car heater on for the entire journey home because she was cold, fair enough but by the time we'd reached the end of the motorway my eyes were as dry as sand and they scratched every time I blinked. This upset me somewhat as dry eyes are really rubbish. We bid each other good night without even a peck on the cheek and I said/threatened that I'd catch up with her upon returning from distant lands, well, France is quite distant from where I lived, much more compared to somebody who lives in a place such as Dover for example.

Guildford

1999

I was due to start work at nine the following morning manning the phones and being shouted at by irate customers because they'd gone over their agreed overdraft limit, of course in their opinion it was my fault and not theirs that they'd overspent their weekly shopping budget buying premium dog food and not the stores own brand. After work I was traveling down south as I was going on holiday by myself. I'd invited Lucy but it was a bit too last minute for her and maybe it would have appeared a bit full on for her to have spent a week with me in a two man tent which of course only really fits one person. Initially a few of my mates were up for going away with me, Charles and Steve included but as the months went by and the holiday drew ever closer my friends all pulled out one by one, all with different excuses. To say that I developed a bit of a complex would be an understatement; however, I'd decided that I wasn't going to let other people spoil my fun so I carried on with the holiday plans regardless.

The ferry was due to leave Portsmouth on the Sunday night bound for Caen but for some reason or other I'd already planned to travel down on the Saturday and camp somewhere although I still hadn't given too much thought into exactly where, I'd considered the possibility that I might end up camping in an isolated layby, a bit risky though as Dogging was starting to take off in a big way. A crazy, wild voodoo kind of thought popped into my head. James were due to headline on the Saturday night at the Guildford Festival (now known as 'Guilfest'). I considered the option of heading to the festival instead of a dodgy layby and seeing my favourite band again which would also mean that I'd have a place to camp. I applauded myself at what I perceived to be a very good idea indeed and I high-fived myself in congratulation. The idea was easily up there with the brave concept of solar power, wind turbines and green tomato ketchup.

My battered old car was packed very early on Saturday morning. It included my tent, provisions for a week or so, but no road map, I wouldn't need one I was quite sure. Okay, so I was heading for a remote viaduct in northern France where I would hopefully spend the week bungee jumping which in a way was like looking for a needle in a foreign haystack, but I was sure that I'd find the viaduct no problem because God himself was on my side. I waved goodbye to my mum and drove off to work and spent three laborious hours answering calls and been given dirty looks by the team leaders whenever I needed to put my computer on hold and use the toilet. But when twelve o'clock came around I leapt out of my chair like a salmon heading up stream at the prospect of going on holiday, by myself, and of course seeing James in Guildford. I left work and headed south down the M1 Motorway before eventually reaching the M25 and travelling anticlockwise until I saw the signs for Guildford.

By the time I reached the Surrey town the windscreen and bonnet of my car was blood red due to the shear amount of bugs that had met their maker via my rusty light blue car whilst it hurtled down the motorway at brakeneck speed. I bowed my head in respect and saluted the poor little mites who'd perished in such an undignified manner and I even shed a small tear too. It was a sad moment, but then I remembered that I was off to see James and I soon forgot about the massacre that had taken place a few inches away from my nose. I parked up near the town centre and asked a local where I could buy tickets from, they pointed me in the direction of HMV and I ended up buying a Saturday ticket and an overnight camping pass before racing back to my car and driving to the festival.

Guildford Festival, well, it was nothing like the Reading Festival that was for sure. The festival was sponsored by Radio 2 back in the days when Radio 2 wasn't as cool as it is these days, or maybe my current age has something to do with the fact that I listen to it more so now than any other radio station. The festival was festooned with families enjoying picnics and the local vicar's wife sold freshly made lemonade by the paper cup full. Very civilised, just the kind of live event I expected the Mancunian Rock Gods to take over and utterly annihilate with their unconquerable back catalogue and their future hits. It was going to be a sonic bloodbath that would change Guildford forever. I was absolutely gasping for an ice cold beer after the furious long hot drive but I decided to erect my tent first. It was a bit/lot of a struggle, I should have practised at home and in the end a kind and attractive hippy looking woman helped me sort things out after she saw me making a comical hash out of trying to erect it by myself. When the red material based habitat was finally up I thanked her by giving her a high-five although she didn't partake in the act so I ended up looking rather stupid holding one hand up in the air and shouting "WHOO!" She walked away from me in a slow and meticulous manner; I'd obviously unsettled her somewhat with my Americanised display of congratulations and thanks.

Having embarrassed myself as per usual I ran away from the scene and headed across to the bar, bought myself a beer and downed it in one. I toasted the dead bugs too in remembrance. It made me feel kind of special. James weren't due on stage for a little while yet, The Afro Celt Sound System were on the main stage playing a frantic set as I approached the arena. They were a little bit like a polite version of The Prodigy, they were very good and I nodded my head in respect to their flutes and loops, some half naked burnt out old school ravers were throwing shapes in time to the music and I decided to join in with them. The beer had definitely gone to my head but they welcomed me into their chaotic throng for one song at least, then they told me to be on my way as my normalness was making them feel uncomfortable.

The band Ultrasound who at one point were going to be "the next big thing" had cancelled for some reason or other and ex Suede guitarist Bernard Butler played instead; he was a bit boring though, he hardly spoke to the crowd and wore a pair of extremely tight red leggings. He still managed to look extremely butch though. Kristin Hersh was

163

the penultimate act of the day, her mission was to warm up the crowd for James, I knew of Kristin Hersh as she'd recorded and released a song with REM's Michael Stipe called 'Your Ghost', it was and still is a rather wonderful song. By then I was onto my third pint of beer and as she played the haunting song I swayed along to it with my arms raised skywards whilst mouthing the wrong lyrics as I couldn't actually remember what they were.

A round of muted polite applause greeted the song as it ended; I nosily roared my approval and was given several dirty looks for my drunken boisterous show of approval. Feeling embarrassed for the fiftieth time that day I mooched away from where I'd been stood and noticed that a make shift merchandise stall was being erected nearby out of a couple of tables. I staggered across for a bit of a gander and noticed to my astonishment that James t-shirts were for sale! Well, there was only one design for sale, it was a black shirt which in pink writing had "I Know What I'm Here For" emblazoned across it with the 'James' logo on the left arm and a picture of a pigs bum on the reverse. Of course I had to buy one; I dug some cash out of my wallet and paid for the said item before haphazardly racing back across to my tent and hiding the shirt under my sleeping bag in case I ended up being robbed. I didn't take quite as much care though regarding my passport and ferry tickets and simply left them exposed on the lumpy floor of the tent.

I was definitely feeling the effects of the alcohol, the tiredness of the night before and the drive down south and I slowly made my way back into the arena and spent about fifteen minutes rambling away to a security guard trying to persuade him to let me backstage to meet James. Naturally he declined as he had a mortgage and other exciting bills to pay and he didn't want to lose his job because of some drunken northern twerp. Kristin Hersh was still wailing away to a still rather small and uninterested crowd and before her set ended I headed to the toilet, had a massive wee and then made my way towards the barrier to find a position in front of where Tim would be stood. I was quite surprised at how few people were in attendance, I thought I'd really struggle to make it anywhere near the barrier but I simply strolled up to the black metal fence and made myself as comfortable as I possibly could.

It was at this point that a couple of lads started talking to me, I never did find out there names or maybe I was just to drunk to retain that particular bit of information but they were HUGE James fans and had seen them umpteen times. They'd told me that they'd also been to the Blackpool gig the previous night and that they thought it was one the best James gigs that they'd ever attended. Well, these lads were apparently in the know regarding the band. They'd spoken to various band members during the day at Guildford except for Tim and they'd garnered loads of information relating to the new album.

"Do you know the song 'Crash'? Well it's going to be their first number one single you know!" one of them said to me.

"Can you see that woman over there?" one of them said to me pointing towards the mixing desk, "She's involved with the new album". I couldn't tell who they were talking about so I just said "Wow" in amazement.

"*Millionaires* is going to be massive and it's gonna put them in the same league as Oasis" chipped in the other lad.

I agreed with them. The future was James' for the taking. I waffled on to them both, like I do, (which you may have noticed by now) and I quizzed them further regarding James until the warm up music stopped and the crowd started to wolf whistle and clap. I turned around and was shocked but pleased at how big the crowd had grown. James then marched onto the politest stage of the politest festival in the land.

The band looked hungry to rock. Saul in particular had an air of rage about him as he prowled around the stage, raising his fists at the audience in a threatening manner whilst Tim strutted about like a heated up meerkat. New material was played in a similar vein to the Blackpool gig. The audience lapped it up but of course the biggest cheers of the night were for 'The Hits'. However, it was the new material that the two lads and I went really nuts for, except perhaps for 'Someone's Got It In For Me' which still sounded overblown and pompous. When the band played their new single I went particularly bananas and threw myself about like a rag doll. Tim sang the lyric, "*The band are sharp but the singers slow, everything must go*", and I must have caught his eye because when he sang the first bit, *"The band are sharp but the singers slow"* I started making hand gestures arguing this particular point whilst shouting "NO!" very loudly and Tim put his hand to his chest and smiled as if to say, "Really, you're too kind". I burst into a maniacal fit of laughter and my bladder leaked a little bit from over excitement.

The varied set continued, dusk settled in but I remained warm due to my rather wild dancing. I'd been shouting out between songs and at one point I embarrassed myself yet again shouting "WE LOVE YOU TIM" causing much mirth and laughter from those around me. Midway through a song Tim jumped off the stage and ran directly across to where the two lads and I were stood and he leapt right over the barrier and stood in front of us. The two lads dropped onto the floor and started to frantically bow like the Messiah himself had made an appearance. I grabbed Tim and had a bit of a feel of his back, (I'm not sure how I'd feel if a random stranger did this to me). Although Tim was of a slight build he felt lean, wiry and strong. He then started to tear off his backstage wristband pass and I grasped it from his hand and stared at it in wonderment. He then spoke to the immediate crowd.

"Hello! Hello? Hello there!" he said with a beaming smile on his face.

I looked in astonishment at the people he was talking to, most of them smiled whilst others literally just stood there and stared at him in complete awe. Tim remained in front of us for a few moments more but as he hadn't been man handled by the crowd (except by myself) he scrambled back across the barrier out of what appeared to be sheer embarrassment and disappeared into another section of the audience stage right who reacted more appropriately and they mobbed, loved and licked him. The two lads and I chinked fists with each other in congratulations as Tim had obviously visited our section of the crowd because of the three us, I'd finally gotten to touch the great man and had a piece of his attire in my hand. I even gave it a gentle sniff.

Tim finally clambered back on the stage and the band finished the song, the set was drawing to a close, Saul kept urging the crowd to "COME ON!!!!" and he angrily threw his plectrum at the crowd, it could have easily taken someone's eye out however the small piece of plastic fell short by several meters and it landed in front of me like a butterfly. I quickly gained the attention of a security guard begging him for the piece of memorabilia, he passed it to me and it went straight into my pocket along with Tim's wristband. What a night! The set unsurprisingly ended with 'Sit Down' and then the band all buggered off and the audience began to disperse. I said farewell to the two lads and headed towards my tent, after of course I went for another massive wee.

I slept and I dreamt. I dreamt that I was a carrot being chased by a large donkey. It was quite a frightening dream and I awoke with a sudden start. It was about eight in the morning and I had a bit of a hangover from the fizzy alcohol that I'd consumed the night before. I nakedly scurried around the floor like a filthy sweaty little beetle and I found my jeans and dug deep into the pockets and prised out Tim's wristband and Saul's plectrum. I stared thoughtfully at them for about an hour before deciding to sober up by eating the largest bacon, egg, sausage, mushroom and tomato sandwich the world had ever seen. Later in the morning I bid farewell to Guildford and set off south arriving in Portsmouth after midday. My ferry wasn't due to sail until midnight so I chilled out on the stony beach for the remainder of the afternoon until I headed back to my car to listen to the chart run down on the radio, I was desperate to hear where in the top ten the new single had reached. I expected it to jump in at around number five or six but the fine and wonderful song 'I Know What I'm Here For' crawled into the Top Forty at a disastrous number twenty two! My heart was broken. How? Why? It was a cruel world and a bitter end to a fantastic weekend, maybe it was my own stupid fault for purchasing the single early. Maybe the official chart people had gotten wind that copies were being sold early so they knocked the actual chart placing down twenty places! If there is any truth in this then I apologise. Sorry James.

Still feeling pained with disappointment I caught the ferry later that night and had a great time in France and I rewardingly managed to find the viaduct without any navigation equipment at all which I have to say was a major fluke! I think I freaked the locals out a bit driving around the *Wickerman* themed villages in my old banger of a car. I got wind of the fact that the people who owned the camp site also thought that I was a bit odd. A lone British guy who'd travelled down from the north of England specifically to spend a week bungee jumping off a viaduct in northern France. The people who worked at the bungee site thought I rocked though; I did thirteen jumps that week. It took my mind off the major disappointment that was *that* shocking chart position. Well, maybe the general record buying public were holding off until the new album came out I thought to myself. Maybe the band members would indeed be millionaires before the year was out.

The Curse of Sinead O'Connor

1999

The remainder of the not too stifling hot but still rather pleasant summer was spent anxiously looking forward to the release of the new James album, well, other stuff was going on in my life of course, I'd hate to give the impression that I was a tad obsessed with either the release date of the new album or the band itself! God that would be just so embarrassing! The Sinead O'Connor thing still irked me somewhat, was the angry Irish woman with the rather beautiful voice cursed after ripping up the picture of The Pope live on television? I wasn't too sure but after the death knell had been sounded upon Marxman's career following her input I tried to put it to the back of my mind. Surely lighting couldn't strike twice?

My 'I Know What I'm Here For' t-shirt garnered a bit of attention on a few occasions, one of the most notable times was when I was doing a bit of shopping in my local supermarket. I'd bought some fresh vegetables and some processed meat based products for eating and generally enjoying. The guy serving me was a slimly built, bespectacled beardy fellow. He greeted me as all checkout people should, with politeness and courtesy. His eyes were soon drawn to the large pink font on my shirt.

"Aha, so, what *are* you here for then?"

"Ha, I can't tell you I'm afraid, it's a secret" I said and then I gave him one of my weird winks.

"Hmmm, so, a secret you say. Well I certainly know what I'm here for". He then started to ramble on for about a minute or so about Eastern

Zen Buddhism, although it was rather interesting it probably wasn't the most ideal time or location to start up such an in-depth conversation and the queue of shoppers behind me weren't too pleased as it delayed them from purchasing their cut price spaghetti.

On a rainy Sunday morning a passer by in the street stopped me.

"I'm really sorry, this is going to come across as being a bit odd but I really feel drawn towards you and I feel that we need to speak to one another" the rain sodden man said to me.

"Err, right, well, hello" I said, also rain sodden, I'd not worn a coat and I was wearing nothing more than my James t-shirt and a pair of jeans, plus all of the other essential stuff such as underpants, not Y-Fronts though I hasten to add.

"You're t-shirt. Tell me more"

"I'm sorry, I'm not with you."

"Sorry, it's just that I'm sure I dreamt this sequence of events where we met and you were wearing this t-shirt, it's a message for me. It has to be".

He was damn right; he was coming across as a bit odd and coming from me that is quite a thing to say.

"Sorry but I really need to go" I nervously said to him.

"Oh, okay" he said sounding disappointed. "But before you go, I want you to do something for me".

"Riiiiiight. What?"

"Say 'Gouranga'".

"What?"

"Say 'Gournaga', go on, it won't hurt".

"Sorry mate, I've really gotta go" and I marched on feeling a bit psyched out by the strange man. After a while I turned around and noticed that the man was still stood in the same place staring back at me. I was a little bit unnerved to say the least.

I was pleased when James were announced as the headliners for a Radio One 'Big Day Out' Festival event that was taking place in

Manchester the following September. Support came from the slightly overrated Supergrass and the rather fantastic Doves. The 'Big Day Out' Festival, not to be confused with the Australian festival of the same name had been set up to modernise the radio stations summer of live events such as the Radio One Road Show that used to trundle around various seaside towns over the summer. If you were lucky enough to be able to attend one of the Road Show's then you could experience a variety of acts playing and definitely not miming to backing tracks. The acts usually comprised of the latest 'Boy Bands' with a couple of 'Indie' bands chucked in to keep all the Indie Kids happy. The show would be broadcast live on the radio and hosted by some pretending to be interested presenters who probably all secretly hated each other, the bands and all attending. I wasn't going to be able to get to the show in Manchester though as trying to secure a ticket for the event was difficult unless you lived in Manchester itself.

The second release from *Millionaires* was announced as the rather wonderful and beautiful 'Just Like Fred Astaire', the title of the song had been changed at the insistence of the Fred Astaire Estate who'd threatened to kill the band if they didn't change it and of course no one wants to face the wrath of an American Estate unless that's your kind of thing of course. The single was going to feature another song that featured a duet with Sinead O'Connor. Arghh!!! Again, like the previous single I can't remember the first time I heard the studio version of it, I do however remember an interview on Radio One with Jo Whiley. The gist of the interview went something like this…..

"Tim, tell us about the new single!"

"Thanks Jo, well, it's a beautiful song about a man who goes to the doctor because he feels unwell, but it turns out that he's actually suffering the symptoms of being in love. It's the first time that I've made a real conscious effort to write a love song".

"Wow, it sounds fantastic, okay thanks very much Tim Booth from James, and now let's play some music by the Manchester legends, here's 'Sit Down'!"

How annoying! A similar thing happened to the Liverpudlian band The Boo Radleys who had the weighty millstone that was 'Wake Up Boo!' hanging around their neck, the DJ on that occasion announced that their new single 'Find The Answer Within' was being released on that particular day. Then he said,

"Anyway, here's 'Wake Up Boo!'" before the annoying jingly jangly song was spun.

Anyway, I digress back to 'FRED ASTAIRE'. (It'll always be 'Fred Astaire'!)

It really was a fine song, very pretty with loved up boy meets girl lyrics that were sweet on the ear and not at all mushy. The music itself was dreamy, warm and snug with just the right amount of sharpness and edge created by the bands guitarists. Of course I bought the single on the day of release, or should I say singles as it was released on two different discs, the first one featured the Sinead O'Connor song, it was and still is a very popular song amongst the hardcore James fan base out there but I have to say that I didn't like it at all. It didn't sound like it was going anywhere in particular to me. 'Long To See' was okay although a bit melancholy and Enoesque whilst the second disc featured 'Mary' which was rather excellent and 'Goal, Goal, Goal' which was the absolutely hysterical 1994 World Cup football anthem that never was.

It was quite weird in the fact that the bands profile was huge at the time, there was an awful lot of expectancy from the band by the record company, the fans and the public at large yet I only managed to hear the single twice on the radio that week and I spent an awful lot of time in my car driving to and from work. The band performed their new single on the Saturday morning kids music show CD:UK hosted by the annoying and frankly droll television presenters Ant & Dec but thankfully supported by the rather attractive Cat Deeley.

"Quick Mum, come and have a look who's on the telly, it's James!!" I yelled at my mum who was smoking a cigarette and drinking a cup of tea in the kitchen. She came in and watched the band for a few moments in a bored kind of manner.

"He looks very gay doesn't he?" Mum said in reference to Tim Booth.

172

Now I must mention that everybody looked "very gay" in my mum's eyes, this even included Mr T from The A-Team and Phil Mitchell from Eastenders.

"Err, I think you'll find that he's not gay, he's married with kids and all sorts" I said in a rather defensive tone.

"Well, that means nothing these days does it!" was her reply. "They're all at it, men and women! And why is he singing about Fred Astaire? He's played out; nobody's interested in Fred Astaire these days. They're out of touch they are. Didn't they sing that sitting song? Now that was a nice song, and that 'Roll With It' song was good, oh, that was Oasis wasn't it? They love their mum do those two boys", she said in reference to the Gallagher's and then she angrily stormed out of the room and back into the kitchen. My mum was the harshest of critics, even more so than Charles.

The song should have been an enormous hit for the band but as you may have already guessed by now it wasn't, the song entered the chart that following weekend at number seventeen which was higher than the previous single but still not high enough and the single then proceeded to drop out of the charts like a freefalling skydiver. In hindsight releasing the single the week before the album was released may have been a mistake, maybe the single should have been released to coincide with the Radio One gig? The disappointment though was dampened slightly by the fact that *Millionaires* was released the following week. I'd read a Stuart Maconie review for it a few weeks prior in Q magazine and he'd given it an absolutely stonking review. He boldly stated that when the round-up of the best albums of the last decade of the twentieth century was released then *Millionaires* would be able to stand toe to toe with *Urban Hymns* and *Ok Computer*.

Millionaires was being released with a second disc of live tracks too, naturally on that cold, grey and damp Monday lunchtime I ran from my place of work skidding several times on the gravelly path and headed towards HMV. The album was thankfully sat in a prominent position, right in front of the entrance and I desperately grabbed a copy of the two disc version with sweaty palms, handed over my cash to the pretty female member who was serving and ran back to my car, again skidding on the gravelly path and this time actually ending up on my backside which ended up muddy which is not a good look when working for a professional organisation such as a bank. As I didn't have a CD player in my car I spent the rest of my lunch break carefully admiring the rather spartan artwork which featured a rather large pig wearing jewellery against a rich blue background whilst I tried not to cover it in grease and crumbs from my packed lunch. The rest of the afternoon was spent dreaming about listening to the album; even the most annoying of customers didn't faze me.

A few hours later I was sat on my green 1970's carpeted bedroom floor with the album held in my shaking hands like an unpinned hand grenade. I nervously turned on the stereo and slid in the precious silver disc and promptly sat in an awkward cross legged position (because I can't actually cross my legs properly!) The first track was 'Crash', it was meant to be the song that was going to be the bands first number one single according to those two lads from Guildford, and it really could have been. However, the song didn't sound anything near as good recorded as it had live, it was in fact rather tinny, wobbly, and way too fast. The guitar part towards the end of the song was horrible, grinding and tuneless, Marilyn Manson would have whimpered at it. With a bit more work or maybe with a little less work the song could have been much improved. Perhaps if the tempo had been slowed down and the bass turned up a few notches then 'Crash' would have been an absolute killer of a song.

'Fred Astaire' was next followed by 'I Know What I'm Here For', so far so good. 'Shooting My Mouth Off' started off quiet enough and then built up into something that sounded close to electronica, it was a fine song although I felt Tim's vocal during the latter part of the song sounded off key, however I loved the song it was joyful and spirited to say the least. Nothing could have prepared me for 'We're Going To Miss You'. I'd heard it live already but the recorded version just blew me away. I can honestly say that when the first chorus erupted my eyes welled with tears and my jaw dropped wide open, it was stunning, absolutely stunning and the song just got better and better throughout, it's pinnacle was when Adrian Oxalls' multi-tracked Cellos' sang out in the most beautiful mesmeric manner possible. I was utterly gobsmacked and had the rest of the songs on the album ended up being crap then it wouldn't have really mattered, however this would not be the case.

'Strangers' stirred up, it's looped drums clicked and a clacked away, the song sounded like a Neil Young song, it was a pretty little number. 'Hello' followed, sparse beyond belief with Tim singing over a simple backing track where less definitely meant more. 'Afro Lover' followed, the song was produced by the guys from Faithless and it was a very silly song that at the same time was great fun and lively. It sounded a million miles away from the James of old. I ended up jumping around my bedroom to it causing my mum to shout at me for scaring Waz-Waz the cat. 'Surprise' followed, I'm sure I could drop in a joke about how surprised I was by it but there's no need to is there? As for the song itself, it was one of those songs that I didn't like initially from the intro but the song certainly improved as it went along and I loved the chorus.

'Dumb Jam' was yet another classic James song, short, bouncy and extremely self-depreciating regarding its title, had a band such as Oasis released it as their own then it would have been one of those songs that they would definitely have had to play each time they performed live. The guitar work actually sounded a bit like Gallagher Senior. My old favourite, the rather pompous 'Someone's Got It In For Me' sounded like a big song played as a small song. I'm not too sure if that makes any sense, another way to put it is that it was obviously meant to be an epic sounding song but it felt like it had been short changed somewhat, maybe the song should have been a minute or two longer in length to really play on the over the top drama further. Tim had described the song as a "victim song", because apparently "everyone is a victim" or something like that. I kind of knew where he was coming from; at least I think I did.

The final song was the odd yet quite beautiful cascading beast 'Vervaceous', the song morphed from initially starting off as a fairly pleasant shimmering little number into a galactic sized beast that featured a certain Irish singer towards the end of the song, her voice had been processed so that it sounded as if Arcee from *The Transformers* was singing/speaking the closing lines of the song. It was a rather fitting end to a fantastic album, possibly in my humble opinion the bands best and certainly most commercial work to date.

Once the stereos green light emitting diode reset itself to show the albums length in its entirety I reached across and pressed play again and listened to the album right through. The album was joyous, uplifting and warm in sound and production, a proper pop album that was still weird enough to be a James album. It came at just the right time too, my life felt like it was unravelling to a degree, I was in a job that I'd really grown to hate, friends had come and gone including Lucy who'd been what I could only describe as a complete bitch towards me on a night out in Manchester. My alcoholic mother had absolutely driven me to despair, actually it went beyond despair if truth be told, the whole sorry saga is discussed in my previous book 'Their Spirits, My Demons' which can be picked up in all good bargain book shops, if you're interested. (Actually this isn't true, but I've got a few dozen copies sat all lost and lonely in my loft). I embraced the optimism of *Millionaires* as tightly as I possibly could and no matter how depressing other things in my life felt I knew that I had a reliable talisman in the album and the band itself. As for the second disc, it was pretty good although I cringed when I heard myself shout "WE LOVE YOU TIM!" at the start of one of the live tracks from Guildford.

Millionaires unsurprisingly received another mixed bag of reviews, naturally the weeklies hated it, the NME had a field day of slagging it off describing it as *"deathly average"* and giving it 4/10. Slightly hilarious in my opinion and the 'Monotony Maker' featured another cheap shot at mocking and making fun of the band. It said an awful lot more about the journalists own failings than it did about James. Other more sensible and slightly less self obsessed journalists from a range of publications gave the album a big thumbs up, it proudly arrived at number three in the album chart the following weekend.

Once again though disappointment was going to spoil everybody's party including mine. And the reason was this, the following week the album plummeted in a way not to dissimilar to that of *Laid*. It became painfully obvious that the only people who'd bought the album were the hardcore James fans and the odd person who'd discovered them from the *Best Of*. Even though the album had received positive reviews in the mainstream press the album refused to bloody sell. Perhaps everyone had been spending their money on plastic tarpaulin, bottled water and cans of baked beans in preparation for the end of the world that was due to happen in less than two months following the release of *Millionaires* as the Millennium Bug was about to be unleashed destroying mankind and all of its work. For me *Millionaires* summed up the existing pre-millennium tension perfectly, so perfectly in fact that the government should maybe have made it compulsory listening for each and every person in the Kingdom. It really was the last great album released in the Twentieth Century.

Inbal was a very pretty Israeli girl I'd befriended whilst in New Zealand back in 1998. We'd kept in touch through the medium of writing letters and she wanted me to visit her but I couldn't really afford to as my salary wasn't anything to write home about, plus I was spending all of my money on music. It was her birthday in October so I decided to send her a present which was the 'Just Like Fred Astaire' single. In her birthday card I wrote, *"May your eyes be opened by the wonderful"* in reference to the lyrics from 'Waltzing Along'. She wrote back a few weeks later....

"Thank you so very, very, very much for the wonderful song. It really is the most beautiful song that I have heard in such a long time, it made me cry but it is so happy too. My mother also likes it and she dances with my father to it in our apartment. Thank you from all of us! I need to point out something though, I think you made a bad spelling mistake or missed a word out in my birthday card as it does not make any sense to me or anybody else here. What is the "wonderful"? Is this an English thing? If you can tell me what the "wonderful" is then this would make some sense to me because this does not sound like good English to me and I am surprised by you. Anyway, thank you again and I hope to see you soon enough.

Inbal

xxxxx

I laughed out loud when I read her reply; it was hilarious yet kind of cute and very sweet. I had images of her parents waltzing in time to the music in their home in Tel Aviv, romance and love filling the air. It was a perfect introduction to the band for Inbal and her family and I made a mental note to send her some more material at a later date.

Charles had been a great support to me regarding loads of crap that had been taking place in my home life which I've hinted at earlier. He visited me at home most nights and took me out for a beer from time to time. Charles obviously had an interest in James but was notoriously difficult to please or impress. I played him the album one evening when he was around.

"It's such an awful song" he said in relation to 'I Know What I'm Here For'.

"Not bad" in reference to 'Just Like Fred Astaire'.

"Oh my, this is really embarrassing" he said when 'We're Going To Miss You' started. I was really angry with him.

"Just wait until the chorus!" I said my voice filled with panic, and when it came to the chorus he actually raised his eyebrows somewhat.

"Hmm, not too bad" Charles said, I knew that in 'The World Of Charles' that "not too bad" was a compliment of the highest order.

Charles and I moved to Leeds a week later, he'd wanted to move there for some time as he also worked in the city, life for me was intolerable in my family home and I was going to crack up if I stayed a moment longer so we ended up renting a 'back to back' house in Burley, Leeds. It was a triumphant move in every possible way. My stress levels lessened and we became 'kwazy party animals'. The television was hardly ever on and instead a couple of albums took up residency on the stereo, *Golden Greats* by the enigmatic Ian Brown and *Millionaires* by James. Charles had grown to love the album and he requested his own copy for Christmas even if it was simply to learn all of the lyrics from the album to make me jealous. We had a ton of visitors to the household and each and every one of them was subjected to *Millionaires* in a way that could only ever be described as brain washing. It was a simple task, get them drunk on cans of Carlsberg and then play the album on repeat until they'd succumbed to its charm and magic or they died. Then they were ordered to go out and buy the album themselves, some of them actually did this, except the dead ones of course.

The third single from the album was going to be released in December, I was really hoping that it was going to be a remixed version of 'Crash' but instead 'We're Going To Miss You' was the song of choice, I thought it was quite a poor choice as a single but I had faith in the band and their record company that it was going to be the song that tipped the balance for them. One of the DJ's on Radio One had selected the single as his 'Single of the Week' the week prior to it's release and he was extremely enthusiastic about the song, however the version that was released was slightly different to the album version and it had lost something special in the translation. Tim's voice sounded odd during certain parts of the song which I really didn't like. It was the first and the last time that I'd hear the song played on the radio, ever. The single ended up being released on the 6th December and I popped into HMV in Leeds city centre to buy the two compact discs which of course featured some extra tracks, I was extremely interested to hear the Brian Eno version of the title track. Upon returning home I was a tad disappointed in all of the tracks barring a live version of 'Top Of The World' from Gold Mother. Even the Brian Eno version of the song was a huge disappointment to me.

On the following Saturday I was off to see James play at the Manchester Evening News Arena which back in 1999 was called the NYNEX Arena. I was driving across to Manchester mid-afternoon with Steve who'd bizarrely enough decided that he wanted to go and see James live again. He'd even bought a copy of Millionaires which surprised yet pleased me. Charles was also attending the show, he was going to be driving across later in the day as he was going along with another friend, they had seated tickets so it didn't really make much sense for us all to travel across together as I wanted to make sure that Steve and I were stood right by the barrier. Thankfully this time around he didn't have injured feet like he had done some six years earlier where he ended up missing the gig that was eventually cancelled and rescheduled anyway.

I'd never been to such a big venue in my life, it was actually quite frightening to be in such a large enclosed space and I felt pangs of panic as we walked down the steps to the arena floor, a sizeable crowd was stood by the barrier already which meant that we wouldn't be by the barrier itself but still close enough to be within throwing distance of the band, not that we would be throwing anything at them.

Although come to think of it I once threw a packet of cheese and onion crisps at Suede's front man Brett Anderson at a gig in Bradford, the packet missed him and I ended up regretting the act as I was actually quite hungry. The support act for James was Cast who's popularity had somewhat diminished represented by ever decreasing record sales. They came across as surly, uninterested and going through the motions simply to get paid; it wouldn't have surprised me if they didn't even like James. They played an okay set which consisted mainly of their singles and we jumped about a fair bit particularly to 'Free Me' which was and still is a ferocious song which held many a good memory for me. The audience behind us had grown enormously and as I turned around and panned around the arena I felt pretty awed at the fact that the band had managed to fill such a vast space. When Cast eventually plodded off stage the usual air of excitement and expectancy really built up. Even Steve was very excited and stomped from foot to foot in a merry little way. This might however have been due to the fact that the floor was bloody freezing as the venue was then used as an Ice Hockey arena and the coldness of the ice underneath the boards chilled our veruca infected feet.

The lights shut down, the arena was plunged into semi darkness and all seventeen thousand people made a sound that roared like thunder. James made their entrance, the "Boothy, Boothy" chant rose up, fists and fingers pointed towards him like it was a friendly Nuremburg Rally and the band opened their set with 'Laid', the crush from the audience and the sound system was immediate and we danced like an electric current was rippling through the ice beneath our feet. 'Ring the Bells' followed and again the audience really went for it, the band had raised their game due to being on home ground and they played with all of their might. Two songs from *Millionaires* came next, 'I Know What I'm Here For' and 'Crash'. 'Crash' sounded fantastic and only emphasised the disappointment of the recorded version. 'Say Something' followed and the biggest shock of the evening was 'Sit Down' being played mid set. I couldn't believe it, quite a daring move in their home town but definitely the right decision, the band gave the impression that they wanted once more to unshackle their past and show off their present. The fans favourite 'Johnny Yen' followed, the place went absolutely wild, in some ways more wild than they had for 'Sit Down' and in my opinion deservedly so. The rest of the set was a mixture of old and new, 'Someone's Got It In For Me', Shooting My Mouth Off', 'Waltzing Along', 'Sometimes' and a strange version of 'We're Going To Miss You'.

"This is our new single; it's been released this week. It's probably going to go straight into the charts at number fifty five", joked Tim causing much mirth and laughter from the audience and the band.

I was sure 'We're Going To Miss You' wouch reach a higher position than fifty five which for a band the size of James and their tight following was a non position as far as a single was concerned. We'd find out the following evening when the chart run down was announced. The set continued with 'Vervaceous', 'Stutter', 'Just Like Fred Astaire', 'Out To Get You', 'Destiny Calling', 'Tomorrow' and 'Sound'. The band then played 'Top Of The World' and Tim appeared onstage with a glittery coat before flying right across the crowd suspended by wires as he held a balloon in his hand. A ripple of laughter spread throughout the arena, it was quite sweet with just a touch of Tim Burton creepiness mixed in for good measure. 'Come Home' followed and the show ended with the big sing along that was 'She's A Star'. It was a triumphant set and a great end to an unpredictable and mixed year as far as success was concerned. We left the arena with the droves of fans and had a few beers with Charles et al at our gaff in Leeds.

"They absolutely murdered 'We're Going To Miss You', it sounded totally shite" moaned Charles, I tried to argue the point somewhat but I realised that I was fighting a losing battle and instead I cracked open a can of Carlsberg, necked it and gave out a dinosaur sized belch for good measure. As for the chart position of 'We're Going To Miss You', well, it didn't even make the top forty although it did reach a few places higher than Tim predicted at a whopping number forty eight in the top one hundred singles of that week. Still crap though but sometimes in life you just have to take it on the chin. I still blame Sinead O'Connor to this very day.

By the way, I posted a copy of 'We're Going To Miss You', to Inbal in Tel Aviv. She wrote back and said that she didn't like it. I never contacted her again.

Footnote: I've since learnt Gouranga is a harmless word that those Hare Krishna lot use quite a lot. They're a nice bunch of people, I like their use of miniature percussion instruments too.

Armageddon then

2000

The year 2000 arrived with a bit, actually a lot of a whimper, the Millennium Bug had miserably failed to materialise, my pocket calculator still worked and Armageddon sadly hadn't commenced in a 'War Games' manner. It was actually a very good thing indeed, particularly in relation to my calculator. It was one of those scientific calculators that I couldn't actually work out how to use or what the actual point of it was. 'Cos', 'Sin' and 'Tan', it's a completely foreign language to me. I was settling down somewhat in my new life in Leeds, the problems that existed less than twenty miles away felt thankfully way out of reach. I had a new bunch of friends and an absolutely fantastic social life. The many parties at our house never got out of hand though, in reality it was normally just a case of drinking lots of cheap lager, eating take away pizzas, playing darts and listening to music, lots of music.

Millionaires was still on very heavy rotation although Charles would often annoyingly skip past 'Hello' as he thought it brought the mood down somewhat. Sometimes we'd end up listening to The Bloodhound Gang and pretend that we were Frat Boys laughing at the childish insensitive lyrics from the album *One Fierce Beer Coaster*, it's a terrible album that somehow ended up being played an awful lot along with *Beaucoup Fish* by Underworld. We didn't have an actual stereo in the lounge, instead my Sony Playstation was used to play music, the sound quality was less than perfect though as it was piped through the mono speaker of our mid-eighties portable television. By this point you may have gathered that I had a bit of a soft spot for James' latest offering; however, amongst the hardcore James fan base I appeared to be a minority of sorts. A lot of the feedback that I read on the internet namely on the official James website was actually quite damning. The words *"over produced"* *"pop"*, *"camp"* and *"pompous"* appeared rife. Fans appeared to feel let down by the band for some reason or other. If you compare *Millionaires* alongside *Whiplash* then I think you'll find that there is a league or two's difference in the quality of the albums as a whole. I'm probably not making much sense; this however is not unusual.

As the excitement of the album release faded away my musical interest shifted in line with the rest of my life and soon enough *Millionaires* was played less and less whilst other bands took hold of my interest. And for me at least the first six months of the new millennium were quiet ones as far as James was concerned. *Golden Greats* ended up being played more than anything for the first part of the year, Charles and I were pretty much obsessed with the first six tracks of the album, it did kind of tail off towards the end though and the last tracks were what we would call 'Duffers' as in they were a bit duff. The muted fourth single from *Millionaires* was also abandoned, it was meant to be 'Crash' but after the bomb that was their last single the record company wisely decided against wasting any more of their money on the commercially misfiring band.

My life changed forever though in May of that year as I ended up meeting a woman who'd become my girlfriend and five years later she'd end up becoming my wife, (the poor thing). It's a bit of an embarrassing story but we met during a very drunken karaoke night where I serenaded her by singing 'Stupid Girl' by Garbage. Anyway if it wasn't for her then I wouldn't be writing these very words and would have probably have ended up as a directionless filthy drunk and feeling quite hard done by with the cards that life had dealt me so far. She'll feature a fair bit from now on throughout the rest of this book so to avoid confusing people any further than I may possibly have done already I'll simply refer to her as my 'wife' from here on in. Okay? Cheers.

Now as lovely, caring and as thoughtful as my wife is she has a major problem, and the problem is that her interest in music is pretty much zero. Okay, so she had The Stone Roses first album in the small collection of albums that she owned but some of the other albums that featured in her collection included an album by Gerry Halliwell, both albums by Steps and the musical Les Miserables that I'm not over keen on which of course probably makes me a bit of a sub-cultured philistine. And those albums were believe it or not the best of a bad bunch! Something definitely had to be done about this and I was especially irked when she described James as being "cheesy".

"Cheesy????" I said to her, absolutely horrified and shocked at her comment.

"Yeah, you know, 'Laid' and 'Sit Down' always get played in cheesy night clubs, good to dance to and all that" was her reply.

She was probably right though.

I was aghast. The relationship almost ended there and then however I gave her the benefit of the doubt because I *quite* liked her. Her saving grace was that she'd seen a few live bands before as she'd worked at V97 in Leeds which I'd also attended and it turned out as a result of my questioning her that we were possibly stood quite close to each other during The Prodigy's set. I knew that I had to try and influence her tastes somewhat but whenever I played any of my music she turned her nose up stating that,

"It's just noise."

The albums by the Australian band Tism went down particularly badly especially when their single 'He'll Never Be An Old Man River' was aired for the first time in her presence. I was a tad surprised at this but in retrospect maybe it wasn't the most romantic of songs to play to her and she commented that she'd actually quite fancied River Phoenix so found the song rather offensive. The guy who lived next door to Charles and I owned quite a well known music venue in Leeds called The Cockpit and he often used to let us in for free. A large group of us were sat outside the front of our house one sunny Saturday afternoon listening to The Avalanches wonderful *Since I Left You* album on repeat whilst drinking tremendous amounts of lager when our neighbour asked if any of us fancied coming down to The Cockpit that evening to see a live band.

"We've got Crashland playing this evening if you're interested at all?" he said.

Everybody was drunk and not too bothered but I leapt at the opportunity of seeing a live band, also I thought it might be a good opportunity for my wife to experience a proper gig. We arrived at the dingy, dark atmospheric venue relatively early because the band was playing an early evening show. Being a gentleman I bought drinks for the two of us as well as one for our neighbour as a thank you for the free club entry. I wasn't too sure what to expect but I'd heard promising things about Crashland in the NME. It only took one song though to realise that the band were exceptionally bad. My wife was polite enough and she gently nodded her head and tapped her foot to the tuneless dirge the band was creating. The most interesting thing about the set was watching some guy with a rucksack on his back nodding his head completely out of time with the music throughout the entire gig whilst he stood only about two foot away from the stage. If I'd been in the band I'd have been a bit freaked out by him. The attendance of the gig was about ten at a push. I was so disgusted with the mediocrity that we'd experienced I insisted that we simply had to leave so we went home and resumed listening to The Avalanches along with everybody else who were much more inebriated than they'd been when we'd left them, the shot glasses were in full swing along with cheap bottles of dirty convenience store vodka.

Back to James, well they'd actually continued to perform live during the first half of the year, mainly overseas including a fairly high profile gig in Beijing. I never went of course, in fact I didn't even know about the gig until some time afterwards plus as cool as it would have been to have travelled so far to see my favourite band Beijing was just a tad out of reach. Had it have been Brussels then maybe but I wasn't really in a financially sound situation at the time to be able to afford such treats. Darts and lager in my bedroom was as frivolous as it ever got, plus the odd free gig at The Cockpit of course.

James also performed at that years V2000 festival which took place over my birthday weekend. I never went to that one either, the reason was that Charles and I had actually bought the house two doors up from the one we'd been renting since moving to Leeds so pennies were a tad thin on the ground. I did manage to read a review for James' performance though, the band had given a lively interview afterwards which pretty much comprised of a tirade of cranky four letter words particularly from Saul who appeared quite aggrieved at the attitude shown towards the band, not just by the music industry but I feared from the record buying public who'd pretty much shunned not only the bands last album but the majority of their fine work apart from the *Best Of*. Casual music buyers, don't you just hate them? The band also played a couple of new songs including one song described by the NME as *"sounding like The Specials playing Pac Man"*. Confused? So was I.

On a happier note the band had announced that they'd demoed plenty of new material which they'd be road testing on a tour in October. Now this was the kind of news that made me sit up straight and make Gangsta Rapper poses. I announced to my wife that she'd be bursting her 'James Cherry' in October as the first night of the tour would be at the world famous Leeds University refectory where The Who had recorded their live masterpiece *Live In Leeds*. Tickets were swiftly purchased and I excitedly kept up to date with the latest news and updates via the internet.

On Saturday the 21st October my wife and I spent the afternoon roaming around Leeds market in search of a cheap roll of carpet. It was to replace the one I'd ripped up from the stairs in an act that would have made a hallucinating Julian Cope cringe with embarrassment and remorse. A friendly facially tattooed market trader sold me a piece of off-cut for £15 and there was much cheering from the three of us, my wife and I were happy because it would dampen the sound of marching feet up and down the wooden staircase and the market trader was happy because he had some money to spend on Pork Scratchings and ale at the social club later that night. I was obviously extremely excited about going to see James that evening, more so than normal as I couldn't wait to see my wife's reaction to the band.

"Seriously, you're going to love it, they'll change your life forever!!!!"

"Right, cool" she politely replied over a pint of Guinness in an Irish bar we'd ended up in with my new roll of carpet for company.

We drank up, headed home and grabbed something to eat before heading to the venue leaving behind a living room full of people drinking dodgy cocktails and playing the popular and somewhat dangerous card game 'Chase The Ace'. Well, the version that we played was pretty dangerous anyway, you'd easily end up absolutely annihilated on vodka within fifteen minutes if you were unlucky enough or if Charles cheated which he did each and every time. He'd issue a caveat prior to beginning a game which was the decent thing to do, however bravado and machismo ruined many a person foolish enough to play.

My wife and I arrived at the venue, it was only a twenty minute walk from where I lived, we entered the university building, it was already heaving with gig goers. For anybody who's never been to the refectory all I can say is that it's easily the most horrible venue in the land, the reason for this is down to the appalling acoustics plus the venue is long and narrow with whacking great stone pillars down the sides obscuring the view. I hated the place, James in my opinion deserved much better but any opportunity to see the band was of course alright by me. Plus the Town and Country Club had closed down and had been turned into an awful nightclub. The other problem was that my wife is only just over five foot tall, she was going to struggle to see the band unless we were stood right by the barrier and this wasn't really an option by that point in the evening. I snaked us through the crowd as much as I possibly could and we ended up stood by one of the pillars on the right side of the room.

The audience appeared to be much more rowdy than usual and there was a lot of people dressed up in posh attire who were blatantly going out clubbing in the city afterwards. The chitter-chatter was deafening; it was difficult to have any real kind of meaningful conversation with my wife so we just silently waited in anticipation. The warm up act made their appearance onstage to a polite round of applause, the support was a woman called Shea Seger. She and her band were alright but nothing too special and I was quite pleased when they made their exit.

The warm up music rose up and we carried on waiting, and waiting and waiting........

After several hours the house lights finally dropped and the boisterous audience which was comprised of students, young loved up couples, lonely misunderstood weirdoes, night clubbers, 'Sit Down' fans and football hooligans tore the roof down with their deafening roar which was heard as far away as Bradford. Tim was sporting a rather nice Trilby hat; he looked a bit like a sinister magician. The rest of the band was dressed down as per usual in Sports Casual chic that would have made Alan Partridge proud.

"Boothy, Boothy, Boothy"

"Hello, were going to do something a bit different tonight" announced Tim to the crowd, "we're going back to how James used to be, taking risks with the audience, so bear with us!"

The short hairs stood up on the back of my short neck; it wasn't going to be a greatest hits set! I wondered if they'd play 'Sit Down' though. The band started with a lovely new song called 'What Is It Good For?' It ambled along nicely enough, quite subdued and understated in its magnificence and by the reaction of the audience it appeared to be fairly well received and my wife and I clapped along with everybody else. 'Stand', another new song began, the keyboards appeared to be too high in the mix but it was another pleasant song that also received a positive reaction from the beery audience. Once the song had finished Tim made a reference to the fact that some of the songs were less than a week old.

"Even Dave's not heard these songs before, Dave's our Number One fan" said Tim with a big smile on his face and he appeared to acknowledge somebody in the crowd who was out of my eyesight. I wondered who Dave was and what made him their Number One fan. I thought I was their Number One fan not this supposed Dave person whoever the hell he thought he blummin' well was making out he was something that only I could possibly be! I felt a rage of jealousy in the pit of my stomach but just to distract me from my annoyance the band launched into 'Senorita' which was yet another new song, the best one of the evening so far and number one fan Dave was soon forgotten about. However, an air of restlessness was apparent, the audience wanted to hear material that they knew and the talking and general noise amongst people stood around us grew in intensity. Maybe the band sensed that the audience was growing a tad restless so to appease them the band played a fairly middle of the road version of 'Say Something', it certainly did the job though, the audience sang along as if it was The National Anthem, not the Radiohead version I hasten to add.

'Sometimes' was equally well received and was swiftly followed by a rather lovely version of 'Just Like Fred Astaire'. Half the audience blatantly didn't know James' most successful single from recent years. The band were on a roll though, my wife appeared to be enjoying herself and had been bopping along whilst straining her neck so that she could see what was happening on stage. The "Boothy, Boothy, Boothy" chant continued after pretty much every song, it was almost a bit embarrassing but I was always intrigued that a front man who was hardly Liam Gallagher in the attitude stakes had developed such respect and love from big burly blokes in a way that was not too dissimilar to how Morrissey was fawned upon by the most masculine of men. Maybe Tim Booth tapped into these blokes internal homoerotic thoughts and desires. Not mine of course even though I'd had a feel of his back and arms at Guildford. Come to think of it the Manic Street Preachers once had a t-shirt with the classic "All Rock And Roll Is Homosexual" slogan on it. It was a t-shirt they'd had made for when they supported Bon Jovi back in the early nineties. It apparently sold quite well on the day of the performance.

'Johnny Yen' shook the very foundations of the building, it's furious tribal drumming and Tim's mesmeric dancing worked in perfect symbiosis, it's sing along factor equalled some of the bands more familiar hits and misses. The band followed with three new songs, 'Scratch Card' which was okay, the brilliantly titled 'Daniels Saving Grace' which was rather excellent and 'Coffee and Toast' which had a wonderful swirling keyboard riff throughout, it was probably the best new song of the evening so far. My 'favourite' James song 'Someone's Got It In For Me' still sounded pompous and overblown but it appeared to go down well with the majority of the audience at least. In truth I'd grown to really like the song but still couldn't get Frankie Goes To Hollywood out of my mind.

And still the new songs came. 'Give It Away', was a fairly jolly excursion into 'folk pop', 'Gaudi' an up-tempo stomp along and 'The Shining', was a piano heavy ballad. Although it was the first time that I'd heard these songs I was very impressed, they were all fairly immediate to the ear and if any of them made it onto their next album then it was sure to be the album that *definitely* made them Millionaires! The band though had probably pushed their luck and the audiences patience as far as they could, in fact for some people they'd pushed it too far and I noticed that the audience around where we'd been stood had thinned considerably as people either went to the bar or headed into the city for alcohol related fun. As a treat for being so patient the band ended the evening with some of their sizeable hits, 'Destiny Calling', 'She's a Star' and 'Born of Frustration'. The audience sang and clapped along in gratitude.

After a brief encore/toilet/cigarette break the band returned to the stage and played their final new song of the evening, a slow burning number called 'Junkie'. I wasn't too keen to be honest but I was sure that I'd grow to love it if I heard a recorded version of it. The last two songs were 'Laid' and 'Ring the Bells'. During the final song a strange thing happened, the song built and climbed in a similar way to how the recorded version does, the instrumental end section strung out into a psychedelic and hypnotic groove, Tim danced with such passion and fury that it captivated everybody's attention.

Then suddenly out of nowhere a lone red balloon rose up into the air from the audience about midway down the refectory hall, the balloon then started to slowly make its way across the heads of the audience heading straight towards Tim Booth. The balloon caught his attention and he stopped his wild dancing as the music thundered on. Still the balloon made its journey heading ever closer to him. People were stood very still staring up at the balloon, a few people tried to jump up and catch it but it was just a bit too far out of reach. And then the balloon stopped right in front of Tim. He looked in awe at the most simple of children's toys as it hovered right in front of his face, barely moving. He moved his hands around the balloon without actually touching it, a red globe that appeared to be driven by something unearthly and unseen, and then the balloon decided to slowly drift away from Tim and 'Ring The Bells' came to a cataclysmic end. What had piloted the balloon is still a mystery.

The audience went wild with delight, they were however awaiting their final gift of the night from the band, 'Sit Down', but it never came. Instead the band thanked us all for coming and then slowly sauntered off stage. The distinctive sound of 'Sit Down's chorus being sung by the audience still couldn't bring the band back onstage and then the house lights powered back up and recorded music poured out of the PA system, the definitive sign the gig was over.

"Well, what did you think then??"

"Yes, very good indeed" replied my wife, she sounded genuine enough and I grabbed her by the hand and dragged her (not literally) towards the merchandise stall. A young girl who was dressed up to the nines suddenly spoke to me,

"They didn't play 'Sit Down'" she said to me in a sad sounding voice.

"Yeah, good eh!" I replied to her in a caustic tone annoyed that the girl who looked no more than eighteen had probably stood there all night waiting for that one particular song.

"But, but I really wanted to hear it" she replied with a definite look of disappointment and sadness upon her face.

I suddenly felt very sorry for her, by the looks of it she was by herself and she looked genuinely downbeat and forlorn that she'd not heard the song she obviously loved so very much.

"Maybe they'll play it next time you see them" I said in what I hoped was a more optimistic and not too patronising manner.

"Yes, maybe" she said before walking off by herself towards the exit of the refectory.

I remember at the time thinking that it was probably the most disappointing James gig that I'd attended. The band had been on very good form no doubt about that. The new songs sounded really good but the venue ruined the experience for me. My wife could hardly see anything during the show, the acoustics were all over the place and the audience appeared to have been more leery than usual. When we arrived back home the raggedly drunken mob all cheered and started to sing 'Sit Down', as I was stone cold sober I felt embarrassed and very awkward indeed.

"Did you have a good time?" asked Louise who was a close friend of ours; she was the most sober compared to the rest.

"Yes, it was pretty good" I replied.

She looked at me in a funny manner.

"Oh, well that's not the usual kind of response that we get from you when it's related to James! You're normally falling about the place in excitement and awe"

I pondered her words for a moment or two, I had had a great night, but something just hadn't felt right at the gig, I didn't really know what it was, maybe it was me. I grabbed a can of lager and joined in with the frivolities taking place around me.

Footnote: The 'Pac-Man' song was actually 'Coffe and Toast' two consumables that I quite enjoy although coffee does send me ever so slightly manic.

Event horizon

2000/2001

My wife bought me the most brilliant Christmas present that I could have ever dreamt of, (at my request I must add), I realise this rather bold statement may sound a tad over the top in hindsight. The brilliant present was the first and only official book regarding James written by media maestro and culture connoisseur Stuart Maconie. *Folklore* was an in-depth read that documented the bands rise from poverty, medical experimentation, religious cults, football hooliganism, drug usage and questionable clothing into misunderstood musical globe boys. The book was a rather excellent read and I've have read it many a time since, in fact the book pretty much lives in my bathroom alongside Stuart's other book about Blur. Stuart, if you ever read this which I'm sure you won't, (you probably won't even be aware that this book exists) but if you do all I can say is that the fact that your books reside in my bathroom is a compliment of the highest order. My wife also bought me an imitation lava lamp, it didn't work properly, the lava wasn't viscous enough and it would turn into a milky residue but I appreciated her kind thought anyway. Charles bought me a couple of fantastic albums, *Felt Mountain* by Goldfrapp and *The Sophtware Slump* by Granddaddy, both of them were pretty fantastic, particularly the latter. The albums were chosen at random from a list that I'd given him as potential presents, something we've been doing for years now. It means you get what you want but there's still a bit of an element of surprise involved.

A few weeks earlier I'd received an email from someone called Dave Brown. It was an invite to visit his new James website called oneofthethree.co.uk. It transpired that this was the same Dave that

194

Tim had mentioned at the Leeds gig, not sure how he found my email address but I was pleased to receive the invite and the site was pretty good too, it also became quite obvious that he really was their number one fan and I forgave him. So, the old year ended, a space odyssey was prophesised and I was hopeful in fact certain that a new James album would be on the horizon soon enough although I didn't want to hold my breath regarding this one, to attempt such an act of foolishness would have resulted in certain death.

In early spring an article in the NME confirmed that James would be releasing their new album in the summer. The album was once again being produced by Brian Eno which was reassuring although they were yet to taste enormo-success regarding any of the wonderful material that they'd done with him so far, except perhaps for *Laid* in The States all those years ago. Brian stated that *"James are a band who've undergone a rebirth of sorts"*, now this sounded very promising indeed, if the material they were going to release was even better than the magnificent (to me at least) *Millionaires* then we were all in for a treat and a rollicking good time. The band were going to be back on the road in the summer in support of the new album which had at one point been called *Space*, then *We Want Our Money Back* before finally settling on the rather drearily titled *Pleased To Meet You*. Brit Pop semi-legends Sleeper had named their final album *Pleased To Meet You*. It wasn't meant to be Sleeper's swan song at the time of release; I hoped the album's title didn't have a hex upon it.

A gig was going to take place in Grimsby in Lincolnshire, I'd never been to Grimsby before, all I knew about the place was that it apparently smelt quite strongly of fish and that the gig itself was a rescheduled show from the autumn tour of 2000 as the roof of the venue had been badly damaged during a storm. The gig was taking place on the 6th July which would be the very week that *Pleased To Meet You* was due to be released. A solitary ticket was bought for me as my wife wasn't too fussed about going and neither were any of my other friends, the fools. I'd told, not asked but told my wife that we were definitely going to the Guildford Festival at the beginning of August as James were once again headlining the Saturday night, she was pretty keen to go anyway as the

195

ABBA tribute band Bjorn Again were going to be playing on the same bill. She'd seen them before at her university graduation ball and rated them quite highly.

The first single from the new album started to gain a bit of radio airplay, unfortunately the main station Radio One who'd given intermittent support to the band over the years didn't get behind the song one iota. The majority of the commercial stations as per usual would only ever play 'Sit Down' however Virgin Radio played the song a fair bit. As for the song 'Getting Away With It (All Messed Up)' it was a fairly edgy affair with a "don't mess with us" kind of attitude. The song should be applauded for referencing John Travolta and Richard Burton. I'd heard the song the year before at the Leeds gig although at the time it had been known as 'Daniels Saving Grace'. Even though the song had undergone a name change the *"Daniels saving grace…."* lyric was used in abundance throughout the song.

During a request show on Virgin Radio some woman rang up and practically begged that Chris Evans who was presenting at the time played the song which he did with as much enthusiasm as he had for the band when he was presenting his *TFI Friday* show back in the nineties. I was driving at the time and the single sounded excellent on the car stereo, I quickly wound the windows down as far as I could and pumped up the volume excessively to the point where somebody shouted "KNOB HEAD" at me whilst they crossed the road. I wasn't the "knob head" wearing the Sunday supplement cargo pants my friend.

James were guests on BBC 2's *Later… With Jules Holland*, it was and still is probably the best if not the only music television programme worth watching on the terrestrial channels. My wife and I were away for the weekend as it was our first anniversary and we'd travelled down to Warwickshire for a weekend of romance, fine food and of course scrumptious ale. James performed some of their new material on the programme including a new song called 'Falling Down'.

It,

was,

simply,

stunning.

Tim alternated between falsetto and his usual vocal delivery, compressed drums were mashed out by Dave, amazing guitar twiddling came forth from Adrian, the band looked moody and played as a tight unit. Tim had grown his hair back although it wasn't such a great look for him; he looked like a doppelganger for Art Garfunkel. Once the song had finished my wife insisted that we turned the television off but an Audley Harrison fight was being shown on ITV and I insisted that we simply had to watch it, just for the sheer fun of watching Audley becoming defensive and cross when being interviewed post fight as he was given his usual and well deserved critical mauling. Then and only then did I turn off the television...........

Dave Brown from the website oneofthethree.co.uk had been given a promo of the new James album and he posted a review of the album on his website in early June of that year. It was an intriguing review, quite positive in content, as much as he loves the band Mr Brown is no sycophant and he's well known for speaking his mind. The comment about the album that really caught my attention though was this,

"Whilst it, (the album) will sell well it won't sell millions".

Hmmm, my anxiety levels started to bubble away like a cauldron. Perhaps the band members were never destined to be millionaires after all or perhaps Dave was wrong, very wrong. I printed off the review at work and brought it home to show Charles and our friend Louise who loved James. She seemed pretty intrigued by the review, Charles less so.

"The problem with James mate is that they lack consistency, people reckon that they're on a par with U2 or REM but they are so not. They're a good band and that's it" was Charles' opening gambit for an argument that I simply couldn't be bothered to rise to. The single had been released in two disc format again and although the songs were all pretty good the production appeared to lack any warmth, the material hardly invited the casual listener in and I guessed this was due to the way it had been recorded, produced and mixed. Brian Eno himself had commented that all of the faders in the studio were set in a single straight line. Even Louise wasn't too keen on it.

"Ooh, it's nothing like anything from *Millionaires* is it?"

I tried to explain that the production was less poppy and was more akin to a 'live' recording.

"Well, to be honest I prefer poppy sounding stuff. Songs you can sing along to like 'Strangers' from their last album".

I rolled my eyes in annoyance and exasperation. I guessed that she wouldn't be buying the new album. In fairness, I knew what she was saying. The band featured on *CD:UK* again, I thought they looked fairly surly throughout, Saul grumpily playing the guitar instead of the wonderful violin part towards the end of the song. Tim's thinning hair had been cut short again, he now reminded me of Neil Tennant from the Pet Shop Boys.

Would it come as a surprise if I was to tell you that the single bombed? Probably not I guess. With minimal airplay and a song that once again sounded totally out of synch with the rest of the charts it only managed to reach a paltry number twenty two in the hit parade. Maybe, just maybe everyone was waiting to buy the album instead I optimistically thought to myself about yet another James album. Further bad news came to me in the form of an album review I read in Q magazine. The album was pretty much slammed and was only given two stars out of five. I winced in particular at the quote that the album was a *"self-parodying splunge of limp-wristed anti-materialism"* I didn't actually know what this meant, but it obviously sounded dreadful beyond words.

Pleased To Meet You was released on the 2nd July 2001, to this day I'll always wonder why but I didn't buy the album on the day of release. It was probably because money for me was as tight as a slugs bum hole and I had to make do with admiring the album on the shelves in the local supermarket instead. The cover featured an unusual looking gentleman who turned out to be a composition of all of the bands faces merged together. The reason being that James is often referred to as a person with Tim Booth often being mistaken for being 'James', the band decided to play up with this belief and created a character who would truly be 'James'. He looked like the kind of man who smoked Dunhill cigarettes, drank Martini Rosso and carried a briefcase around with him wherever he went, a self indulgent moody individual who broke women's hearts and made other men jealous by being so perfect. I didn't like the look of him one little bit. On the Wednesday after the album release my wife bought me the new album as a treat for being good and rather pleasant. She'd recently moved into a friend's house for a short while as her tenancy had come to an end and it was at her friend's house in Chapel Allerton, Leeds that I heard the album for the first time. It was hard to really concentrate and focus fully on the album as my wife and her friend were gassing away to each other whilst drinking cups of hot Ribena out of season, (it's a winter drink and a winter drink only!)

The opening track 'Space' was a song that I hadn't heard before. It was a slow burner, initially ambient in mood before the song suddenly burst into life; Tim screaming the lyrics towards the end of the song with some nice 'Enoesque' choir singing from the rest of the band members. Upon first listen I thought it was okay, but nothing special. 'Falling Down' was next, now this was a song that I immediately got very excited about, Dave Brown had commented upon the fact that it sounded like 'Material Girl' by Madonna and I understood what he was talking about. Now, if this wasn't the song to really take James back into the mainstream then nothing ever would!

The bizarrely titled 'English Beefcake' was the next song. I immediately found it very annoying with a violin part that really got my back up for some reason. The song was in two parts. The first section I really didn't like at all with Tim singing/talking about magicians at one point but after a musical breakdown the song slowly built up again over a beautiful refrain of *"There's nothing to say, I get in the way, unable to break obsession"* repeated over and over, the guitars built into a flurry of noise with Tim doing a bit of his wonderful yodelling over the top. This section of the song should have been a separate song in its own right, it could even have possibly been a flukey hit single!

'Junkie' followed, the drums appeared too high in the mix, a deathly violin struck up and Tim referenced Pokemon in the lyrics. The song though was fairly uninteresting for the first two minutes forty seconds and then built up in a similar way to the previous song. Again, like 'English

Beefcake' it should have been split in half and kept as a separate song. According to Tim "everyone's a junkie". I suppose there is some truth in this. I quite like coffee, not so keen on heroin though, (I've never tried it of course!) The title track was next, it sounded extremely maudlin and it immediately put up a defensive barrier around itself. Once again the song slowly built up and the end of the song was pretty fantastic but like the previous two songs it should have been split in half and I'd have erased the whimsy backing vocals too. Needless to say, I wasn't a fan. The songs were desperately trying to sound epic but missed by quite a larger than usual mile.

'The Shining' followed, I'd heard it before in Leeds, a pleasant enough piano ballad that didn't push any of my buttons. Once again I felt the drums were too high in the mix and overbearing. 'Senorita' livened things up a bit though, a short punchy song that would have made a great single however the song was ruined by some absolutely terrible backing vocals during the chorus and I felt embarrassed as they squawked their way out of the speaker. 'Gaudi' I'd also heard before in Leeds, it was the best song on the album so far, Tim's delivery was fantastic, amazing instrumentation and the backing vocals from Michael really made the song. I played the song on repeat at least four times in a row before my wife's friend said, "Okay, that'll do", with a forced pained smile upon her face.

Sadly though the albums tempo dropped right back down again with a song they'd opened the Leeds show with the year before. 'What Is It Good For' was a nice enough song but certainly nothing more and nothing less. 'Give It Away' followed, it was a jolly piece of folk pop music with a hummable chorus that could have passed for another misfiring near hit single. I was side stepped by the next song though which was called 'Fine'. It was such an odd little song, I'd never heard a song like it which has happened many a time regarding James' back catalogue. It bopped along with the most simple of tunes and choruses which was encased around a sweet almost electronic shuffling break beat from Dave. It was a highlight for sure. The single followed, the version released as a single had been mixed to make it more immediate, and the album version was more brooding which was of course a good thing. Then came 'Alaskan Pipeline'. It was quite a melancholy piece of work that ended the album on a despairingly glum note and vibe.

My overall feeling was of great, great disappointment. Sure, the songs overall were very good but the album felt glacial and distant to me. It felt like bumping into an old lover and trying to strike up a normal conversation whilst knowing each other's deepest darkest secrets, it was for me an unfriendly unlovable album that came across as awkward, with a sense of trying too hard to rekindle something that had possibly already passed by. I thanked my wife though for the purchase before ejecting the disc and replacing it with At The Drive Inn's excellent *Relationship Of Command* album which cheered me up a bit. Oh well, I was heading off to Grimsby a couple of days later to see James perform, I was sure that the songs would take on a new lease of life when performed live.

It was late afternoon on Friday; I set off east bound along the M62 motorway before taking the M18 and finally the M180 to the coastal town of Grimsby. The journey wasn't in my trusty Vauxhall Astra though, sadly that particular car had finally conked out and I was instead in my wife's trusty red Fiesta. As per usual I didn't have a map and I didn't know where the venue was either but I knew that it couldn't be too hard to find. Sure enough, as I drove along a main road into the seaside town there was a distinctive smell of fish in the air, it wasn't an urban myth after all. The radio was tuned into Chris Moyles on his afternoon/teatime slot, he was talking to a chirpy Welsh lad called BB Aled who was discussing who was and wasn't his favourite housemates in the Big Brother house. Thankfully I parked up before the moribund conversation persecuted me any further and I asked for directions to the venue from a passerby. The venue was just out of the centre of the town and I soon found myself parked up outside it along with 75,000 other cars. Actually my car was the only car there and it was after five in the afternoon, the doors were opening in less than two hours. I wondered if I was at the wrong venue or had the dates wrong. I ran across to the venues doors and was reassured the gig was taking place that evening by an A4 piece of paper stuck to the inside of the glass door.

"James: doors open at 19:00".

I stood alone admiring the empty car park like it was a miniature grey tarmac National Park, it was quite beautiful in its ugliness. After a while there was movement, I suddenly felt like I was a hunter being stalked by a wild animal except this wild animal was instead a short man with long wild wavy hair. He approached me with a smile.

"Hey, are you here to see James?"

I was wearing a blue t-shirt with 'Ja-m-es' spread across the front and back of it in bright yellow font whilst stood outside the venue where James were going to play. A hundred sarcastic answers flashed before my eyes. Then, as quick as a flash I said,

"Yes, are you?" (He was also wearing a 'Ja-m-es' shirt although it was a different colour to mine).

"Yes I am, wow, so, this is where they're playing tonight? I thought that it would be a big arena, this looks like a sports hall." he said obviously very disappointed with the venue and its spanking new roof.

His accent was either American or Canadian, I never could tell the difference so I asked him where he was from and he said that he was an American and that he'd travelled all the way from California to see the show. I was mightily impressed with him and slapped him extremely hard on his back; in comparison Guildford was as far as I'd travelled to see James. Conversation was struck up, he was a pleasant enough chap, a bit odd though and his eyes bulged heavily, I feared he had problems with his thyroid gland but I didn't feel brave enough to ask him. A couple of other lads queued up behind the two of us and introduced themselves in thick North Eastern accents. Graham and Carl were from Sunderland; it transpired that they did a lot of travelling when it came to seeing James and they'd seen them many more times than I. I suddenly felt like a little fish compared to the three James fanatics that I was stood talking to. As conversation continued it turned out that we all recognised each other from the James forum we used to frequent daily so we had a gossip and a slag off regarding comments that other users had posted on the forum. The forum was quite a 'catty' place to communicate with others, full of sarcastic vitriolic replies to polite questions that users often posted. I'd already grown to dislike it and much preferred the family friendly oneofthethree forum that Dave Brown hosted, it was a welcoming place of kindness, gentleness and love for small animals, particularly stoats.

The queue behind us had grown but it still wasn't that big. Suddenly, a figure that we all recognised casually walked past us heading towards the back of the venue, it was Saul Davies looking very small with a rucksack on his back. I fought off an urge to run across and speak to him as it would only end in embarrassment for all considered and instead I watched him disappear out of sight before refocusing on the entrance to the venue that still remained shut with little signs of movement from deep within its bowels. Time ticked along, it was approaching the hour yet the queue behind us was still relatively small. The security bods were now stood behind the glass doors, taunting us with their power that only they knew when they would be opening the doors to our miniature utopia and before we knew it the doors were opened, tickets were handed over and the four of us ran like rabid greyhounds towards the barrier. It was going to be a fantastic night.

Grimsby and Guildford

2001

Tim Booth cradled a large mug of coffee on stage whilst appearing deep in thought.

"FUCK Q MAGAZINE, TIM!" an emotive fan shouted out clearly as upset as I'd been with the magazines review of the new album. Tim must have heard the comment but he didn't bother to respond to it, instead he took a large gulp from his steaming mug.

James opened with 'Space' which set the scene for the evening ahead. Its trippy intro sounding excellent pumped through a decent sound system, the band appeared poised and confident in manner, because it was a new and relatively unknown song the usual surge and push from those behind me was absent and I stood in relative comfort. I struggled throughout to remember the lyrics to 'Space' which caused me some irritation and paranoia; I really wanted the band to recognise that some of us didn't go to see James just to experience 'the hits'. Once 'Space' finished the audience showed its appreciation with a polite round of applause even if less than half of those in attendance appeared to recognise the song. James swiftly followed on with 'Waltzing Along' and 'Sometimes' to keep the *Best Of* fans happy. The atmosphere warmed considerably, 'Senorita', 'English Beefcake' and the new albums opening track 'Space' sounded a hell of a lot better than what I'd experienced when listening to the album, hearing those songs live further compounded my disappointment at what I perceived to be a lost opportunity with some of the bands best songs to date. Even 'Junkie' sounded really impressive, especially the grinding guitar section of the song, I could even overlook Saul's backing vocals which had grated me somewhat on the recorded version.

'Destiny Calling' and 'Fred Astaire' followed, the latter sounded like a lost classic British single overlooked upon release by the majority who had chosen to jump on the bandwagon and follow the latest flavour of the month, I was still outraged by the fact that the single had nose dived so badly. I looked over to my right and saw the American guy I'd spoken to outside the venue; he was bellowing along to the songs with so much gusto that I thought his eyes were going to fly right out of their sockets.

"This'll hopefully be our next single, that's if the record company want to release another single of course" Tim said with both humour and apparent frustration before the band played a striking version of 'Fine', the off timed drums clattered away, the bass reverberated around the gymnasium and into my lungs in a choking manner. 'Getting Away With It' was the best song the band had released in aeons, why had it been ignored by the British public? Maybe, I thought to myself that other more appreciating people in foreign lands would take to the song more favourably than it had been received in our little green island surrounded by grey cold water. Perhaps the song suited warmer climates? Perhaps the band did? My mind was cast back to the interview Tim had given in 1994 where he stated that the band had seriously considered not releasing any more music in the UK due to a lack of appreciation and a sense of being taken for granted. Sadness gripped me before I was immediately thrust back into the present time and place, I was at a James gig, they were without a doubt the best band in the world and there I was stood only a few feet away from them.

'I Know What I'm Here For' and 'Ring The Bells' concluded the main set and the encore was made up of 'What Is It Good For?', 'Say Something' and 'Laid'. The band left the stage to much applause, Dave threw his drum sticks into the audience and I caught one mid-flight which most probably prevented somebody from being blinded and the band being sued for billions. I held onto it like my life depended on it. It was something else for the mantelpiece back home alongside Tim's wristband and Saul's plectrum. Once again, 'Sit Down' hadn't been played much to the annoyance of a large section of the audience who sang the song until the house lights were switched on and the roadies came onstage to dismantle the equipment. My mind was cast back to the sad young lady who I'd so cruelly scorned back in Leeds the year before and I wondered if she'd made the trip to Grimsby and what her reaction would have been regarding the songs omission. I'd certainly enjoyed the show. It was as good as any other James performance I'd seen; at least, I thought it was. During the evening Tim had looked thoughtful and at times quite distant; something didn't seem right with the band at all during the gig. I couldn't quite put my finger on it but I felt a sense of unrest.

Outside the venue I met up with Carl and Graham for a chat, Graham had a bottle of water with him.

"Here, take a drink of this water, this was Tim's own bottle of water" Graham rather excitedly said to me.

My stomach leapt about in a sheer orgy of excitement, I took a huge swig of the water and let it wash across my parched mouth. Drinking from Tim's bottle was as good as meeting the man himself, well kind of. The crowd dispersed and soon there was only a few of us hanging about the venue talking to one another hoping that we might have an opportunity to meet some of the band members. After a while we realised this was not going to be the case, the closest we got was when Adrian walked past with what appeared to be his elderly parents, Adrian had grown up in nearby Hull and his parents apparently continued to live in the vicinity. I bid farewell to Carl and Graham, I never saw the American guy with the bulging eyes again and before I knew it I was driving along the motorway bound for Leeds and upon reaching Leeds I met my wife outside The Elbow Rooms nightclub and the two of us headed home, both of us content having enoyed two very different nights out.

Sunday, album chart run down day. Where oh where would the new James album *Pleased To Meet You* enter the charts? Number one? I didn't think so. Number five? That would have been a great achievement. It had to be in the top ten at the very least. But, no, the album entered the album chart at number eleven. I was down hearted as per usual; it felt like the wheels were starting to come undone on the James Express and somebody was going to get hurt. I knew it was highly unlikely that the album would climb any higher in the charts and I was right. Although I'd been disappointed by the album judging by the reaction of the fans using the online forums and the positive reviews the album had received even in *Heat* magazine I was apparently in the minority. It seemed obvious to me that someone else's star was on the ascent whilst James' star was fading, well at least in the UK.

Less than a month later my wife and I were heading for Guildford to experience James headlining the family friendly festival I'd visited two years earlier. My wife had been on a night out the evening before, she's terrible when it comes to hangovers and I suggested she didn't go too crazy as we had a long drive the following morning. When I went to collect her from her friend's house I found a very hung over, pale and clammy looking young woman sat on the kerb with a dimple pint glass of water in her hand. I wasn't pleased. I was hoping that we were going to share some of the driving but from the state she was in this clearly wasn't going to be the case. The passenger side window was partially wound down the entire journey from Leeds to Guildford; she said she needed constant fresh air to stop herself from throwing up. The droning sound of the open window gave me a headache and it meant that I couldn't enjoy listening to any music either. Then, just to liven up the journey even further the car boot door suddenly blew open whilst travelling at seventy miles per hour in the fast lane of the motorway. The sudden frightening noise was deafening, I panicked at the prospect of the tent and the rest of our belongings escaping from the car and causing a motorway pileup however I'd packed everything in such a tight and clever way that we didn't even lose a packet of crisps! I slid the car onto the hard shoulder and closed the boot whilst my wife heaved up her pints of water. I looked at her with a pitying look in my eyes and patted her gently on her head.

Now, as mentioned apart from James my wife was really looking forward to seeing Bjorn Again so she was pretty disappointed when we parked up at the festival car park and there carried on the wind was the sound of the ABBA impersonators themselves already on the main stage. We'd been caught up in some awful Saturday morning traffic on the M25 which resulted in us missing their performance. Never mind though because after setting up the tent, (well I set it up whilst she lay on the grass nursing her sore head) we managed to catch the beginning of The Wurzels who were playing to a criminally small crowd inside a tiny tent. Songs about drinking cider and driving combine harvesters certainly put a smile on the faces of those who were witnessing the performance from a wily bunch of pensioners. The Wurzels should have been playing the main stage but there they were hidden away from the masses, it was a real shame as they were rather good. The rest of the day was spent sitting near the main stage or wandering around checking out the most polite and decent festival of the summer. It was a cold overcast kind of day, a contrast to how it had been two years before. On the main stage we witnessed The Chameleons who were excellent as were Chumbawamaba who'd gone from being another cult act to a band who had a number one single with the rather irritating but catchy 'Tubthumping'. Whilst I'd been in Australia I simply couldn't get away from the song, it had been played to death all around the world and now there I was watching the band mid afternoon in front of an audience made up of parents and children. Goodness knows what they made of the abundance of foul language that the band used throughout their set, and I'm pretty sure that they didn't play 'Tubthumping' either!

Cast were due to play on the main stage before James. I'd seen them support James in Manchester on the Millionaires Tour and on that occasion they'd appeared surly but it was nothing compared to how they came across at Guildford. The band didn't greet the audience at all and instead they played five new songs in a row from their new album *Beetroot* (terrible name!) which had only reached something like number seventy eight in the charts.

"Here's another song that you probably won't be interested in" snarled front man John Power to the bewildered crowd. And the songs were crap, too much crazy flute action for my liking, now if I want to hear flutes and rock then I'd dig out *Hocus Pocus* by Focus. Once Cast had gotten their new material out of the way they played a greatest hits set which managed to liven the place up a bit and my wife and I sang along to their rather wonderful back catalogue until the band angrily trudged off stage never to be seen again, well, not literally but the band called it a day and split before the month was out, (of course they'd reform years later).

A light drizzle fell from the dark leaden sky. The roadies started to prepare the stage for James. My wife and I eased our way over to the barrier left of the stage standing in front of where 'Mr James' himself Jim Glennie would be strumming his bass. A sense of unease lay in the pit of my stomach, it didn't feel like the usual nerves I'd have before James came on stage, this was something quite different but I couldn't quite put my finger on it. The band then made their presence to a rapturous applause from the festival crowd, Jim, Adrian and Mike all looked fairly jolly and upbeat whilst the rest of the band sauntered on rather casually, Tim included.

James were quick to fire into some of their greatest hits, 'Say Something', 'Sometimes' and 'Laid' were played straight through, I didn't feel the usual magic from the stage though, James appeared to be going through the motions, it was the first time I'd experienced it and I didn't like it one little bit. 'English Beefcake' followed and confused the majority of the crowd to the point where a large proportion of the crowd started to mutely applaud during the mid-section of the song thinking it had finished, the song built up again and climaxed to an almost Everest sized peak with the most wonderful mix of yodelled vocals and guitars. 'Senorita' sounded extremely sexy; Tim danced slowly throughout writhing like a snake, sex oozed off stage although by this I mean metaphorically not literally as that would have been rather disgusting. 'Johnny Yen' fired up the crowd somewhat; and the band suddenly seemed less tired than they'd appeared at the beginning of the show.

'Waltzing Along' followed before 'Stutter' was given a rare live outing. The majority of the crowd had never heard of the song, it's never officially been released as a recorded track and it showed a different side of the band compared to the 'greatest hits' outfit they'd slowly and disappointingly started to become. Mike joined in on the vocals appearing to have a whale of a time before he sauntered off stage for a while mid song presumably heading towards the toilet. And then the band dished out further festival friendly hits, 'Out To Get You', 'Destiny Calling', and 'She's A Star'.

'Falling Down', probably the best track on *Pleased To Meet You* was played next but it just sounded wooden and under rehearsed, a bit of a mess really although within its chaotic structure was one of James' best songs, a wasted opportunity letting that one get away was all I could think. James ended their festival performance with 'Born of Frustration', 'Getting Away With It (All Messed Up)', 'Sit Down' and finally 'Ring the Bells'. As the band disappeared offstage a very kind woman who'd been stood on the other side of the barrier throughout the show ran over towards me with a big smile upon her face and handed me a piece of A4 paper.

"Here, you'd better have this".

The piece of paper was the bands set list which included times when photographers could and couldn't take photographs, another souvenir. I thanked the woman and we slowly vacated the area we'd been stood in. I just felt really, really sad. My wife and I headed back towards our tent, the drizzle becoming heavier; it certainly didn't feel like summer anymore, autumn had crept upon us in the blink of an eye.

"Did you enjoy it then? You've been very quiet" she asked.

I paused and then spoke.

"I think James are in big trouble, something's not right, their presence on stage was weird, and they didn't seem to be connecting with one another like they normally do. I'm not sure if they're just really tired because I know that they played at Benicassim last night but I'm really worried for them".

She just looked at me and smiled.

"Don't worry; I'm sure all they need is a good night's kip".

I didn't know if she was right or not but storm clouds were definitely on the horizon.

End days

2001

Charles unsurprisingly absolutely detested *Pleased To Meet You*.

"Sorry mate, I know that James is your favourite band and all that but this new album of theirs isn't that great. I think you're blinded by the love you have for the band. They could probably release an album of each of the band members farting and you'd say it was fantastic".

I didn't bother arguing with him, there was no point, plus he was probably right, at least in relation to the farting album anyway. The well-known saying relating to death and taxes being the only things certain in life should also include that people will always find farting amusing. I'd listened to *Pleased To Meet You* on repeat but I still hadn't developed any real love for it. But I did try, honest. My mood was lifted somewhat when the announcement of a December tour was made and I secured a single ticket to see the band in Manchester. None of my friends were at all interested in going, even my wife turned her nose up at the offer. It was going to be a painful waiting game until December; in the meantime I was enjoying albums by other artists. I'd bought their album sometime after its release but *Enjoy The Melodic Sunshine* by the Cosmic Rough Riders became my proper summer album alongside Graham Coxon's wonderful album *Crow Sit On Blood Tree*. My wife and I had a weekend in France in late August, I'd driven there pretty much in a single stint which might not sound like anything truly epic but on the very same day we'd set of we foolishly decided to go waterskiing for the first time ever, needless to say the extremely tiring activity was not a good move before such a long drive. I was as stiff as an ironing board and had to be hammered into shape to fit into the car. Thankfully those two albums

211

kept me sane and awake during the journey to, around France and back home. Whilst over there I managed to squeeze in some more bungee jumps at the same site I'd been to a couple of years earlier and I watched a disabled guy perform a bungee jump whilst he was strapped into his wheelchair. It really was one of the most incredible and awe inspiring things I've ever witnessed in my entire life.

It was September when I found myself in HMV in Leeds being surprised but also very excited to hear 'Falling Down' being played on the stores radio station. The DJ spoke at the end of the song.

"And that was James with 'Falling Down' taken from their latest album *Pleased To Meet You*, that's going to be their next single; the boys from Manchester have apparently been working with electro legends Orbital and they should be releasing some material together at some point soon".

Well, I was thrilled at the possibility of a new single and mystified at the prospect of the Orbital collaboration. However, sadly none of this would ever happen, or at least see any kind of release......

October 2001, bad news was announced. James left their record label after fulfilling their record contract of six albums and a greatest hits compilation. One of the UK's biggest bands was without a record deal, an unsigned band. It seemed totally preposterous, I was sure one of the other major labels would snap them up quick as a flash. It was by all accounts an amicable decision and certainly not a case of the band being dropped. So, where was this going to leave James? It was quite an exciting prospect, I wondered what they'd do next, perhaps it would gee them up a bit into flying by the seats of their pants again I thought. Or perhaps not......

October 2001. TERRIBLE NEWS WAS RELEASED OF INTERGALACTIC SUPERNOVA SIZED PROPORTIONS THAT WAS GOING TO BREAK HEARTS, CHANGE LIVES AND SHATTER DREAMS..........

Tim Booth announced that he was leaving James after the December tour. I found out about the disastrous news one lunch time at work when I popped onto the internet for my daily James update. To paraphrase Tim's long and rather touching statement he commented that for him it was *"the right time to leave"*, and that he *"wanted to leave on a high"*. I was crestfallen; I had to reread the statement several times through eyes that stung with salty tears. I printed off the statement and sat back down at my desk before pinning it up so that I could reread it and depress myself throughout the rest of the day.

I called my wife and told her the news.

"Oh, that's a shame isn't it?" she said as if we were discussing a pet goldfish that had passed on to the great fish tank in the sky.

"A shame? A SHAME? IT'S A BLOODY DISASTER!!!!"

She sighed a large sigh down the phone and told me that she'd take me out for something to eat that night to cheer me up. I definitely needed some comfort even if it was simply going to come in the guise of a chiminchanga and a pint of John Smiths.

Numerous statements were published in various formats, it was a medium news story in the music world and I felt sadness in that it had taken the announcement of Tim leaving James to bring people's attention back to the band and to the forefront of their minds. An extra tour date was announced at the dreadful Leeds University Refectory but wild horses wouldn't stop me from attending the gig. I knew it was going to be one of the last times I'd get to see them again, at least with its charismatic and distinctive front man anyway, you see the band wasn't splitting up, it was simply a case that Tim was leaving. That's all. Nothing really.

I therefore decided it would only be right that I should make a pilgrimage up north to Newcastle and catch the band when they played there too. It would mean three James gigs in a week, Leeds on Monday, Newcastle on Tuesday and Manchester on the Friday. My wife then decided that she did want to go and see James in Manchester however the standing tickets had already long sold out so my wife, her sister and a friend of theirs bought seated tickets for the final ever Manchester show.

So, what next?

Well, in what seemed like sheer desperation by the record company to wring out as much money as possible from the band James' albums that

I hasten to add had already been released by Mercury Records ended up being re-released, all of them re-mastered with extra tracks. I definitely wasn't going to end up buying all of the albums again, I couldn't really afford to although *Seven* was the only album I didn't own on compact disc, apart from *One Man Clapping* of course. Another new album was to be released as well. It was going to be a collection of the bands best 'b-sides' that James fans were asked to contribute suggestions to for the release. The album was to be released in December just in time for the Christmas farewell tour. It was originally going to be called *Now That's What I Call B-Sides* until the band were threatened with death by electrocution for a breach of copyright, instead they opted for the so awful it's actually not too bad name of *Ultra*, the cover of the album looked like a box of washing powder.

3rd December 2001. I was feeling quite unwell, another case of 'Man Flu', a bit like what I'd experienced at the Carter USM gig all those years ago but I genuinely felt quite unwell with a horrible sore throat. It didn't bode well for three nights of tomfoolery and singing at the top of my voice. To add insult to injury I was on a training course during the week in the main offices of the bank I worked for based on Park Row in Leeds. It was to be a week of dullness that would be brightened by seeing my favourite band in various venues throughout the country.

"Right, I want each person in the room to tell us something about themselves that nobody else knows" said the guy leading the course in his cheap pinstriped Burtons suit.

Each person gave an interesting or amusing anecdote, except none of them were either interesting or amusing.

"I've got a tabby cat at home called Fluffy".

"I'm going to buy a new car next year".

"My husband spilt a glass of red wine last night all over our white carpet".

"I love *Big Brother*".

"I'm a closet transvestite".

And those were the more interesting facts, all except the last one because I've made that one up however that *would* have been an interesting fact.

Then it was my turn.

"Err, right, well, do you know the band James? You know, Oh Sit Down, Oh Sit Down, Oh Sit Down, Sit Down next to me? Well, I'm going to see them live three times this week" I stated and everyone and I do mean everyone smiled and commented upon my interesting fact, they all seemed very impressed indeed and I felt fairly proud of my disclosure.

"What? Are they still going? I thought they'd split up years ago?" said the course leader. I therefore punched him and gave him a dead leg for his insolence and then I blathered on for quite a bit about the history of the band, what they'd been up to, what was going to happen until somebody said,

"Okay, I think that's quite enough".

The team leader hobbled around to his laptop to begin the Powerpoint presentation regarding the week ahead and I drifted off, lost in my thoughts about attending the gigs.

Monday evening: Leeds Refectory. Once again I was the first in the queue outside the venue. It was a very cold night, typical for the time of year and as I didn't feel very well I felt the cold even more than normal. It didn't help that I was only wearing a James t-shirt and jeans; I knew that it was a horrible sweaty venue and I didn't want a repeat of the Carter USM gig regarding almost passing out from the heat and lurgee combination. A face I recognised came into view, Graham from the Grimsby gig turned up with some lass. We greeted each other with a whoop and a high five (we didn't of course) and we engaged in chat regarding the band. A bloke called Ian introduced himself to us, it was to be his first James experience and he was very excited.

"Seriously mate, you're in for a hell of a treat!" I croaked to him through dry sore lips. Over time the queue built up, a fairly noisy boisterous crowd as excited as Graham, Ian and I.

And then suddenly the doors next to where I was stood swung wide open and all seven members of James walked past us, no more than three feet away, I could have reached out and grabbed them all and briskly stroked their backs, I didn't of course and the band members all headed away from the venue. They looked like a dressed down version of the characters from Reservoir Dogs, In fact I'm sure I could hear 'Little Green Bag' playing inside the venue. The band members had smiled at the people waiting in the queue but not one person appeared to acknowledge them, strange really as I thought the band would have been mobbed, maybe it was just the cold that had momentarily blinded everybody.

"Did you see who just walked past?"

"Shit, yeah, ah we should have asked if we could have gone with them, they've probably gone to the pub up the road" said Graham.

Once the doors opened I ran as fast as my legs would carry me, (along with everybody else) towards the stage and propped myself up against the barrier far right in front of where Mr Kulas and Mr Oxall would be strutting their stuff. I felt sick, tired and in reality I should have been tucked up in bed with a hot water bottle and a Lemsip but it was important to put aside such wimpy gestures as succumbing to bugs and bogeys, it was to be the last time I'd see James in their second home of Leeds. The support slot was provided by a band I'd not heard of before called Haven. It speaks volumes when all I can say is that I remember nothing about them whatsoever. I do remember being quite pleased when they'd finished their drollness and the stage was vacated for the greatest rock and roll band this side of Wisconsin.

The place was boiling hot, or it could have been just my ill health that was making me feel so woozy. The noise from the audience was overbearing, the pushing and a shoving had already started and this was before James had even arrived onstage. And then quite suddenly the music stopped, the lights dropped and the audience roared like a murderous pack of lions. The band were all smiles, the usual "Boothy, Boothy, Boothy" chant rose up and Tim bowed in recognition before the band literally fell into their set of greatest hits and misses much to the pleasure of the audience. The big problem though was the sound quality, it was awful. When Tim sang his yodelling bit during 'Laid' he sounded like a Dyson Hoover that was malfunctioning and the look on Jim's face was absolutely priceless, he looked like he was in severe pain due to the deafening droning sound! Saul appeared really cranky throughout the entire set, I wondered if he was angry with Tim for leaving the band, at one point he started berating some of the audience and trying to goad someone into a fight after the show. By the fourth song my voice no longer worked properly from bellowing along at full volume through battered vocal chords.

The set comprised of the usual crowd pleasers but with a smattering of less familiar material including the Sinead O'Connor duet 'I Defeat' which I still didn't like, Sinead obviously didn't bother to turn up on the occasion either which resulted in Mike taking her place instead. Material from *Pleased To Meet You* was aired and was well received by the boisterous audience even if the majority of them probably hadn't bought the album. The evening ended with 'Sit Down', well, it had to really. As the band were exiting the stage I shouted/croaked/yelled out and caught Jim's attention,

"SEE YOU TOMORROW NIGHT IN NEWCASTLE JIM!!!!!!"

Jim smiled and gave me a big thumbs up. I was surprised he could actually understand me; my voice sounded like it was being beamed in from another planet. It was the last straw, the exertion meant that my voice pretty much shut up shop and I felt absolutely dreadful. Again, the girl who I'd been rude to the year before came into my mind, had she attended the show, and if so how did she feel when the band finally played her song? I hoped that she was there and that all of her dreams had come true. I hobbled out of the refectory, my head was spinning, bile rose up and caused further discomfort as I headed into the freezing cold night in a soaking wet t-shirt side stepping the bootleggers and the rest of the gig goers who were congregating like a Catholic Mass outside the white stone building.

Ian who I'd spoken to before the gig was sat next to me on the bus.

"My god that was one of the most amazing experiences of my life" he said to me with a dumbstruck look upon his face.

I tried to speak to him but my voice simply didn't function. It was as if I'd necked two litres of vodka, I sounded intoxicated and couldn't really formulate any words at all that made any sense. I was desperately trying to tell him that as brilliant a gig as it had been the sound quality had been ruined due to the crappy venue and a number of technical problems the band had experienced throughout the evening, he just looked at me in a bewildered manner as if I was a complete idiot, it was obvious that he'd been touched by a greater power throughout the evening, for him there simply wasn't a negative aspect to the evening in any way, shape or form. As the bus pulled up near The Original Oak pub I bid him farewell and staggered home before I collapsed into bed and fell into a restless haunted sleep.

My alarm clock woke me up tormenting me in the fact that it was time to go to work. I groggily showered, dressed and headed to Park Row for another day of Powerpoint presentations and role plays.

"How was last night then? Did they play 'Sit Down'?" one of my colleagues asked me. I croaked back to them that yes it had been a good night and that yes, they had played 'Sit Down'. Except that when I spoke it sounded more like,

"Nyesh, grudd noyt out, nyesy vey playid shit darn".

Thankfully my poorly vocal chords resulted in me not having to participate much during the day and by lunch time I actually felt a lot better though I didn't reveal this to the rest of the group. In fact I felt so good that I called into Jumbo Records during the lunch hour and bought the re-mastered version of *Seven* with the extra live tracks that were included. I didn't bother buying *Ultra* though; I thought I'd save that for another time. After a laborious day in the office talking about "developing a helicopter view of the current banking situation", "thinking outside the box" and "what else could you offer the customer?" I had a 100 mile trip to Newcastle to see James at the Telewest Arena. The journey was rather unpleasant, I was immediately caught up in rush hour traffic and just getting out of Leeds took the cunningness of several foxes as well as driving across roundabouts and performing the odd somersault too. The A1 motorway is a horrible road, extremely dull and dreary with too many heavy goods vehicles for my liking. I drove as quickly as I possibly and legally could past Dishforth and Catterick, heading deeper into the cold night, the red glow of Newcastle lighting up the sky in the distance. When I reached the arena some time later I thought I was done for regarding getting near the barrier but I was rather alarmed yet pleased at the same time in the fact that there was hardly any bugger there and I walked straight up to the barrier right of the stage. I kept my eye out for Graham knowing that he would be attending but I couldn't see him at all.

The support slot was Turin Brakes who arrived onstage to muted polite applause. The songs 'Underdog' and 'Mind Over Money' were fantastic, (they still are), and the acoustic duo was backed by session players to recreate the best tracks from their album *The Optimist LP*. The songs that were good were great; the songs that weren't good were just plain boring. However it was the first time since seeing Radiohead support James back in 1993 that I'd actually enjoyed one of James' support bands. After twenty minutes or so the band trooped off to an appreciative audience, the house lights came back on and music rose up from the sound system.

I was fatigued and I prayed that I didn't pass out when the crush commenced like Steve had, except there was to be no crush at all. When James arrived onstage the audience showed their appreciation but it was nothing compared to the night before in Leeds. There was no crowd surge, my ribs didn't end up being squashed and bruised against the barrier, it felt like I was attending the Last Night of The Proms except without the stupid bobbing up and down thing the audience participate in. The band kicked off with some of their sizeable hits, well, you couldn't have it any other way really on a final tour now could you? The Newcastle audience were treated to straight versions of 'Say Something', 'Waltzing Along', 'Sometimes' and 'Laid', so far so good, the band appeared on good form playing very professionally, too professionally some might say, they'd perfected their art and craft by playing these songs a million times already. I turned around and had a panoramic view of the arena, I was sad to see so many empty seats particularly towards the back of the venue, and for an arena it's quite small too. A couple of years earlier and the band would have played to a packed venue; sadly this wasn't the case on that particular cold December night.

Thankfully the next set of songs made up for the tame start to the evening in that James played excellent renditions of 'I Know What I'm Here For', a ferocious 'God Only Knows', a really pretty acoustic version of 'Protect Me' and 'Walking The Ghost', it sent shivers down my spine before being followed by a spunky version of 'Hymn From A Village', during which cowbells were bashed about like they'd upset the band somewhat. Only two songs from *Pleased To Meet You* were played, 'Space' sounded pretty good but it should have been dropped for another song such as 'Senorita', but 'Getting Away With It' sounded brilliant. The rest of the set was made up by 'Tomorrow', 'Born Of Frustration', 'Destiny Calling', 'Ring The Bells', 'Someone's Got It In For Me', 'Sound', 'Out To Get You' and of course 'Sit Down'.

Now, that was all well and good, but something very, VERY cool happened during 'Sit Down'. No, we didn't all sit down, heaven forbid. No, what happened was some guy ran back and forth the other side of the barrier handing out what appeared to be stickers to audience members and I instinctively reached out to grab one, we made eye contact, he paused a moment or two before passing one of the stickers to me. I examined the sticker only to realise that it wasn't a sticker as such. In bold writing it stated,

"Guest: After Show".

Oh My God!!!

An after show pass!!!!!

Backstage!!!

James!!!!

By The Lord Harry!!!!!!!!!!!!!!!!!

I was still in shock when riotous applause broke out signalling the end of 'Sit Down', Tim thanked the audience for attending before the band members trooped off stage. I held the priceless object in shaking sweating hands unsure what I was supposed to do next. I was certain to find out though soon enough.

As a footnote I've just realised reading back through this book that I used to sweat an awful lot, I've mentioned it at least 100 times up to this point.

Never meet your heroes,
you'll only be disappointed

2001

When the house lights were turned back on the audience took the hint and proceeded to make their way towards the exits dotted around the arena except those who were hawking for set lists and other souvenirs from the evening. The security boys and girls started to order and boss people about whilst brushes and brooms skidded around the slippery wet floor clearing up all of the debris which mainly consisted of plastic beer glasses. I held my ground and figured that somebody would make an announcement regarding the back stage passes. There was at least thirty other people hovering about with identical green circular passes in hand and I was well chuffed when I noticed Graham and Carl amongst them. I marched across to them with an enormous grin on my face.

"Alright lads! I'm guessing you've got back stage passes then?"

"Alright! Yeah, a bit of luck the three of us getting them eh!" said Graham, Carl shook my hand as if greeting a long lost relative almost dislocating my arm in the process. Carl hadn't attended the Leeds gig the night before and I hadn't managed to catch up with Graham after the gig so I quizzed him on what he thought of it, he too thought that the sound quality had been pretty rubbish but of course he'd enjoyed the experience as much as ever.

We continued to wait until a band official made himself known, he ordered the excited crowd to follow him as if he was The Pied Piper minus the wind instrument. I felt extremely anxious, I wasn't sure what

222

to expect, Graham reckoned there'd be loads of free booze and food, I obviously wasn't going to be able to drink anything alcoholic as I was driving home but I was ravenous due to the fact that I hadn't eaten anything since lunch time and I relished the prospect of a posh bottle of pop to wet my sore throat.

We reached the top of the stairs and continued through several sets of doors until we all trooped into what appeared to be a function room, the official told us to be patient and that the band would be with us as and when. I scanned the room, the other people appeared to be made up of either more mature in age people with a smattering of young girls and a few kids as well. Graham, Carl and I appeared to be some of the only attendees wearing James t-shirts. It quickly transpired that there wasn't a nice spread of food and drink on offer either, not unless it was all going to be wheeled in at some point later by the hosts of the evening but I had a funny feeling that this wasn't going to be the case. Oh well, I couldn't moan too much, I was about to meet my favourite band, I felt like I knew them all intimately which of course I didn't but anybody who is as touched by a band or a musician as I was (and still am) will know exactly what I mean. Band members become like friends and family to you, rarely letting you down or disappointing you.

Now, I'd heard that it was important to never meet your 'heroes' as you may end up feeling disappointed and this particular thought had been in the back of my mind, I was pretty sure that this wasn't going to happen, the band were going to be very down to earth and friendly I was absolutely sure of it. After about ten restless minutes that seemed like forever a door at the far end of the room swung open and Tim Booth walked in, everybody immediately burst into a massive round of applause which actually startled me a tad and Tim looked very embarrassed and awkward indeed at the reception he'd received. People started to approach him with their arms outstretched, it looked like the scene from Life of Brian where Brian is swamped by people believing that he's the Messiah.

"I'm afflicted by a bald patch" an unknown man said to him reaching out towards Tim who didn't appear to be really enjoying the experience.

He was polite enough but it appeared he wanted to get the meet and greet out of the way somewhat. He did the rounds and agreed to have his photo taken with a few people but it looked like his patience was coming to an end and at one point he snapped at somebody due to the length of time it was taking them to take the photo, and then he was gone. Tim had been in the room for no more than five minutes, I hadn't gotten to say hello or anything, I really wanted to thank him for guiding me through some dark times and to tell him how much James meant to me but I guessed that this opportunity was never going to happen. I also wanted to ask him what happened to his reply to the letter I'd sent him back in 1993.

"Well, I guess he's not coming back then?"

"Probably not, it didn't seem like he really want to be here did it?" said Carl.

"Hmmm, maybe it's all a bit awkward, what with him leaving the band" Graham piped up.

Oh well, what next? The experience of meeting my favourite band had been a bit of a non-event so far. After a few minutes the door reopened, Saul Davies walked into the room and once again everybody bust into a huge round of applause, Saul stopped dead in his tracks. And then he said,

"Shit, I thought my dick was hanging out of my trousers or something".

Everybody burst into laughter the three of us included although I felt a bit embarrassed by his comment as there were quite a few young people in the room including some children.

"What a guy!" said Graham, his face lit with up with a dreamy gaze.

Dave Baynton-Power then entered the room, the round of applause that greeted him appeared to confuse him and he looked behind to see if somebody else was following him into the room, satisfied that the round of applause was for him he smiled and gave a small wave to all.

"Now what?" I asked Graham.

"We wait, they'll probably sign our tickets at the very least, it'll just depend on who else turns up, we just need to wait until the mauling by this lot has lessened" said Graham pointing at the other attendees.

We waited as patiently as we possibly could. Saul and Dave had sat down and were shaking hands with people and signing autographs. The three of us edged ever closer to them, my heart was in my mouth, not literally of course because this isn't humanly possible but I felt very nervous. Before I even realised it the three of us were stood next to Saul and Dave, eye contact was made and I reached out to shake Saul's hand, it felt quite weak which surprised me, maybe he was sick of shaking peoples hands.

"Hiya, great show tonight!" I squeaked in a nervous trembling voice.

"Cheers" Saul replied in a deadpan manner.

"I saw you guys last night in Leeds and I saw you in Guildford too!" I said hoping that he'd be impressed, he didn't really react though.

"Guildford, yeah, great" he yawned.

"Hmmmm, a bit of a funny gig that one wasn't it?" As soon as the words had left my mouth I realised I was treading on thin ice with this notoriously bad tempered multi instrumentalist.

"A funny one?" he scowled at me.

"Err, yes, well you all seemed to be in a bit of a weird mood" I nervously said to him expecting to receive an uppercut as a reward, however Saul did nothing more than just give me a bit of a dirty look. Then, just too really push my luck I asked him if he'd sign my ticket and being a gentleman he did, I thanked him before making a hasty retreat. I'd embarrassed myself yet again. Dave on the other hand was much warmer in manner, he signed our tickets and made small talk with the three of us, well, I actually remained pretty quiet and left the talking to Carl and Graham as I was worried that I'd say something stupid yet again, possibly something similar to "ALRIGHT CAPTAIN!"

Dave said that Jim would probably make an appearance too and then Saul got up out of his chair, waved goodbye and exited the room, I was tempted to chase after him and thank him for everything that he'd contributed towards the band and my life over the years and give him an alarmingly big bear hug and a lick of his forehead but this would have resulted in certain death so I remained rooted where I was. Dave then bid us farewell and the three of us discussed whether that was it as far as the evening was concerned. After another fifteen minutes and with no other band members making an appearance we left the room through the door we entered and made our way out of the venue, it was late, very late and I had a long drive back to Leeds down the unlit A1. I offered the guys a lift into the city centre although I somehow managed to lose my bearings in the car park and at one point we ended up in the loading bay of the venue.

"So, what did you reckon to that then?" Graham asked.

"Great, brilliant, I wish Tim had stayed a bit longer though but it was cool to meet Saul and Dave, I think I may have offended Saul or at the very least he must have thought I was a bit of a knob" I replied.

The others laughed out loud and we chatted about the evening in general. The gig had been pretty good, a decent mix of songs but I thought the atmosphere wasn't that fantastic, in retrospect maybe it was just where I'd been stood. I dropped the guys off and wished them well, I wasn't sure if our paths would ever cross again, I hoped that they would but without James it was unlikely we'd ever meet again. The drive back down the A1 flew past in a cloud of thoughts relating to the evening and by the time I'd parked my car up outside my house it was two in the morning.

Wednesday and Thursday were recovery days of sorts, I was still feeling under the weather and the two very late nights, the crowd noise and sheer exhilaration and punishment of the gigs had severely depleted my energy levels. Hot broths and warm baths soothed my aching bug ridden bones which felt like they'd aged at least five years, but in a somehow satisfying and quite a nice way if such a way exists. The reviews for the gigs on the James forums were very positive; everybody appeared to have had a great time. An announcement was made by a forumite that the Friday gig in Manchester was to be filmed! I had to be at the front by the barrier, I just had to be! I couldn't concentrate properly at work throughout the whole of Friday and when we were finally released from the shackles of corporate training I ran as fast as I could down Park Row skilfully avoiding the Big Issue sellers, the Christmas Shoppers and the drunken idiots spilling out of the Becketts Bank Pub.

The train journey to Manchester was uneventful; my mind remained focused upon the evening ahead. Upon arrival on a busy cold winters evening in Manchester I braced myself for the run through the city towards the venue. Again, as I had earlier in Leeds I ran and dodged pedestrians and traffic as if I was on a death wish, knackered upon arrival at the venue I almost collapsed running up the large set of steps leading up to the entrance before I crashed through the glass doors and bolted down the stairs to the arena floor. I was gutted though when I saw that there was already a sizeable crowd congregating by the barrier as if they were at the Wailing Wall, but without the wailing or pieces of paper with prayers on them I hasten to add.

Support was once again supplied by Turin Brakes. The atmosphere was buzzing, the last ever James hometown gig, the seats around the venue had filled up quickly, the crowd behind me was expanding by the minute like an inflatable mattress. I wasn't sure how I was going to react to seeing my favourite band one last time, I thought that perhaps I'd cry, it was going to be a bereavement of sorts. Part of my life was kind of coming to an end, sure, other bands would eventually fill the gap but I couldn't imagine another band meaning so very much to me in the way that James had done for so long. The lights dimmed, Turin Brakes marched on stage, plugged in all of their own instruments and proceeded to aggresively point them at the audience before playing a few of their songs for us. Nice lads with nice happy songs. After Turin Brakes finished with their polite noise terrorism the lights came back on and the roadies prepared the stage for James' last ever Manchester show. A curtain obstructed our view of the stage, all we could see were spooky shadows and silhouettes carrying out their evil yet magnificent deeds.

Stage time, the lights dimmed, the place erupted with a thunderous roar and the curtain on stage dropped to the floor revealing the band in all of their glory, Mike and Adrian were stood in front of me, Mark was stood behind them sweating heavily at the prospect of performing to his devoted fans. 'Say Something' opened proceedings and was played straight through, the audience sang the song back to the band equalling them in the noise stakes. Tim thanked the audience after the song had finished for the support they'd given the band over the years; I raised my arms in exultation and punched the air in sheer joy. 'Waltzing Along', 'Sometimes', 'Laid' were played through in a 'James by numbers' style but the set really livened up with 'I Know What I'm Here For', the lyrics about *"holding on till late December"* finally making perfect sense due to the circumstances and timing that they were being sung under. Tim described 'God Only Knows' as "an old regurgitated James song for the old regurgitated James fans", I'd never thought all those years ago when I listened to the song for the first time in my bedroom that I'd end up being "an old regurgitated James fan", my chest swelled with pride and I threw myself into the song as much as the band did.

'Someone's Got It In For Me' was aired to an appreciative reception followed by the rather gorgeous 'Vervaceous'; Sinead didn't turn up again though the cheeky little Irish mare. Once it had finished the majority of the band marched off stage leaving Tim and Jim alone, but not for long as a bald headed man made his appearance, it was none other than Larry Gott himself. Although he wasn't James' original guitarist he was probably their most well known after serving with the band until the middle of the nineties when he decided to quit music and focus on furniture making, a wise choice it seemed now. There was apparently a bidding war for him for a while between MFI and Ikea! The three 'original' members of James performed a beautiful rendition of the *Seven* song 'Protect Me', a gentle and beautiful song which sounded all the more better being played in its stripped down format in the aircraft hangar venue that all of us James fans were housed in together as one.

'Out To Get You' had a bit of a bumpy start and the song collapsed in on itself, Tim joked with the audience making light of the technical malfunction which appeared to be almost symbiotic with James gigs, stuff was always conking out and blowing up causing much mirth and sometimes a fair bit of annoyance usually from Saul of course the fiery mischievous little fox. A superb version of 'Hymn from a Village' followed where cowbells were once again knocked and brayed by various band members, this was followed by the *last* ever James single 'Getting Away With It'. As the song built towards it's destructive climax a cameraman filming the show pointed his camera in my direction, I immediately started to point into the camera screaming the lyrics to the song into the lens, the red light on the camera lit up and I knew that I was being filmed and the cameraman's face was filled with a knowing smile.

The song finished, 'Tomorrow' lifted the gig up to another level, I could feel the veins in my neck and forehead sticking out and throbbing whilst I howled the song almost as loud as Tim. 'Born of Frustration' was next, sixteen thousand sets of vocal chords whooped and hollered the American Indian signature sound of the song that had been rubbished by Ulrika Johnson so many years before, Tim dropped off the stage and headed up the steps towards the bands adoring fans, everybody else's necks craned towards Tim, the rest of the band included. He didn't return to the stage until the end of the song, the fans respected him throughout; he didn't end up being inappropriately touched up or have beer chucked all over him.

'Ring The Bells' closed the set, the band left the stage to the usual rapturous adoration that the band had gotten used to but had never taken for granted over the years. Once toileting was carried out and sandwiches had been eaten the band returned to the stage, all except Tim and Saul. 'Top Of The World' created a ethereal ambience to the venue and hushed the audience with it's wonderful delicately played instrumentation and then Tim made his presence known from way up high amongst the seated audience, the song sung beautifully, Saul parallel to him at the other side of the arena amongst the seated audience, his violin playing layering the song with such beauty that I had a lump in my throat. The band reconvened on stage and played a version of 'Sound' that seemed like it would have gone on forever, the song continuously spiralled out of control before it was reined in time and time again, Adrian's guitar playing proved to be an integral part of James in ways that I hadn't sadly realised up until this point. And then, they were gone. In some ways the house lights should have come back on and the gig should have finished at that point. Of course it was blatantly obvious that one particular song hadn't been played, the band therefore had to return and return they did.

James being James had to be awkward though, instead of hammering out one of their hits they decided to play 'Space'. A hushed audience showed their appreciation for the song but it kind of felt that the pace and tempo of the gig had slipped back a gear or two, fair play to the band though for once again throwing a curve ball to the fans who expected the band to return to the stage with 'a hit'. The night drew to an end with bouncy versions of 'She's A Star', 'Come Home' and finally 'Sit Down' with Mark playing an extended version of the songs intro on the piano.

And,

then,

they,

were,

gone,

forever.....

There would be no more James albums, singles, live appearances or anything really. Part of my life was drawing to an unwanted conclusion. Before the gig I thought that at some point in the evening I might have started to cry, but I never did. Instead I celebrated the end of something rather beautiful along with the rest of the people who were in attendance by clapping till my hands bled. Somewhere at the back of the arena high up in the gods my wife was sat with her sister and their friend, I wondered how it had been for them and did they truly understand the enormity and magnitude of the event. Or perhaps they were just happy to have enjoyed an evening of cheesy pop songs to sing along too.

Joseph's Well

2002/2003/2004

The year 2002 had arrived and on a personal level it was to be the year that everything starting to unravel for me before slowly, very slowly realigning itself. My favourite band was no more, longstanding friendships were really being put to the test and the already poor relationship I had with my immediate blood related family was turning ever more sour. I felt quite lost; I was questioning who I was and where I was in life. I hated my job, in fact I really hated my job, it was soul destroying, when you start work at 09:00 and by 09:15 you're looking at the clock whilst holding back tears of boredom then you know you're in the deepest of poo. The only person who could do anything to change my life was me and I'd lost any motivation I'd previously had, I felt an overwhelming sense of apathy and anhedonia.

On a positive forward thinking note I managed to persuade my wife to buy a house using a graduate mortgage on the proviso that I'd pay half of the mortgage and bills so that we could live together properly instead of swapping between each others houses as it was starting to become tiresome for a number of different reasons. Charles and I had definitely drifted apart, I'd love to say that it was because of his comments regarding *Pleased To Meet You* but this wasn't the case, we were just heading in different directions, I was sure we'd reconvene though when the time was right and the stars held a certain position in the cosmos. True friendships always find a way of restoring lost equilibrium.

Early in the year Tim Booth's own website was launched although frustratingly hardly any of the links worked on it so access to information was therefore quite limited. New solo material was briefly mentioned as was a project Tim was involved with called 'Dancing With Dolphins'. I had visions of the sexy aquatic based beasts mincing about in frocks and tutus to 'The Macarena' whilst Tim threw himself about in one of his usual manic but controlled frenzies. I laughed out loud when someone on the James forum stated that Tim was apparently going to be "tangoing with tigers" the following year although I gulped in panic at the prospect of Tim scaring the beautiful beasts before being torn to bits by them as a show of approval of his funky moves. That would have been a bad career move although record sales do tend to increase dramatically when an artist passes onto the afterlife.

Some further light relief came later in the year via the release of the live DVD and CD of their last Manchester gig. Being particularly curious and probably a tad vain I headed straight for the 'Getting Away With It (All Messed Up)' option and watched to see if I'd made it past the cutting room floor. I still cringed with utter embarrassment when there I was pointing into the camera singing and looking as aggressive as a National Front lout. The pause and rewind function on the remote control was soon worn down as each and every time a visitor came around to the house (including the window cleaner) they were forced to watch the clip umpteen times causing them to be bored to death by my excited ramblings regarding my miniature claim to fame, although to me it was more than that, it was a moment in time and history that would exist forever, possibly. The NME gave the album of the gig a massive 0/10, a waste of ink and paper really. A tree died for that review you sons of bitches!

I really thought that was it, the final nail in the James coffin of sorts. The last ever James release. Their music still stayed with me, it was like a running commentary in my head. I was experiencing James withdrawals and musical schizophrenia, thankfully without any other delusional thoughts. The year continued to drift along, my wife and I moved into our new house in Tingley and we settled down into a perfectly happy life with our two cats Cosmic and Ziggy until they were both run over by cars on the busy A650. That was a very sad time. I won't bore you any further with 2002 though except for this....

Now, 'Noughties' television was slowly being strangulated by the cultural phenomenon known as 'Reality TV' which in reality is as far away from reality as you can probably get, and that my fine feathered friends is the actual bonefied reality that exists. That sentence made little sense but you'll probably get the gist of what I'm talking about. *Fame Academy* was the BBC's attempt at rivalling ITV's *Pop Idol*. Desperate for fame and slightly deluded and mentally on the edge individuals tried to carve out a musical career for themselves by singing MOR songs in front of an audience of millions whilst being bullied and ridiculed by the so called experienced judges of taste and musical knowledge.

It really is atrocious television and not that far away from the days of public executions, with hungry mobs baying for blood so it was a surprise to hear that Saul and Mark would be assisting one of the contestants on *Fame Academy* in writing a song. I obviously had to watch the show to see what the hell they were playing at, I felt a bit let down that two people who I really respected and looked up to had ended up in a situation where they were embroiled in such nonsense, but to my surprise the material that they were involved in with a young chap called Ainslie was actually rather good. One particular song reminded me of 'Chunney Chops' with Ainslie adlibbing quite a fantastic phonetic melody over the top of it, Mark and Saul appeared to be particularly impressed with him; he definitely had some sort of talent that could possibly be tapped into. I was concerned at the prospect that Mark and Saul might ask him to join James and take over from Tim. Now, if that had happened then I think I may have left the country for God, I mean good. Ainslie was eventually voted off the show and although he'd release a few records and keep in contact with Saul via later projects that Saul was involved in he faded from the public conscious just like everybody else does who appears on those shows, even when they end up winning them.

2003 was an eventful year from many reasons, Charles and I sold our house and called it a day as far as that part of our lives was concerned. I went to Glastonbury for the first time and spent the majority of it drunk on Somerset Cider. The acts that impressed me the most were

Sigur Ros, Mogwai, The Flaming Lips and the legendary Julian Cope. Although I enjoyed the weekend Glastonbury felt just too big. I tried to avoid the main stage as much as I could and investigate the weird and the wonderful but I still managed to spend too much time by the large pyramid.

I'd saved up all of my annual leave from work that year so that I could have December off as my wife and I were going to Australia for a month. I simply couldn't wait to return to a place that felt like a second home to me, little did my wife know that I was going to propose to her in Australia. But first of all let me tell you about the next 'blip' on the James radar which happened in November of 2003. Towards the back end of the month I went to see one of my favourite new bands in Leeds with a friend from work called James, (this section of the book might end up becoming even more confusing, the thing was that I had loads of friends called James.) He was a top bloke who loved XTRNTR era Primal Scream. British Sea Power were a rather odd band who'd initially caught my eye because of their bizarre name, I'd wanted to see them live earlier on in the year at the same venue (Josephs Well) but I hadn't made it because I was too tired and hung over after going to a wedding the day before. I'd seen British Sea Power at the Leeds Festival in the summer with my brother in law who'd never been to a gig let alone a festival and we decided to watch them instead of Metallica who were bashing out their hits on the main stage whilst being paid mega bucks. British Sea Power blew me away and the free Kendal Mint Cake they gave out to the audience was very tasty indeed.

Now, the only problem was the gig in November had sold out but James had a friend who worked there behind the bar who was sure to be able to let us in for free. James' friend was a guy called Simon Rix who played in a band called Parva, they'd later change their name to the Kaiser Chiefs and sell quite a few records, undeservedly in my opinion but once again that's yet another story for another time! As it happened Simon couldn't get us in for free but the guy on the door told us that if some people on the guest list didn't bother to turn up then we could pay and go in. James and I hung around the bar chatting and enjoying a couple of beverages whilst we patiently waited. The support band was an unknown band called The Killers, they sounded okay as far as I could tell from the bar but I didn't think I'd ever hear of them again.

As we drank our ale I realised I was stood next to a bloke who was accompanied by a very attractive woman, she'd caught my eye initially but I didn't want to get a smack off the man for staring at his female companion so I'd politely looked away. She then left to go and apparently use the toilet as she was clutching her stomach, it was then that I realised that I recognised the man. It was Jim Glennie! I looked at him, looked away, looked again, looked away and almost did a little wee in my pants. He must have realised that he'd been recognised because he then walked away from me and stood next to the fruit machine.

"Mate, guess who that was stood next to me? It was Jim from James!!!"

"Jim from James?" said James.

"Yes, the bass player from James!"

"James?" said James.

"Yes James, 'James'. Oh my God!!! What should I do? Should I say something to him?"

"Course you should, if you don't you'll regret it" said James and then he downed his drink and shouted angrily at Simon demanding more ale. I looked over at Jim who looked much taller than I remembered; he looked like he was trying to remain anonymous in the packed bar. He was doing too good a job as far as I was concerned. I ummmed and ahhed for ages until I plucked up the courage and walked across to him my heart once again beating like a drum.

"Err, hi, is it Jim?"

Jim barely made eye contact.

"Yes".

"Jim Glennie, from James?"

He made eye contact but didn't really smile or anything.

"Yeah".

"Oh, wow, hiya I'm really *pleased to meet you*, I've been a massive James fan for years".

Jim smiled at me.

Then I really embarrassed myself.

"Hey, Jim, I'm on the Manchester DVD you know! During Getting Away With It I'm pointing into the camera and singing!"

"Wow, well I'll have to keep my eyes open for that one next time I watch it" Jim quietly said.

I cringed at my stupid comment (chalking up another moment of self embarrassment). What a waste of an opportunity! Then I really put my foot in it.

"So, are you still in touch with the rest of the guys then?" Jim had commented in the past that James were not finished and would continue without Tim Booth.

"Yes" he simply replied without looking at me. There was an awkward moment or two until I decided to change the subject.

"So, British Sea Power eh!"

"Yes, did you see them the last time they played here?" Jim asked me, the mood warmed up somewhat.

"Err, no I didn't, I was going to but I was unable due to being too tired from a wedding I'd attended in Oldham the night before, I think I'd been disco dancing way too much which was why I was probably so knackered!"

Jim looked at me like I was even more of an oddball than he probably already thought I was.

"Ah, you should have made it, there was only about fifteen of us there".

My heart sank. His comment made it clearly obvious that I'd missed an amazing opportunity to meet probably the most important member of my favourite band in an intimate surrounding with an amazing band all because I had a hangover from drinking cheap lager all night at my wife's cousins wedding.

"Oh, right" I mumbled.

There were a few moments of awkward silence, it seemed conversation had run as dry as the Sahara. I admitted defeat and decided I should leave the poor man alone.

"Right Jim, well, I think I've probably embarrassed myself enough, nice meeting you though, all the best mate!" I said to him knowing I'd probably never get another chance to speak to him again.

"Cool, have a good night" replied Jim and I walked back towards James, grabbed my beer and drank it in one gulp cursing myself for being such an idiot.

James and I finally made it into the gig just as the members of British Sea Power were walking onto the stage. Even though we'd been let in via guest passes that hadn't been used the guy still charged us for the gig, a bit tight really considering that we missed the warm up and as the gig had sold out by the time we'd entered our view of the band was minimal to say the least. The band played their environmentally friendly eclectic collection of songs which climaxed with the wonderful 'Lately', the band performing the song demonstrated a full ensemble of acrobatics including climbing to the top of the PA system, jumping off into the crowd and sitting on each others shoulders whilst playing their instruments. Jim had been stood a couple of meters away from me during the gig; due to his height he'd been able to see a lot more of it than I did. As the final piece of feedback squawked and wailed and people started to leave the room I approached Jim on the way out and daringly spoke to him one last time.

"See you later Jim, all the best!"

"Oh, you made it in then did you!" he said with a friendly smile upon his face.

"Yeah, they let me and my mate in with some unused guest passes, but you know what, the tight bugger still charged us £11 pound each!" I said whilst realising that Jim probably wasn't too interested in the minor detail of how we'd paid for the experience.

"Okay, well nice to have met you, see you" Jim replied and before I could say anything further James and I were buffeted out of the venue by the thirsty crowd heading towards the bar.

So Jim had said that the band were in touch but he'd remained tight lipped about any details. I announced the contact I'd made with Jim on the official James forum to muted interest, the forum was starting to resemble a Wild West Ghost Town with just a handful of survivors flying the flag for James, the most regular participant was somebody known only as 'Adrian Oxalls Jazz Master', my goodness this person could rant like there was no tomorrow. Adrian Oxall's Jazz Master was convinced that James would reform at some point and they were mocked on a regular basis for their delusionary belief. It also transpired that the interest Jim had in British Sea Power was due to the fact that he co-produced some of the material on their debut album *The Decline Of British Sea Power*.

Next came Australia, it's such a beautiful place that holds so many wonderful memories for me. My wife absolutely loved the time we spent there together and proposing to her went down a storm. I embarrassingly quoted Rocky Balboa and asked my wife what she had planned for the next fifty years or so. Although where I proposed to her was somewhere more picturesque than a zoo, it was on top of a cliff but maybe she felt she didn't have much choice in the matter. Whilst we enjoyed the scorching hot weather I still found time to have a nosey around the music shops. There weren't any James items for sale in Red Eye Records or Fish Records, in fact I didn't find one album or single for sale even in the second hand shops. I was excited though when I found 'Getting Away With It (All Messed Up)' on a digital juke box in a pub on Kangaroo Island, a nice reminder of home and my past, the song had apparently made it on to a compilation album called *Triple J's Hottest 100* as the song had been an alternative hit in Australia so the lack of any James albums was a puzzle.

In January 2004 we bid Australia farewell and returned home slightly sunburnt and engaged to be married, with a new chapter in our lives about to unfold. I was on the verge of quitting my job at the bank and in March of 2004 I started my nurse training at university specialising in mental health, it was make or break time, I knew that if I didn't give it a go then I'd end up at the age of forty bitter and angry for not taking the plunge, who cared whether I succeeded or failed, better to be a failure at something than to always have wondered what might have been.

Bone

2004

In 2004 a new James album was released! It was a simple affair; a compilation that the great man Dave Brown himself had compiled called *The Collection*. The more obvious hits were included along with a few rarities such as 'Lazy', 'So Long Marianne' and 'Coffee and Toast' which harked back to the *Pleased To Meet You* era. 'Coffee and Toast' had sounded pretty good played live but the recorded version I wasn't too fussed about. I didn't buy the album; I'm not sure why even when it was in the "two for £10" section in HMV! Tsk, and there was me claiming to be such a fan of the band! I'll certainly rectify this at some point in the future.

Rumour had it Tim was going to release a solo album in the summer of 2004; I was naturally very excited at the prospect of further Tim Booth action and I vibrated at random moments in celebration. A new Tim Booth website was set up by Dave Brown, its mission was to keep the believers in touch and up to speed with developments regarding the project that Tim had rustled up with a guy called Lee "Muddy" Baker and a mysteriously named individual called 'KK'. By all accounts the album was to be a proper bargain bin classic, cheaply produced and recorded in their prospective homes on the south coast of England. The album would eventually be given the title of *Bone*; to this day I'm unclear why the album was named after something that I could find inside various parts of my body, but bones are very useful things to have, I'm sure the same thought must have crossed Tim's mind which is possibly one of the reasons why he chose it as the album title.

The album was set for a June release and the lead single was to be 'Down To The Sea' which was such a gorgeous title for a song and to top it all live dates were announced for the month of April. As soon as the tickets went on sale I purchased three tickets, one for my wife, a friend of ours called Edward and of course one for yours truly. The closest venue to where we lived was Liverpool which was a bit of a trek but I couldn't pass up on the opportunity of seeing the legendary Mr Booth in action, and I was very curious to hear what the new material would sound like.

On the 19th April the three of us set off from Tingley westbound along the motorway until we finally reached Liverpool, I hadn't been there in years, since I was a kid in fact and I hate to say it but driving through the outskirts of the city I thought the place looked like something out of a post apocalyptic movie, lots of boarded up and burnt out buildings dotted around, I told the others to lock their doors. After hitting the city centre and finding a respectable place to park we used dead reckoning and found the venue for the gig, entered and headed directly towards the bar. Drinks were bought, (soft drinks for me) and we entered the small auditorium and waited in anticipation for the action to begin. To be honest, it's all a bit of a blur now looking back; I can remember details much clearer from gigs some ten years before hand. However, this is what I remember most about that evening...

The support was from Tim's mate Lee, just him and an acoustic guitar. Lee was just too good looking to be honest, thick jet black hair with a cool trim of beard to boot. A friendly chap he was too, chatting away to the audience who were settled in and very polite. His songs were okay however there was one song that irked me somewhat as it featured a lyric about emails and for some reason it just really got my back up. Lee eventually finished his set and we waited, and waited and waited. Tim was meant to be on stage for about 21:00 but by 21:40 we were still listening to the warm up music (*Faded Seaside Glamour* by the Delays) and the crowd was becoming increasingly inpatient, my wife in particular was really moaning and whining about where the hell Tim was. I told her to hang on and was sure that Tim would make an appearance soon enough. It was alright her moaning but it was me who was going to be driving home after the gig! 21:45 the lights finally dimmed and the small audience cried out their appreciation and respect towards Tim and his cohort of musicians who he'd later label as 'The Individuals'.

"Look, do us a favour and don't be the first stupid fucker to ask for 'Sit Down'", voiced Tim resulting in much laughter from those in attendance.

"Tim, do 'Sit Down'" some fool shouted which received even more laughter.

"Typical fucking Scousers" Tim humorously replied, it appeared that we were in for an evening of comedy. The set opened with a song called 'Careful What You Say'. Lee's Middle Eastern phonetic line created a beautiful haunting ambience, the song began slowly enough before bursting open like an exotic flower showering us all with it's polyphonic pollen, before the song finished my jaw was already aching from having the worlds biggest smile upon my face and when the song finally finished to a massive round of applause I screamed out in absolute pleasure and joy, it was and probably still is one of the finest musical experiences of my life. If Tim and the rest of the band had walked off stage and ended the set after that one song then I would still have driven home in utter amazement and extreme happiness. Of course that wasn't the case, the band played some of the most amazing music that Tim had ever been involved in, I was in utter ecstasy and the at times heavy heart I'd experienced with James when they'd turned into a bit of a greatest hit dinosaur stomping from Enormodome to Enormodome in their latter days was exorcised from my psyche.

The new material sounded so fresh and invigorated; Tim appeared extremely relaxed and comfortable. The other highlight of the night was 'Butterfly's Dream' from the Booth and the Bad Angel album that held so many warm memories for me, I'd never heard a live rendition before and Tim's band conjured up a dirty, sexy little minx of a song that had me swaying my hips in unison with Tim.

The main set finished and then the band returned for an encore which featured 'Fall In Love With Me', a song from the Bad Angel album.

"Please, I really do need absolute silence for this song, I can't do it if there is any noise" Tim politely said.

Of course it initially had the reverse effect and people started to wolf whistle and call out, Tim looked annoyed. Lee stepped in.

"C'mon guys, seriously, this song is so delicate that it really needs your undivided attention".

The noise swiftly abated, there was the odd murmur and then the audience calmed and fell silent. All except some young girl who was stood in front of me!

"Yum Yum" she said loud enough to be heard by those in close proximity including the band.

"SHUT UP!" I hissed at her, she turned around at me and I gave her an evil look, she looked embarrassed and turned back round and remained quiet. The song began; it was as delicate as a sea horse, quiet to the point where the hum from the sound system could be heard above the band. The original song hadn't initially been my favourite on the *Bad Angel* album but I much preferred it to the new version the band played that night. The song finished, Tim and the rest of the band thanked the audience, invited everybody back for future gigs and of course insisted that everyone bought his new album.

I drove us back to Tingley full of excitement from the evening, I'd been blown away by the new songs and the James song 'Five-o' that the band had performed was a reminder of the past that seemed to stem from another lifetime. My wife and Edward had been enthusiastic about the evening although I don't think they'd been as moved by the experience as I had. There was still a couple of months to go before the release of the album however Dave Brown must have received a copy as he posted a fine review for it online, the word that leapt out at me from the review was *"fun"*, the night in Liverpool had certainly been fun and as I mentioned earlier there was a sense of lightness to what I had heard, Tim visibly breathing new life again and unshackled from the past.

I bought *Bone* from HMV in Bradford, the city where Tim Booth had been born back in 1960, the very same city where I was forging a new identity and a promising future from studying nursing. The album cover was great, a family photo of Tim and his wife (who appeared to be exposing her chest although it was cunningly hidden by masking tape with the album title written in marker pen on it). I dashed home and slapped the compact disc into my stereo. 'Wave Hello' the first track had me laughing, it's a jolly little number with some great guitar playing throughout, Tim sounded so happy, in fact in some ways it didn't sound like him at all, I certainly didn't recognise him as the same Tim that I remembered from 2001 or perhaps even some of the years prior to the end of the last century. The only let down regarding the song was that it ended as abruptly as a song from the 1960's in that it sounded like it had been edited short to please American Juke Box owners. The title track was a murky little number with a slow burning groove throughout, the song featured the classic lyric *"One born rich, one born poor, life's a bitch and I'm her whore"*. The song ended in a way not too dissimilar to 'Karma Police' by Radiohead in that it sounded as if all of the musical instruments had started to disintegrate.

'Monkey God' was next, a galloping beast of a song with a bass line that bobbed like a cork on a rampant ocean. The song questioned man's evolution from slime to ape to God. It was a fine, fine song. 'Redneck' bubbled along; Tim mentioned his favourite food product (Ice Cream) before the song ended with Tim's vocal slowing down to the speed of dust motes. 'Love hard', was next, a filthy dirty sounding song, oozing sex and tension whilst clickety beats, warm synth lines and a tune bashed out against what sounded like a posh set of wine glasses added a sinister sense of humour. A squelchy choppy guitar part played by Lee overpowered the songs final bars but in a good way.

'Discover' featured abandoned lyrics from the James song 'The Shining' regarding Nazis and Jews which I'm guessing had originally been edited and replaced at the insistence of either Brian Eno or the record company in that they may have been too emotive to feature on a major label release. It was yet another great song that chilled the mood of the album somewhat further due to its beautiful strings and Lee's finely strummed guitar. 'Fall In Love' was a stripped down version of the *Booth And The Bad Angel* song from 1996, Tim obviously felt the song deserved to be given a second chance and I hate to say it but the version on *Bone* felt out of place somewhat, it was extremely slow and sparse to the point where the only place I could really imagine it working was in a wine bar at four o'clock in the morning (of course I'm making an assumption, I'm not the kind of person who hangs around wine bars at any time of the day, I'm more of a real ale pub kind of bloke). I could imagine Seal performing it, not sure if that's a compliment or an insult. Perhaps it should have been one of those 'hidden tracks' that are often tagged onto albums. 'Falling Down', not to be confused with the excellent *Pleased To Meet You* song was a pleasant enough tune, no more and no less.

'Down To The Sea', the lead single from the album is perhaps one of the saddest sounding songs that Tim had ever penned; seriously, the lyrics are so desperate that they hurt. It's a wonderful song, it was never going to be a big hit single in this lifetime though, the song was just too darn good for the 'hit parade'. It had been released as a single but where indeed if it had charted was a mystery to me, an official video had even been made for it and Edward told me that he'd seen it on one of the Satellite music channels. It's definitely one of Tim's finest moments and I smile to myself now due to the fact that the first time I heard 'Down To The Sea' I thought it was rather bland. 'In The Darkness's distorted bass line was absolutely blinding, a proper groovy stonker of a song with Tim name-checking Ipod's back when they were kind of fresh on the scene. 'Eh Mamma' is for me perhaps the best song on the album; seriously, I can't fault the song in any way whatsoever. Once again a distorted bass line created a groove that made me want to shake my booty; in fact this is something that I've done many a time to this delightful song. Further suspect lyrics of a sexual nature featured this time referencing fellatio in which pardon the pun could only be described as a very tongue in cheek manner. The album ended with the song that had opened the Liverpool gig, 'Careful What You Say'. I can't think of any more superlatives to describe the song; it's quite simply stunning in every way shape and form.

Bone had exceeded all of my expectations; I was blown away. It made the last James album seem even more cold and oppressive than before. *Bone* evoked warm sandy beaches and strawberry ice cream. Even the more serious tracks felt light and airy without a hint of pretentiousness. Reviews were generally positive, *"An unexpected but welcome return of the former James singer"* Q magazine commented upon the release of Tim's new album. The NME gave the album 3/10 which in NME land is quite good. *Bone* was wedged inside my stereo for ages, repeated plays revealed further hidden depths and secrets, the James community or what was left of it anyway were favourable too. I wondered to myself what *Pleased To Meet You* would have sounded like had it have been produced by Lee instead of Brian Eno.

August 2004. My wife and I had travelled to Spain for a couple of week's holiday; amazingly I'd managed to persuade her to let me buy tickets for the festival at Benicassim. The festival had an amazing line up, Kraftwerk, Pet Shop Boys, Morrissey, Lou Reed, Primal Scream, Brian Wilson, The Chemical Brothers, Spiritualized and Love to name but a few. The festival properly began on the Friday but on the Thursday a number of bands played the main stage as a bit of a warm up, headlining the Thursday night was the legendary Paul Weller. I couldn't wait; even my wife was excited which made a change for her regarding live music. It was scorching hot and we arrived at the festival site on the Tuesday. We had to endure truly ferocious heat inside our tent, it was nearly impossible to sleep, during the day tired and weary bodies found any piece of shade they could, the town looked like a scene from a disaster movie. I felt particularly ignorant as I knew zero Spanish apart from "si" and "dos dedos mis amigos" and none of the locals spoke English; I was too used to the popular resorts that resembled Bridlington or Blackpool but with sunshine.

On the Wednesday I received a text message from my mate James. He was also heading to the festival with a group of his mates. The text read as follows...

GOOD NEWZ 4 U MATE, PAUL WELLER NOT PLAYING, TIM BOOTH PLAYING INSTEAD, C U ON THURSDAY.

I danced a merry little dance of happiness, skipping wildly like a child in a meadow chasing butterflies.

"Tim's playing, Tim's playing, oh my god, oh my god. Tim's playing, Tim's playing, oh my god, oh my god". I sang over and over again causing my poor wife to feel rather embarrassed as the locals stared at the pasty looking mad English man. I was as you might have guessed by now, rather pleased.

Thursday evening couldn't come quick enough, although Tim was the headlining act other bands would be playing after him, in fact Ash were due to follow after Tim's set had finished. Come show time and I was drunk on the expensive ale served in the corporate sponsored paper cups. My wife and I were stood stage left, plenty of space around us, I was wearing my blue Ja-m-es t-shirt that I'd had the wisdom and foresight to bring with me to Spain. Tim and his band walked on stage to much applause.

"LISA!!!!" I drunkenly shouted out towards the attractive keyboard player on stage, Lisa smiled and waved down at me, my wife poked me in the back. A couple of British girls behind me started to make fun of me thinking that I was one of the locals.

"Oooh, he's a bit over excited isn't he" one of them sarcastically said to the other, both then burst into sniggers of laughter. I turned around very slowly with just one eye open.

"I may well be over excited but that bald bloke on stage is a bloody hero to me" I slurred at them.

The look on their faces was priceless and they scarpered away from us.

"Right, we're going to do something a bit different tonight" Tim said to the audience and the band chaotically started with 'Eh Mamma' in what appeared to be a miniature sound check. It sounded wonderful; I jumped and thrashed around as if I was watching Rage Against The Machine. My wife told me to simmer down; I didn't so she moved away from me which was a good thing as it gave me more space to dance.

"We'd really like to thank Ash and Snow Patrol, our equipment hasn't turned up so they're loaning us their stuff for the night" Tim announced,

I started to whoop and holler, my wife told me again to simmer, it was like a red rag to a bull in that my jigging about became wilder as the set went on. The band played the James song 'Sometimes', a slow burning version that was as stripped down as 'Fall In Love With Me' had been on *Bone*. A wonderful moment in time, even my wife sang along and before I knew it the amazing set came to an end, Tim and The Individuals left the stage to much appreciative noise from the audience. As the crowds dispersed I noticed a couple of lads wearing the same Ja-m-es t-shirt as mine. I ran across to them and started to enthuse wildly about the set; they looked overjoyed but clearly didn't speak English so the three of us tried to communicate in a non verbal form. One of their friends had a camera and lined the three of us up, one of the Spanish lads stood facing the camera, I stood side on and the other Spanish lad stood with his back to the camera whilst peering over his shoulder. It made a wonderful photograph, my wife took one too, three brothers from different mothers spelling out "Ja-m-es" across the three shirts. We shook hands, bid each other farewell and then they were gone. During Ash's set I bumped into my mate James from back home, he was as drunk as a lord and didn't make a right lot of sense. He'd also annoyingly missed Tim's set. I told him I'd catch up with him later on but the next time I'd actually see him would be back in the UK. The rest of the festival was amazing, the only bum note was when Morrissey didn't attend for reasons that to this day have never been fully explained.

Whilst at the festival in Benicassim I managed to find the CD single for 'Sometimes' and I threw my euros at the stall holder before racing away with the CD in my hand whilst screaming very loudly indeed. It was one of those wonderfully reassuring moments in life where you just knew even though you were quite small good things could happen to you. That once again probably makes no sense at all and I fear I am possibly wandering into confusing waffle mode again. However, confusing waffle mode is a nice cosy place to visit on occasion, except on Wednesdays between the hours of 14:00 and 16:00 of course.

Anyway...

... after the festival had finished my wife and I headed back to Barcelona and booked ourselves into a swanky yet cheap hotel.

The room had a half decent stereo and upon playing the single I was swiftly and non-violently transported back to 1993 when I'd originally bought the 12" vinyl from Virgin Records in Leeds. The B-sides for the 'Sometimes' single featured a lovely acoustic live version of 'America', it had been shorn of the colossal screaming synths that had been on the recorded version I'd enjoyed from the Alton Towers show. But, the crème de la crème was the spirited 'Building a Charge'. Initially a tad twee but as the song progressed hidden beauty revealed itself, okay, so the song would have possibly sat a tad awkward on *Laid* itself but what an absolute gem. The CD remained on repeat for the majority of the evening yet not for a single moment did I bore of it.

On the 22nd August I managed to attend another Tim Booth gig, this time at the V2004 festival in Staffordshire. It's a funny old festival; actually it's a world away from what festivals used to be about. Sponsorship boards for various companies bombard you with slogans and advertisements for their latest products they're trying to force you into thinking you need in your life. It's often dubbed as being a 'friendly' festival that appeals to young couples who'd faint at the prospect of going to the Leeds Festival but I've actually found 'V' to be quite rough. Lots of inebriated masochistic gangs of lads and the queues for the toilets are astronomical. However, 'V' always manages to feature some excellent bands, (The Pixies, Radiohead, Elbow, Sonic Youth, The Chemical Brothers and James of course) interspersed with some proper dogs dinner bands and artists such as Dido, Big Brovaz, Reel Big Fish, Jamie Cullum and the Red Hot Chilli Peppers to name but a few. So it was a relief to find Tim playing a short set to an appreciative crowd around teatime on the Sunday of the festival in the Music Choice tent; it was rammed solid with a lot of cat calling for James songs. The band played an excellent set, 'Sometimes' went down a storm for those expecting to hear songs from the James repertoire. A couple of mates of mine Kevin and Robin witnessed the spectacle and were taken aback at how good the band was.

"Hey, if Tim plays any other local gigs will you let me know?" Robin asked me. I assured him that I would. We then watched Hope of the States who were quite thrilling.

In fact a November tour was announced, Tim would be playing a gig at Leeds City Varieties on the 8th. I bought four tickets as soon as they went on sale direct from the box office of the venue, two tickets for my wife and me and the other two for Edward and Robin. The venue was gorgeous, all-seated with snug little boxes upstairs along the sides where those with a couple of extra quid could enjoy performances away from the Commoners and Proles. Our seats were near to the stage and the show was as excellent as ever, Tim vacated the stage at one point to climb up to one of the boxes so that he could give his mum who was attending a hug and a kiss, it was quite a sweet moment. A couple of girls who were clearly under the influence of alcohol got up out of their seats and wandered up to the stage to dance, they kept berating the audience for sitting down calling us all "bores", I would have loved to have stood up and danced but would have felt just too self conscious so I remained rooted to my chair head banging violently to the more raucous numbers whilst stroking my chin and thigh during the quieter songs. It was a great evening out, the audience definitely enjoyed the show and when it finally came to an end a genuine buzz of excitement had been created. I hoped the copies of *Bone* that were for sale would have all been bought but sadly as I left the venue I noticed there was still a rather large pile of them waiting to be purchased.

Outside the venue I only went and bumped into Graham! Despite thinking that our paths would never cross again I'd bumped into him at the Leeds Festival in 2002, I was quite drunk at the time even though it was relatively early in the day and it was literally just a case of saying "hello" to one another. I felt quite jealous when Graham announced that he was heading into the city to have drinks with the band, I was driving and had to leave immediately so I couldn't tag along. I had visions of Tim wildly throwing shapes to Franz Ferdinand in Fab Café scaring all of the students in the process, but Graham reported back to me at a later date that Tim never went into town with the rest of the band and he had instead gone back to his hotel for a cup of coffee and a good book, now that's Rock and Roll. The end of an unexpectedly good year in the James/Tim saga, surely that was the end of it all though??

A new beginning

2005/2006/2007

No action regarding Tim Booth for me at least, Tim performed a couple of live dates but nothing more. Although James had dropped off my music radar to an extent I continued to listen to their back catalogue from time to time. *Gold Mother* sounded incredibly dated to me but weirdly enough *Pleased To Meet You* had started to make much more sense probably due to the fact that it was finally distanced from some of the more difficult events in my life that were happening around its release. Some of the spiky edges had begun to smooth off and it felt far less glacial and awkward to me.

In August my wife and I finally married and she therefore officially became my wife in the eyes of the legal system. Our wedding dance was 'Fall In Love With Me' by Booth And The Bad Angel, it seemed such an obvious choice and the beautiful song brought the hotel function room to a standstill, or maybe it was because of my ultra-funky dance moves. I was told afterwards that attempting to break dance during your wedding dance isn't big, clever or dignified. My mum hadn't attended the wedding. Five months later she was dead, in 2005 I signed both a wedding and a death register....

Cyberspace regarding James had dried up, visitors to the James and Tim Booth sites were becoming few and farther between. The year ended and in the New Year I'd discover new bands that'd rock my world again, namely The Brian Jonestown Massacre and Boards Of Canada. Their material was on heavy rotation for the first few months of the year until I somehow managed to get hold of some ultra rare James tracks known only as *The Whiplash Sessions*. I have to say that I honestly can't remember the source where I managed to obtain them from (just in case a record company lawyer ever reads this) and at the time of writing I've since lost the files. But I have to say the material was some of the best music I'd ever heard by James. The one track that really stood out for me was called 'Muscle' it was as far removed from a James song as I could ever have imagined; it was James in pure trip-hop mode. Other noteworthy tracks included 'Hedex', 'Star', 'Orson', 'Maybe Jane' (where Kurt Cobain received a name check) and 'Exma'. My Ipod almost melted from being overused as the material stayed pretty much on repeat; the lack of guitars on the majority of the tracks was unusual, they were obviously from the period when Larry had left the fold. The new material certainly brought James back to the front of my mind and I started to listen to some of their more obscure stuff again purposely avoiding the big hit singles.

Summer once again turned into autumn and of course winter then cantered along like a My Little Pony on crack. It was the end of another busy year studying nursing, I was due to qualify in March 2007, pressure was on to keep my grades up and to find a job however something just as important was announced in January of that year. It started with an email from good old Graham. It simply said,

"HEAD TO ONEOFTHETHREE!"

Blatantly curious I did indeed head to Dave's still lovely website to discover the most amazing bit of news that I'd heard for a long time, (apart from my wife being pregnant of course). James were set to reform for some live dates in the spring, a new 'Best Of' album was to be released including a DVD version of it too. I was mildly excited, ha! Of course I'm underplaying how I really felt, I WAS OVER THE MOON!!!! The planets had realigned themselves and the new Dawning of the Age of Aquarius or something equally important was about to begin. Plus, Larry was back! The icing on the bloody cake I can tell you! However, I wondered where Adrian and Michael fitted into the mix? It turned out that neither of them would be returning as they'd both decided to become fishermen, (this of course isn't true but it's a lovely thought). The 'new' reformed James was to be the *Laid* line up, the line up from their most successful period. Oh sweet child of mine! What a day! What a life! Life does indeed get better as Tim had sung on the song of nearly the same title! I told my wife, in fact I told everybody! I even tried to contact our old window cleaner from a few years back but he was on holiday in Torremelinos and was therefore un-contactable. Never mind, he was sure to hear about it on the BBC World News Service! Forget overseas war, forget unemployment, forget depraved politicians, this was the news the world was really waiting for!

Jim posted a lovely little letter online keeping us abreast of what had and hadn't been happening over the years, it turned out that when I'd spoken to him at Josephs Well he had indeed been in contact with the band hence why he was so tight lipped towards me. Jim and Larry had been jamming away over the years, then Tim was persuaded to get involved and the three of them realised that they still had something very special, an almost telepathic form of communication that materialised itself into something rather wonderful. A reformation was decided, the rest of the James blokes were brought back into the fold and the rest was future history! There was to be one fly in the ointment for me though. A gig was announced at the Manchester Evening News Arena however it was the same date as my wife's best friend's wedding. I was a bit bummed off to be honest, talk about bad timing! Instead I bought a ticket for the gig in Newcastle at the Academy venue. My wife couldn't go as she would be heavily pregnant and was due to give birth to our first child in the first week of May. Knowing my luck the baby would come along early resulting in a non-attendance of that gig too. I asked her to avoid curry and any laxative type food products until after the gig.

The James forums blossomed into life again. The old official website was ripped down and a new one was unveiled, the main image dominating the site was the return of the 'daisy' a multi coloured affair it was too, it was one of the most recognisable images associated with the band and had featured on at least a billion of their t-shirts. The 'oneofthethree' website was where it was really happening though, old characters and names I recognised from years back resurfaced, there was an initial ripple of excitement which transformed into something more akin to a tsunami.

Two new songs were to be on the new 'Best Of', 'Chameleon' and 'Who Are You?' I managed to hear both of the songs before the album was released via, err, the internet and they sounded okay, the latter sounding fairly familiar and very James like. The former was a whirling dirge of a song. With the live dates looming ever closer Lisa, a oneofthethree forum user advertised that she was going to arrange for some one off t-shirts to be printed and she wanted to know who'd be interested in buying one, there was a huge response which of course included myself. For £10 including postage I received a rather wonderful navy blue t-shirt with 'Who Are You?' on the front, the 'o's replaced with daisies and www.oneofthethree.co.uk on the reverse. It looked rather wonderful, as good if not better than some of the official merchandise.

The new 'Best Of' album entitled *Fresh As A Daisy* was released in April just before the live dates; I bought the two disc version which pretty much featured all of James' singles in chronological order. The two new tracks were however a mixed affair, 'Who Are You?' was pretty good but 'Chameleon' wasn't great. The text within the inlay card promised new material, I hoped however that 'Chameleon' wasn't representative of it. I have some very fond memories of being sat in our garden on a red hot day in April 2007, my heavily pregnant wife sat on the door step having a glass of lemonade whilst I enjoyed a cheeky beer. We listened to both discs of the album, happy memories resurfacing. My thoughts turned to poor old Michael and the *Mickey B's* compilation tape that introduced me to James all those years ago (when I was still but a child), it seemed like another lifetime, so much had happened over the years, I'd survived difficult times and ended up in a situation where I had everything I'd ever wanted in life.

Fresh As A Daisy reached number twelve in the charts which was an excellent place for a 'Best Of' when you consider that most fans and casual listeners would already own the original one from 1998. I was as happy as a sand boy. The reviews for the live shows were being posted online, all of them were extremely positive. Fans had travelled from America, Mexico, The Netherlands, Germany and all across the UK. Dave Brown's reviews were a great read, both passionate and honest, his review of the Glasgow gig certainly made interesting reading and I wondered what the band may have felt upon reading his review for that particular show which Dave felt was spoilt by an uninspired set list and a tense aggressive crowd. The set list was alright as far as I could tell, I didn't attend the show so I can't comment upon the atmosphere but I've heard that Glasgow crowds can be quite rowdy and excitable.

On the 23rd April 2007 I headed back up north towards Newcastle, the last time I'd been to this city was in 2001 when I saw James on their supposed final tour. I met up with Graham at the front of the queue on a very cold April evening. We reminisced about the old days then gossiped about the forum members and some of the stupid comments and things that people (including myself) said from time to time, (mine were/are always in jest by the way, particularly in reference to Andrew W.K. circa 2002 which let me tell you I received a bit of earache over). I was proudly wearing my 'Who Are You?' t-shirt and there were others wearing the same t-shirt who either spoke to me or nodded their head in acceptance. It felt like being part of an exclusive club within the existing hardcore James society. Dave Brown said hello and thankfully swapped my balcony ticket for a standing ticket and when the doors were eventually swung open I dashed along with the others to the front of the stage by the barrier praying that my famously poorly bladder would survive the evening.

Support came from The Twang, another so-so James support band; their single 'Wide Awake' was inspiring enough though to remind you of the halcyon days of 'Madchester', not that those days could or would ever really be described as being either calm or serene. I just like the word 'halcyon' and wanted to fit it into my story somewhere. The Twang finished their set and the usual waiting game began. When James finally arrived on stage I thought the venue was going to explode in excitement and I was wearing my usual moronic grin upon my face as the band all still looking rather young and handsome trooped on stage applauding the audience, the set opened with a terrifying and rather ragged version of 'Come Home'. It sounded so good to hear it live again, something I'd dismissed as a possibility for so long but there I was pogoing and jumping like a grasshopper waving my hands in the air as if communicating to the band in semaphore. Before the song had finished I felt somebody or something from behind me pushing forward in an aggressive manner, upon turning around I noticed it was a tiny little skin headed fella in a leather jacket who was furiously trying to push his way to the front. No way mister, I held my ground and wouldn't let him past for love nor money.

The band continued with the greatest hits, 'Waltzing Along' and 'Ring The Bells' caused the crowd to surge and stagger side ways, it took all of my strength to hang onto the barrier, the little fella behind me was trying to use the opportunity to push his way forward except that he lost his grip and was swept away with the crowd never to be seen again. Then the gig shifted up a gear or two, a simply stunning version of 'Play Dead' followed, an ancient 'If Things Were Perfect' a song which I still wasn't over familiar with that had a large section of the audience singing louder than Tim. The new to most 'Who Are You?' was well received as was an amazing version of 'Chain Mail' which featured a different arrangement to the original version, a large screen at the back of the stage showcased giant fish swimming towards the camera in deep black water, quite haunting and eerie yet beautiful in its tranquillity.

The band were sharp, razor sharp in fact and they looked as if they were enjoying themselves, Tim shared banter with the crowd as did Saul, even Larry was fairly chatty. 'Don't Wait That Long' from *Seven* continued the eclectic set list of the gig until it was followed by another new song called 'Upside Downside' which sounded pretty good. The old favourite 'Johnny Yen' raised the atmosphere further, my ribs had begun to really ache but I didn't care one bit, I was having the time of my life.

My arch nemesis 'English Beefcake' started up, I groaned as I still couldn't really find much love for the song but it sounded great, I mean *really* great. The less educated section of the audience did the usual uninformed clapping too early midway through the song where the second section begins to quietly build up and up and up....

At the height of the song when Tim started his yodelling the guitar players all took a step forward in unison and stepped upon their effect pedals and *whoooosshhHHHH!!* The volume levels leapt up and the song burst through the stratosphere into outer space taking me with it. My eyes filled with tears as I held my arms a loft in the air as if God him/herself had made their presence known to me. I was converted, I realised that it was one of James' best songs, it had just been wrapped up in cold packaging for too long and I'd never really gotten a proper feel for it. It was the greatest live moment I had experienced of James up to that point surpassing all of my other 'greatest moments' regarding James gigs. 'Getting Away With It (All Messed Up)' was James' greatest lost single, although it hardly set the charts alight upon release everybody in the venue appeared to know the song and sang along in unifying glory before we were all brought back down to Earth with the throwaway but still rather excellent 'Destiny Calling'. I thought the barrier was actually going to collapse due to the pressure and crush of the audience during 'Tomorrow' and then just to crank it up even further the band played 'Sit Down'.

'Gold Mother' followed, a song I'd never heard live before, it was millimetres away from being nothing more than a rambling wreck of a song but the song ultimately sounded all the better for it. 'She's A Star' was the penultimate song of the evening, James played a slowed down version of the song and I chuckled when I saw Graham bellowing out the *"You've Got It, You've Got It"* lyric towards the end of the song. In my opinion that should have signalled the end of the gig but the band played 'Say Something' instead before calling it a night.

I was in shock, I hadn't seen James play so well before, there was a different dynamic onstage from previous shows, the return of Larry Gott on guitar made a massive difference which isn't a dig at either Adrian or Michael, it just felt like it was the James that I'd fallen in love with so much all of those years back, it was good to have the boys back together again. I knew that each and every time the band played

Newcastle in the future I'd have to attend as the Newcastle crowd was definitely the most up for it crowd I'd ever been a part of, a complete reversal of how it had been back in 2001. I caught up with a few of the guys from the forum afterwards, namely Dave and Graham amongst others I recognised before I began the long journey home listening to a heavy rock show on Radio One.

My wife gave birth a few weeks later, a boy, it was meant to be a home birth but she ended up being transferred into hospital due to the baby being stubborn. I wanted to call the boy James, my wife said no, so I suggested Daniel as the first name, (referencing Getting Away With It) and James as the middle name and she agreed. I hoped that one day I'd be able to take Daniel James to see his daddy's favourite band, the band that had shaped and gloriously sound tracked my life, the band that he'd been named after. Only time would tell.

Charles redeems himself

2007/2008

Our lives had been turned upside down by the squawking and screaming of our new born. It was a bit of a culture shock to say the least. Colic, my goodness, I never knew something could literally sap the life out of me in such a short space of time. A new child was supposed to only bring fun, laughter and joy. Daniel certainly did bring us 'fun' 'laughter' and most definitely a lot of 'joy', however the first five weeks of our life together as a family just seem like a complete blur now, lots of stress and noise, the pooey nappies were fine though.

James' summer was packed full of festival dates, none of them I was able to attend despite being tempted to head to V Festival in Staffordshire for the Saturday as it was the day James were playing on the main stage. Charles went along and I was pretty chuffed for him. He kept encouraging me to buy a day ticket and to head down; I certainly had my eyes open for a cheap ticket but to no avail. By the early afternoon I knew I definitely wasn't going as the best price I could find was still in the eighty pound region. Now as much as I loved James I really couldn't afford such an extravagance. I was given various telephone updates throughout the day from Charles regarding the festival. The main talking point was the weather.

"Mate, the rains coming in sideways here, it's misty and it's absolutely freezing cold! Hey, what's the name of that band from Wakefield you like?" said my dearest friend.

"Oh, The Cribs. Make sure you see them won't you".

"Yeah, they're on next, I'll let you know how they are. Shame you couldn't make it mate, I'll let you know how James are too" Charles kindly said to me.

"Cheers mate, have a great time won't you".

Charles rang again in the evening.

"Ah, mate, I'm gutted for you, James were absolutely amazing, I'd forgotten how brilliant they are. They played some new songs too which sounded excellent".

Part of me was mad for not being there but I was just pleased that Charles had enjoyed their set and not slagged them off for being a bunch of old codgers knocking out the hits (and misses of course) from yesteryear, (which I admit was kind of what I was expecting from him).

Whispers and rumours spread regarding a new James album for 2008, the cynical laughed when a release date was set for early April, even I had my doubts, however guitarist Larry Gott commented on the forum that *"doubters will be pleasantly surprised"*. Plenty of new songs had been played throughout the year at various gigs and festivals, the band seemed to have taken up residency in London at the interestingly titled Hoxton Bar and Grill, James were like a modern day version of Murph and the Magic Tones. I wondered if fresh sirloin and rump was dished up for the hungry fans whilst the band teased them with new material, so new that Tim often read the lyrics from a sheet of paper. I'd have loved to have attended one of the London gigs but of course I had other priorities.

During the early months of 2008 I heard the new single that James were about to release. It was aired on BBC Radio Two during Stuart Maconie and Mark Radcliffe's show, the song was called 'Whiteboy'. To say that I was underwhelmed upon hearing it for the first time would be about correct. It sounded badly produced, a bit ramshackle and not what I'd really expected from the band. Tim was practically spitting out the lyrics over a very fast backing track which appeared to have church bells clanging in the background and a ticking clock acting as percussion. The majority of the comments on the forum were polite enough, some were even quite enthusiastic. My own comment about the song was,

"Y'know, it's alright".

It wasn't until the third or fourth listen that I realised the song was utterly brilliant! Bonkers and charming, fun even! Blimey! What had the guys been consuming during the writing and recording process? Maybe the band members had binned their vegan ways and were off their heads from too much iron from all of the steak they'd been paid for performing back in London? I played the song to death via the link on BBC iPlayer; even my wife had a bit of a boogie whilst our young son stared in fascination at his slightly cuckoo parents. Although the song was meant to be their new single there was bog all promotion for it and no video for MTV either. Not sure on the reasons why to be honest, maybe the record company didn't have the cash for it. I'm sure many a James fan would happily have made a decent enough promo video for them at no cost at all.

So, a promising start one would think. Nothing though prepared me for the first time I heard the next single 'Waterfall'. I had to use the BBC iPlayer to listen to the track which was played at about half past two in the morning, peak listening time of course; it probably is if you work in a chicken packing factory. I had tears of joy in my eyes when the beautiful brass produced by the wonderful Andy Diagram who'd rejoined the band blared out of my tinny laptop speakers. 'Waterfall' should have been a number one single, had it have been released in a different era then maybe it would have been. The song writing sounded refreshed and invigorated. Tim had never sounded so joyful and it seemed like the good vibes from *Bone* had carried across to the new James material. The non single 'single' again had no promotion at all, no video, no nothing. Just a beautiful song that would be sadly lost in time but hopefully rediscovered in a thousand years by a futuristic Alien Death Metal Rap band, only then would the song be fully appreciated although only aliens would be able listen to it because by then mankind will have been wiped out by a nasty comet or an asteroid.

The new James album *Hey, Ma* was to be released in the UK on the 7th April, a tour would take place in the same month. I bought tickets for four shows, Bradford, Newcastle, Sheffield and Blackpool. My good mate Dinalli was going with me to the Newcastle show and my wife would be attending the Blackpool one with me. But before all of this happened something that had been concerning myself and plenty of others from the oneofthethree forum needed addressing. It appeared that there was bugger all promotion for the new album. The majority of people I knew didn't even know the band was still functioning, some of them had forgotten who James were. A controversial album cover had kind of backfired on the band, of course any publicity is seen as good publicity but the cover art of a small baby sat in front of some toy bricks with a hand gun was deemed to be too much for the Advertising Standards Authority and planned posters for the campaign were pulled. Maybe I thought this would stir up the public interest in the band. Well, The Sun newspaper featured the story in its gossip section and that's a fairly popular read isn't it? So a lack of exposure or at least the right kind of exposure, singles that weren't treated like singles and an album that was going to potentially bomb meant only one thing. The fans had to take things into their own hands....

Lisa and Kirsty from the oneofthethree forum posted that they were going to be handing out some home-made flyers for the new album in various cities across the UK. I was impressed by their passion; I knew that I had to do something, but what? I decided to email Leeds United Football Club, BBC Look North and Yorkshire Television to see if they could help at all with the campaign and I mentioned the strong links the band had to this part of the county. Leeds United contacted me back straight away! The guy in charge of media and promotions stated that he was a big fan of the band going back some twenty years and he'd see what he could do to help, he suggested I asked somebody from the bands management to contact him to discuss further. I couldn't believe it! A big football team getting involved with my favourite band! Plus, Tim Booth was a life time fan of the football club which I'd mentioned in my email; surely this was going to be a big opportunity for the band to maximise upon. I emailed Dave Brown and asked him to forward my email onto the band which he stated he would do.

Then a lovely lady from Yorkshire Television contacted me, she also said she was a long term fan and was unaware that the band was about to release a new album, she suggested that I made a brief video clip and uploaded it to their website in their local news section "as long as you don't feature any music" she said. Within the hour I'd uploaded a short clip featuring myself wearing my 'Who Are You? t-shirt discussing the bands recent activities and up coming tour. I posted the link everywhere I possibly could blatantly breaking any spamming etiquette laws that exist in cyberspace. By the end of the week the clip had a thousand views and was the most popular and most viewed clip on the Yorkshire Television website. I really did spam the clip everywhere I possibly could which included loads of other bands websites too. People generally thanked me for alerting them to the news of the new album; the only negative feedback I received was from the Oasis forum where a user replied with "this is so desperate". They were right of course, but desperate times require desperate measures even if you might end up looking like a bit of a plonker in the process. Sadly I never did hear back from the BBC regarding any publicity but at least I had tried! Lisa from the forum contacted me and told me that Larry was really pleased with the viral marketing of the album via the fans; I felt immense pride and a commitment to a beautiful cause.

On the morning of the 7th April 2008 I jumped into my car and drove to HMV at the White Rose Shopping Centre on the outskirts of Leeds to purchase my copy of *Hey, Ma*. The album was on a stand right in front of the main doors, a shoplifters favourite place no doubt. The shop had only been open for fifteen minutes or so but already there was a gap where some of the *Hey, Ma* compact discs were being displayed meaning that purchases had already been made. My heart lit up, maybe the hard work of the fans and of course the band had paid off? I made my purchase, drove home at top speed and within ten minutes the disc was spinning inside the CD tray of my stereo whilst my young son proceeded to stagger about the lounge with his new trick of attempting to walk.

The opening track 'Bubbles' floated out of the speakers. Again, like the rest of the new material it sounded so joyful and spirited, Tim once again visiting the miracle of childbirth whilst the band complimented the positive vibe of the lyrics with musicianship to match. The albums title track followed, an upbeat anti-war song with the shocking powerful lyrics of *"Hey ma, the boy's in body bags, coming home in pieces"*. The song would be adopted by the 'Help For Heroes' charity featuring a very moving video clip. I was astonished that the band that I'd loved for so long had blossomed so far into their career when most bands material deteriorates in quality the older they get. 'Waterfall' followed, three brilliant songs in a row, not many albums these days can boast that I though to myself. 'Oh My Heart' was the fourth track, its fury lifted me off my feet, Andy's trumpet and Dave's drumming taking charge of the inspiring song. Once again, in another lifetime the song would have been a big hit single but this wasn't to be in 2008. 'Boom Boom' was a song that was a great album track, it ticked all of the right boxes yet somehow didn't over excite me at the same time. 'Semaphore' really changed the tempo of the album, sparse in a *Laid* era fashion with a smoky trumpet throughout, a fine song. 'Upside' I'd heard a lot about before I actually heard the song itself. It was destined to be yet another lost James classic single. It was and still is a great song but there was something about it that just irritated me somewhat. I knew that I was in a minority and that the James fans on the forums were passing out from how brilliant they found it.

'Whiteboy' followed on, it still sounded extremely brilliant and it still made me laugh, the *"Ah ah ah ah ah ah ah aah!"* lyric that all parents say to their children when they're being naughty whilst waving a finger back and forth was something that I could relate to, my little boy Daniel would copy me whenever I did it which was extremely cute. '72' continued the up-tempo pace again with its ball breaking bass line, there was something quite sexy about the song, not the lyrics I have to say but the music itself. It reminded me that when James goes 'groovy' they do it very well indeed. 'Of Monsters And Heroes And Men' was the penultimate track on the album, it had a very odd repetitive vocal melody that somehow worked wonders, the song picturing a post apocalyptic landscape something akin to that from *The Running Man*. It was charming and absolutely wonderful. The final song 'I Wanna Go Home' was perhaps the albums high point from an album made of many high points. The song depicting a lonely man sat alone in a bar on the other side of the world from his family, it was poignant indeed. *"Kissing is forbidden, biting leaves marks, sex is overrated, I need to dance"* Tim quietly sang whilst the song slowly built towards its climax, before I knew it the stereo was silent and the digital display showed the running time of the entire album. The band hadn't let either themselves or their fans down, it really was one of James' best albums at a time when nobody in their wildest dreams would have thought that an ancient band from Manchester would be releasing one of their most solid and consistent pieces of work to date. I immediately pressed the play button again and let the experience wash over me a second time, then a smell that I recognised reminded me that a nappy needed changing. An extra track was available to download via Itunes called 'Child To Burn', Tim sang in a falsetto throughout, Larry's chiming guitar and Jim's warm bass created a soothing yet unsettling atmosphere, the song would be classed as being "rubbish" by certain members of the James community but not myself, I thought it was a wonderful song, absolutely wonderful.

As for the album reviews, well, The Sunday Times review was simply hilarious!

"..no fewer than 120 songs were whittled down to the 11 sanctimonious, declamatory, defiantly average and group-huggingly smug tracks featured here, and think, lawks, are they still, this late in the game, strangers to the joys of the traditional song structure; and, if this lot represent the best, what on God's earth were the other 109 like?"

The majority of the reviews were however extremely favourable and welcomed the band back proper. The NME chose to ignore the album, James were still too un-cool for their target audience who thought that The Strokes and the Arctic Monkeys were still going to save the planet from Simon Cowell, this is a fight that never really appears to be winnable. So, Monday was a great day, as for Tuesday, well I was going to be catching a bus from outside of my house to take me to Bradford. I was as ever, rather excited.

Arctic Bradford

2008

The Arriva bus to Bradford picked me up from outside of my house in Tingley, the journey to the steeped in industrial heritage city was no more than twenty five minutes in duration. I've always had a soft spot for Bradford, it's a city that's been kind to me in relation to my chosen vocation and I've a lot to thank it for. It was a very chilly April evening, as per usual I was wearing jeans and a t-shirt without another top on resulting in the piercing cold air digging its daggers into my skinny bones. Although I'd set off early as regards to the door opening time I soon realised I wasn't going to be the first person in the queue, there was at least half a dozen other people already waiting patiently by the doors, all were sensibly wearing hardcore thermal clothing which I guessed possibly included underwear.

The 'Who Are You?' t-shirt I was wearing caught the attention of some of those in attendance and a couple of people asked me who I was (ha!) regarding that of being a forum member. Introductions were made and conversation flowed, unsurprisingly James was the main topic. A guy in a woollen hat introduced himself to me; I recognised him but couldn't remember where from, he then saved me any awkwardness by telling me that he'd spoken to me at the Leeds University gig in December 2001. It was Ian! I smiled and shook his hand and asked how life was for him and we chatted like long lost friends, he still thought that that particular gig had changed his life forever which I thought was a sweet thing to say. Then Graham turned up! Cold numb hands were briskly shook and we had a chat about this and that, asking each other which gigs we'd be attending and what we thought of the new material. We all agreed that it was probably James' best album to date.

"Hey, look, its Dave!! ALRIGHT DAVE!!!!!!!" Graham shouted out in the direction of the bald headed gifted drummer who was walking away from the venue heading worryingly towards the bus station. I hoped that he was just off to buy a bar of chocolate or a bag of crisps and that he hadn't fallen out with the band and was heading home. Dave turned around and gave us all a wave before disappearing around the corner. I was very cold, my shaved head was losing heat rapidly and I prayed for the opening of the doors.

Eventually the kind people guarding the doors decided to let us in and Graham and I did our usual sprint to the front of the crash barrier. The venue, St George's Hall is a beautiful building with terrific acoustics. The last time I'd been to the venue was to see Morrissey back in 2002; it had been an excellent show although I feared for Morrissey's health throughout the evening as he kept putting his hand to his chest and grimacing during the entire performance. Whilst I was being pushed sideways and back and forth in the frenzied mosh pit I'd stretched my hand towards the great man and he leant towards me and shook it. I managed to make a friend of mine who was a massive Morrissey fan cry a few years later when I recounted this anecdote to her. She asked me if she could "buy" my hand off me, this came across as being a bit sinister and I declined her offer but thanked her all the same.

The venue was also where I'd thrown a packet of crisps at Brett Anderson during a Suede performance which I briefly mentioned earlier on. It was at the height of their 'Brit Pop' era (*Coming Up*) and even though I was twenty two years of age I felt very old compared to the rest of the audience that consisted of pubescent boys and girls, in fact I felt so uncomfortable jumping around with them that I decided to enjoy the rest of the gig stood near the bar. I had to for health and safety reasons, due to my height every time I jumped up and down in time to the music my elbows were blackening the kid's eyes causing them to cry.

Support for the evening and indeed for the rest of the 'Hey, Ma Tour' was provided by My Federation which was Lee 'Muddy' Baker's band, they were pretty good, one song in particular really stood out which was 'Don't Wanna Die', a proper gem of a song. Lee was as charming as he'd been back in Liverpool in 2004 and the band was fairly well received although the audience appeared to be quite thin on numbers.

"Hey, are you guys going to come back and see us when we tour by ourselves?" asked Lee, the audience cheered and stated that they would, (at the time of writing in 2012 we're still waiting Lee you naughty little man!)

Show time arrived.

"Hello" Tim warmly said to the audience, the response was deafening.

"Bradford is my home town I was born here you know", now, if the initial response had been deafening then the response to this revelation which was probably unknown to the majority of the audience was deafening to the nth degree.

"Welcome home Tim!" bellowed Ian towards the stage.

My expectations for the evening would be that James would play quite a few new songs; I wasn't going to be disappointed. Out of an eighteen song set list ten of them would be new tracks and they didn't bother to play 'Sit Down' either! I wondered if the Leeds University girl was in attendance, no longer a girl but a woman in her own rights, probably with a mortgage and a Smart Car. The new material went down very well, there's generally more pushing and movement for the more familiar material such as 'Born Of Frustration' and especially 'Ring The Bells', (I've seen grown men crying during that particular song) but throughout the evening the pushing and squashing was pretty much constant, my ribs had begun to ache quite early into the set. When Tim dropped down into the pit and clambered up on to the barrier to sing I thought the wind was going to be totally squeezed out of my lungs as the audience surged forward to touch the Messiah before us. I held Tim's hand as he clambered up and back down at the end of the song and seriously considered how much I'd get for my hand on ebay.

James played an absolute blinder throughout the show, the band members were in very good spirits, Saul kept making cheeky comments towards Tim and the audience, Mark stared at those in attendance with cold calculating eyes. Jim continued to look as young as ever for his sixty three years of age (he wasn't really sixty three). It was great to have Andy back on stage blasting out his trumpet lines whilst he stalked the stage like a praying mantis. Tim advised all of those who hadn't bought it yet to go out and buy the new album which was responded to with much cheering and applause. I wondered if the others who'd been involved in the guerrilla marketing and advertising campaign had increased record sales in any way at all, I knew that the woman from Yorkshire Television was in attendance because of me as she'd emailed me to let me know. As for the songs from *Hey, Ma*, once again the songs sounded so much bigger and more impressive in the live environment than through my stereo. Lee and the band had produced an impressive album but it still never really caught the fire and mystique of the band as a live act even if it was one of their best albums.

During 'Whiteboy' a number of lights attached to ropes dropped down towards the stage and the band members proceeded to swing them wildly throughout the song as if playing an illuminated version of conkers, I laughed out loud in particular at Dave as he leapt off his stool and swung wildly at one of the lights, the little boy in him revealing itself with an excited look upon his face as his own particular light was sent swinging towards the audience. During 'Hey, Ma' a number of people on the side of the stage shone torches skywards as if they were search lights, it appeared that the lighting budget for the tour hadn't been quite as elaborate as it had for the 'Fresh As A Daisy Tour' from the previous year. I guessed for the next tour that the lighting would be supplied by candle only, album sales would probably be the deciding factor I reckoned. A small mirror ball was used to a magical effect during 'Of Monsters And Heroes And Men', Tim held the spinning glittering ball in his hands whilst the reflected light cascaded throughout the venue creating a magical beautiful effect as if we were all trapped inside a huge snow shaker.

The gig ended with a mesmerising version of 'Sound' which seemed to have a mind of its own, the musicians didn't play the song, the song played the musicians and it wouldn't let go until it was ready and by that point the band members looked ragged and knackered. Once finished the exhausted looking band members crawled off stage to a rapturous acknowledgment and we the audience staggered out of the venue into the even colder night air. For me it hadn't been one of my favourite James gigs, not because the band weren't excellent though, it was simply because the quality of the sound was up and down throughout the evening, a shame really as the venue is known for its sound quality but there we go. I bumped in to various oneofthethree forum members outside the venue including Graham and Ian and a member who'd travelled to Bradford from Canada. A girl who I'd been friends with from a few years previous called my name out and reintroduced herself along with a couple of her friends. She told me it was the first time she'd seen James and she was very excited.

"Oh my gosh, they were wonderful, even better than Bloc Party!" she spluttered. I stifled a laugh and agreed with her but sarcastically said that James probably weren't quite as good as Razorlight. It was late; I bid everyone a fond farewell and told them to enjoy the rest of the tour.

"I'll see you next week in Newcastle mate" Graham said as a parting shot and before long I was back on the bus heading towards Tingley. It had been as per usual a great night out with my favourite band, next it was coffee and toast time followed by bed.

The following Sunday and James's wonderful new album *Hey, Ma* entered the UK album charts at number ten! Victory! The album hadn't been available to purchase in any of the supermarkets which was probably due to the controversial album cover but thanks to the hard graft and loyalty of their fan base, (many of whom now had plenty of crows feet and receding hairlines) the album had entered at a respectable chart position. This was without any proper format release for the singles ('Whiteboy' and 'Waterfall') or indeed any other noteworthy marketing or publicity. The following day I was heading back up north again to Newcastle, I'd arranged to meet my friend Dinalli in Wetherby and the two of us were sped up the boring A1 motorway in his rather nifty Volkswagen Beetle which had lovely heated seats to warm up our buttocks. Although he was a keen enough gig goer and a massive music fan (often for obscure French and Japanese pop acts mind you) it was going to be his first James gig and he was extremely excited. We listened to the new James album via his Ipod, as he'd downloaded the album I had an opportunity to listen to the bands track by track commentary which was a rather splendid experience in itself. I'd prearranged to meet Lisa from the forum at the venue as we hadn't met up till that point, the rest of the oneofthethree posse were going to be in attendance too including the unfathomable urban legend known as Dave Brown.

Once we'd reached the as per usual biting cold north east city we found a place to park and hurried to the Carling Academy. There was no way I was going to be able to get anywhere near the front as it was already pretty busy, instead we headed to the bar and bought a couple of pints of lager, the kind of lager that's so cold and fizzy that it actually hurts to drink it, the coldness soon passed through the plastic container into my hand causing extreme frost bite, then my fingers turned black and dropped off. Despite the slight discomfort of losing my digits we managed to meet up with the rest of the oneofthethree crew who were all wearing their 'Who Are You?' t-shirts; we looked like we were part of a Bible Belt cult but without the mass suicide pacts that normally goes hand in hand with cults. The venue was absolutely buzzing; In fact, it was probably the most atmospheric James audience that I'd ever experienced. There was a genuine edgy and excitable feel to the place, not at all intimidating just really upbeat and full of anticipation.

"Wow, I've never seen an audience like it mate! Is it always like this for a James gig?" asked Dinalli.

"Yes, pretty much so, it can be quite full on at times too!" I said looking over at a gang of lads who were already quite drunk and were pulling and tugging at each other's eyebrows.

My Federation ambled on stage, played their songs and then left again. They'd played the same set as the week before and Lee once again asked if people would go along and see them play whenever they returned to the north east and I repeat, we are still ... waiting!.

As the stage crew set up for James the electrically charged atmosphere of the venue intensified, the music pumped out of the venues sound system at an increasingly loud volume causing some difficulty in holding a normal conversation but it appeared to just gee the audience up even further. I tried to make some conversation with Dave Brown but it was nigh on impossible due to the noise level and the jostling that had already begun to take place around us, this was of course before James had even set foot on stage. 'Me Myself and I' by De La Soul was played, I'd loved this song from an early age and De La Soul had been one of my favourite bands of all time, I'd bought *Three Feet High And Rising* from Our Price when I was fourteen using a pocket full of copper and loose change and I'd played the album to death.

"Oh, it'd be great if the band come on stage after this song mate" I shouted into Dinalli's ear.

The song finished.

The lights dropped.

The audience went ape.

I wondered if we were actually in Manchester, it felt more like a home town atmosphere, I pumped my fists into the air and cheered along with everybody else. Like the previous week in Bradford James played 'Born Of Frustration' first which set the tone for the evening of big sounding anthemic tunes. The first half of the gig was great, not amazing but really great nonetheless. However, there was a definite tidal change when 'Of Monsters And Heroes And Men' was played. Tim had his little glitter ball out again and the venue was wonderfully sprinkled in beautiful light, it created a calm and serene ambience which settled the rather raucous but still friendly eyebrow pulling audience. The song was extremely well received and before the final bars of the song were played out the opening bars of 'I Wanna Go Home' picked up, Saul's violin and Jim's warm bass line captivating the audience and those who had been talking aloud to one another stopped to stare at the stage, conversations immediately silenced. As if in some Orwellian nightmare every set of arms suddenly rose aloft and the audience began to clap in time to the beat, myself and Dinalli included. However, it's an unclappable song if such a word exists and after a while we stopped clapping to appreciate the building tension on stage; those who were still clapping were now clapping out of time as their concentration slipped from their arm movements back towards the stage. The brooding atmosphere continued to build, my face tingled and the hairs on my arms stood up on end at the terrifying but beautiful cacophony that was taking place. Dinalli was stood with his mouth wide open.

"I wanna go hommmmmmmme" hollered Tim which caused my lungs to reverberate, I was scared, the last time I'd felt so scared and in awe was the first time I'd heard *Jeff Wayne's Musical Version Of The War Of The Worlds* when I'd been five years old. Saul walked towards the back of the stage, clambered up some steps and stood over a small drum kit biding his time. Several moments passed, Saul and Dave's eyes met, their heads nodded and in unison the two of them broke into a furious tribal drum beat and the place simply exploded, everybody danced the Dance Macabre, fists punched the air and the ground beneath our feet became like a trampoline. It was a unifying moment in time; each and every one of us was as one in the briefest moment of the vast passage called time. I wanted the experience to go on forever, I never realised music could make you feel so very alive. But of course nothing lasts forever and in what felt like a cruel space of time the fury onstage spiralled to a halt.

"In this bar, in this bar, I am dyyyiiinngg, I am dyyyyiiiiiinnnnngggggggggggg" Tim whispered into the microphone.

It's been said that people in Glasgow heard the Newcastle crowd that night. The respect and adulation for the song was magnificent. But after such a high where could the rest of the gig go to? Up, that's where. Crowd favourites were sprinkled in with further *Hey, Ma* tracks, Plaster fell from the ceiling during 'Tomorrow' due to the maelstrom that was taking place beneath it. The band ended the Newcastle gig with 'Sometimes' the crowd sang the song back to the band for at least five minutes after it had actually finished and finally the cheeky chappy that's known as 'Laid' rounded the fantastic evening off with a bit of tongue in cheek sauciness.

As we left the venue Dinalli spoke.

"That was easily one of the best gigs I've ever been to. I thought Saint Etienne were good live but tonight was something else mate!"

"Are you coming along to Sheffield tomorrow night then?"

"Yeah, definitely although I expect it won't be as good as tonight, I mean it'd be nigh on impossible to top tonight mate!" said Dinalli to me. I thought there could be some truth in what he'd said. I knew that within twenty four hours we'd find out. We drove back towards Wetherby where I collected my car, swapping the warm leather seats for my unheated ice cube cold car seats and pondered over what had been one of the best James gigs I'd ever been to.

Sheffield before Blackpool

2008

Dinalli had been right, Sheffield wasn't quite as good as the Newcastle gig but it was still absolutely brilliant anyway. The journey to Sheffield almost ended in absolute carnage though when the sky turned black and an unpredicted and torrential downpour of hail turned the M1 Motorway into an ice rink. A vehicle on the opposite carriage lost control and came hurtling towards us but thankfully it rebounded off the central reservation crash barrier instead of flipping over it and landing on top of my puny Ford Fusion. I could smell Dinalli's fear which managed to leak out of his rear end and I wound the windows down in even further panic.

The gig was taking place at the recently refurbished Sheffield Academy, it was so new that the place had an overwhelming fragrance of fresh paint; I thought it was rather foolish to have carpeted the majority of the venue due to the fact that beverages would undoubtedly be spilt thus creating an unpleasant off-beer odour. The décor was pleasant enough though with a nice ambience created through the mood lighting and lit up beer dispensers; they shone like Carling sponsored beacons of hope and fantasy in the darkness of the room, drawing individuals in with their promise of thirst quenching pleasure for only £3.50 a pint.

Lee and the rest of the hardcore My Federation crew stoked up the crowd into a pandemonium although this might actually be a bit of an exaggeration. Dinalli was rocking in time to the music in an almost delirious state before he voiced to me how much he liked them.

"You know, I think I'll be buying their album on the way out" he said.

Once My Federation finished the crowd swarmed to the bar to refresh and recharge, Dinalli and myself met up with Dave Brown, Lisa and Kirsty as well as a few of the others from the forum, casual chat was made until it was time for them to head back into the middle of the mosh pit. Dinalli, Lisa and I instead stood stage right, there was going to be plenty of space for us to have a jig and a dance and we were only a few feet away from the barrier. Dave Brown managed to sneak up to the barrier where he'd remain for the rest of the gig making notes for when he updated his website. The balcony was packed solid and I felt sorry for the majority of the people up there because unless you were stood next to the barrier you'd struggle to see what was happening on stage. The atmosphere was nothing like it had been up in Newcastle, definitely more reserved in manner. The roadies eventually left the stage after gaffer taping everything up so that Tim wouldn't trip over any loose cables during one of his St Vitus dance episodes. De La Soul's 'Me Myself and I' began to play and I figured that this was possibly the nod to the band to prepare for their entrance on stage and I was right as the band all marched on stage to a round of applause, whoops, cheers but thankfully no vuvuzela's.

James played a similar set to the previous gigs although they surprised us regulars by playing 'Destiny Calling' first, it went down particularly well and we clapped and danced about in sheer delight. The rest of the set was now quite familiar, the band members appeared to be really enjoying themselves as there were plenty of smiles between each other and the audience, it felt like quite an intimate gig compared to Newcastle, The atmosphere was different, not in a bad way though, just different, more sober. Lisa and I jumped around like a couple of electrocuted herrings whilst Dinalli absorbed the atmosphere with his huge beaming smile. Dave Brown was noted to be stood very still indeed.

"I thought he was their biggest fan?" Dinalli shouted in to my ear.

"He's studying the band; it'll make good reading tomorrow!" I shouted back at him.

The gig ticked along, not a note out of place, lights a flashing, mirror balls a twirling and Tim twisting this way and that. The positive energy oozed off the stage, I felt it washing over me and entering my body, a surreal feeling, maybe a bit like taking drugs perhaps. 'I Wanna Go Home' had by this point already earned it's right to nestle in the bosom of James' best songs, in Sheffield it sounded magnificent if not quite as magnificent as the night before, I guessed that this was probably because James always feed off the energy of the audience and the Newcastle audience certainly beat Sheffield's in regards to energy and passion. However, it was night's like that particular one that made me realise I could see James every night of the year and never bore of the experience at all, I'd never ever tire of the emotional journey and exhilaration.

'Sometimes' closed the set, Tim and the rest of the guys looked visibly moved as one and all sang the chorus back to the band for what seemed like forever and then they were gone and the house lights were flipped back on, the sound system carried on with its pre-arranged Itunes playlist. The three of us caught up with the rest of the guys from the forum who were as enthusiastic as a bag of over excited monkeys, a friendly enough bunch to boot and all very hyper and sweaty. Dinalli and I casually made our way over to the merchandise stall where Lee from My Federation was stood chatting to the fans with a huge smile upon his face. Dinalli bought the My Federation album and Lee kindly obliged in signing the album for him, we chatted for a few moments and Lee confirmed that the band would be heading back up north at some point to play their own gigs. He was a vey friendly bloke, I've met many musicians over the years and the majority of them have been lowlife scum like individuals with terrible open sores on their faces. However Lee was quite the opposite which made a nice change. We eventually said goodbye to Lee giving him the opportunity to chat to others but not before he gave us a big handshake and a huge beaming smile.

"Hey, cheers for the support guys!" he cheerfully said as we left him.

Outside the venue mingling with the smokers and the bootleg merchandise sellers were Lisa and Kirsty and we made our presence known to them. Dinalli told them that it was only his second James gig and the girls appeared quite shocked but very pleased when he told them that the last gig he'd attended had been the night before. Before we headed off we gave the girls a hug and I told Lisa I'd hopefully see her at the V festival in Staffordshire that August. It was time to queue up for a ticket for the car park; it would take another forty five minutes until we were heading out of town towards the motorway. Thankfully the weather stayed settled for the drive home and in less than thirty minutes I was back home eating toast and slurping a hot cup of tea. As I sat upon the sofa reflecting upon the evening I knew that in just a week's time I'd be in Blackpool for the last of my gigs on this current tour, this time my ever patient wife would be coming along with me.

A week later and the tires on my car pummelled the tarmac heading towards rickety Blackpool with my wife. It was imperative that we arrived at the venue at a respectable time so that we could try and get as near to the front as possible, this was again due to the fact that my wife is only five foot one in height so she really struggles at gigs to get a decent view of the action unless she's on a balcony or at the side near the front of the stage. I've tried to persuade her to buy some platform boots in the past, the type that miniature Goth's wear but so far she's not playing game. I've always loved Blackpool as a place, sure, its run down and a bit rough but the place still holds a certain kind of romance for me, or is it nostalgia? Lovely beaches too. My wife was familiar with the area as she studied at Lancaster University. As we travelled along the motorway she regaled me with anecdotes relating to her time at university and stories about various field trips, all fascinating stuff of course. Blackpool Tower suddenly poked its head above the hazy blood red horizon, always a comforting sight and a reminder of innocent times as a child. The excitement of the evening ahead of me started to rise up from the pit of my stomach resulting in that wonderful pre-gig buzz.

I also felt a touch of sadness, it was my last gig of the current tour, I was aware that another tour was lined up for the end of the year but that was of course many months away. I think I felt sad as I often do when I visit places I haven't been to for a very long time. The last time I'd been to Blackpool was for a James gig at the same venue nearly ten years esrlier. Returning there reminded me of how much had taken place in my life during that period of time, I'd met many new and wonderful people during that section of my life, but I'd also lost people as well including those who I'll always associate Blackpool with and I think that's probably why I felt the way I did on that particular evening, a gentle ache in my heart for the ones I missed.

We parked the car as close to the tower as possible, locked up and headed towards the venue following the crowds who were taking part in the same pilgrimage as ourselves. Upon entering the historical and ornate venue a couple of people nodded at me, I didn't recognise them but they obviously knew me possibly from my miniature internet campaign to promote *Hey, Ma*. I was absolutely gagging for a drink; my wife was driving us back home so I enjoyed a mountain fresh ice cold beer and I bought her a coke, minus the ice cubes of course so that she got more coke for her money. The balcony was already full, in fact the venue was heaving but I managed to snake us through the audience all the way to the front right of the stage and we thankfully had a fair bit of room around us. My wife had an okay vantage point and said that she could see the stage fine. Some young girl, I say young but she was probably in her twenties started to talk to the two of us about the band, the gigs, the forum, the new album etc. My wife chatted to her like women do, not about hair and make up but about science. Actually, most probably hair and make up but I can imagine this being frowned upon as being a sexist remark.

My Federation did their stuff, they didn't really seem to suit such a big stage but maybe they were just overawed at the large scale of the gig. The Empress Ballroom is a big old venue and it takes balls to play there and not lose your confidence. Not that I've ever played there mind you, actually I'm just making an assumption really. Oh, never mind. Anyway, they sounded pretty good and all that, I'd listened to the album Dinalli had bought and by this I don't mean I borrowed it from him and put it on my own Ipod as this kind of behaviour is destroying the music business and upsetting lots of people.

Right...

"Hello Manchester!" Saul squawked in a helium affected voice into the microphone, from the reaction of the audience it appeared that a large proportion were from the friendly and steeped in musical history city, there were a few boo's near to where we were stood but it all felt friendly enough. The opening chords of 'Upside' were played; the intro went on for quite a while. Tim was already in a trance like state swaying in time to the beautiful music being played, the expectant audience began to sway and swarm like a sea that was about to boil over. The song suited the large space, the acoustics of the inside-out Ferrero Rocher room complemented the gathering sound of James like none of the other venues had truly done on the tour so far, well, the ones that I attended anyway. Of course James played a familiar enough set with the symbiotic pairing of 'Of Monsters And Heroes And Men' followed by 'I Wanna Go Home'.

"Get ready for this" I said to my wife as the opening bars of 'I Wanna Go Home' started up, "the place is going to go absolutely mental with this one!" I was right, the ferocious dual drumming of Dave and Saul shocked those in attendance who hadn't seen the band since the early nineties and only knew them because of 'Sit Down'. The noise from the audience was deafening, they'd been beaten into submission by the song and as a special treat the band followed with 'Out To Get You', it was a truly magical moment to be part of the James fan choir towards the end of the song as we all screamed the *"what I need"* lyric back to the band as if we were an echo.

The evening ended with a barrage of their most well known tunes and 'Sometimes' was once again sung back for several minutes like it had been on other occasions. After the band had left the stage and the hoards started to leave en mass my wife and I caught up with some of the guys from the forum.

"Hey! Chris!!!" my wife said to one of the guys and then the two of them started chatting to one another like old friends! Well, I was a tad confused, how did she know him, what was going on? It turned out that it was 'DJ Chris' from the oneofthethree forum and my wife worked with him in Leeds! She then reminded me that Chris had been the DJ at the wedding of the friend she'd been living with in Chapel Allerton in Leeds, the same friend whose house it was where I'd listened to *Pleased To Meet You* for the first time. A small world! My mind was cast back to the wedding, her friend and her new husband still hadn't decided on a wedding dance and they'd only gone and asked me what James song would make a good wedding dance song and I'd suggested 'Sometimes'! Chris had played it followed by 'This Is The One' by The Stone Roses. It had been a great wedding, none of your Rick Astley or Kylie Minogue; instead Chris conjured up a miniature indie disco heaven.

We all had a bit of a chat and then I managed to persuade my wife to let me buy a new James t-shirt, an electric blue shirt with lyrics from different James songs on the front of it, rather gorgeous I thought. We said our goodbyes and then left the building and walked along to where the car was parked, the atmosphere was still rather boisterous and loud, lots of very drunk people singing the lyrics to 'Sit Down' and in the process strangling the song to death but it was all very good natured. I waved goodbye to Blackpool Tower, hopped in the car and my wife drove us back to our little home in Tingley.

The following weekend my wife and I went to Wales for a romantic break, it was the first time her parents would be looking after our son who was nearly a year old giving us a bit of 'us time'. Llandudno was our choice of destination on the north coast of the beautiful country; it was nice to have a gentle reminder of who we were and what had brought us together in the first place. *Hey, Ma* had remained on repeat throughout the entire journey and the songs just wouldn't leave my head at all, particularly 'I Wanna Go Home'. I was stood on the beach on the south west of the town lost in my own thoughts about my life in general, the wind was howling around the two of us and we stood motionless taking in the breathtaking landscape whilst the song played in the background of my mind, it's one of those moments that I'll always remember.

Over the next couple of months I decided to revisit my entire James back catalogue via my Ipod. *Stutter* sounded like an album created by a bunch of crazy guys, it was all sea shanties, froth and pullovers,

Strip Mine felt like an album created on the brink of personal chaos and collapse, 'Vulture' and 'Not There' still gave me goose bumps. *Gold Mother* had for a while sounded very dated indeed but the album held so many memories for me of holidays in Bridlington, long lost friends and starting college. *Seven* sounded less pompous than it had for a while, the lead singles from it are perhaps some of the finest pop songs of all time, I know that it sounds like a rather bold statement but I truly believe this to be the case, fancy releasing 'Sound' as your next single after Sit Down! I'm sure the record company must have had a fit at the preposterous suggestion!!

Laid glowed a melancholy sadness, *Wah Wah* was pure magic, an ambient trippy unsettling journey that caught the mid nineties zeitgeist perfectly. *Whiplash* reminded me of happy yet demanding times, *Millionaires* still reminded me of that sense of pre-millennium tension although in a much less unsettling way than *Ok Computer* had. As for *Pleased To Meet You*, I'd struggled with the album for a long time, it had at times annoyed me in that for a supposed swan song of an album it had been so unlovable and had left a bitter metallic taste in my mouth. However, over time I'd started to see and hear the album in a different light. The songs were sound solid structures, it felt like an album created by a band that no longer really cared what others thought of them except perhaps their fans. The album is often cited by hardcore James fans as being their best album, although I don't hold it in the same light I know what they're saying. In a weird way the more throwaway pop moments and the really weird stuff makes more sense to me, perhaps this says a lot more about me than it does of James.

The cavernous sound

2008

Winter time and another end of year tour, tickets were once again purchased this time for the Leeds Academy and Manchester Central which was formerly the GMEX, I still had the video of the James GMEX concert that took place nearly twenty years earlier although I hadn't watched it in a very long time mainly due to the fact that I no longer owned a video player. Dinalli, Edward, his other half Debs and our old red headed pal Robin (who'd gone along to the Tim Booth gig back in 2004) were also attending at the recently renovated venue that used to be The Town and Country Club years ago. My wife would not be attending, she was instead sorting out a large pile of ironing at home and watching *Location, Location, Location* on Channel 4.

I'd been to the venue only a few weeks prior to the James gig and experienced one of the greatest gigs I'd ever had the pleasure to attend. I'd gone along to see Mercury Rev by myself, I had a spare ticket that I couldn't even give away and during the gig I felt like crying at the fact that I wasn't able to share the experience with anybody I knew. I'd left the venue that night spellbound and overcome at the awesome live show, the band had recently released a mostly electronic album *Snowflake Midnight* and they'd come across like an Americana band mashed up with the Aphex Twin. If you weren't able to experience Mercury Rev live in 2008 then you missed out on something very special indeed.

James had released a new album just in time for the winter tour. It was a live album limited to only five thousand copies and it was a compilation of some of the best performances from 2008. They'd imaginatively called the album *Live in 2008*. I'd heard that some people were buying quite a few copies and then selling them online for over inflated prices which I thought was a bit of a crappy thing to do, but that's people for you. We met up with a few of the guys from the oneofthethree forum at the Northern Monkey pub and we had some friendly banter with them. By the time we all arrived at the venue it was absolutely heaving, you could hardly move and there was no way that I was going to be able get anywhere near the front. We wandered around trying to locate a decent vantage point to little avail. A camera crew caught my attention, it quickly became apparent that they were interviewing people, asking them a question that went something like "What would you do to create world peace?" The idea was that the individual's answers would be shown on a large screen at the back of the venue prior to the bands entrance. Another film crew was filming people dancing to use during the show. Edward, Debs, Robin and I volunteered ourselves and ended up being ushered off to a side area, a cheap stereo was turned on and we had to dance for about thirty seconds to 'I Know What I'm Here For' whilst the camera man zoomed in on us in an assortment of crazy angles. I threw my best shapes and really gave it some in a manner that would have made Tim Booth proud, the other three gave a fairly sober performance which obviously wouldn't be used whilst my art would make the whole venue erupt with joy once shown on the large screen.

Come show time and we were squashed middle back left of the stage, the view was going to be okay though and as the light dropped the audience heaved and shoved about as everybody craned their necks around towards the back of the venue, the reason was that Tim and Larry made their entrance from way back near the bar. Larry was playing an acoustic version of 'Lose Control' whilst some guy held a massive big spotlight over Tim and Larry as they weaved forward towards the stage. It was like a miniature version of U2's Rattle and Hum but without the pretension's or flag waving. We cheered and clapped until our hands exploded, Tim and Larry managed to make their way through the burly audience before scurrying onto the stage and then the show began proper. The usual barrage of songs was hurled at the audience, crowd surfers were ejected from the venue, the heat was unbearable and somebody who wouldn't admit it destroyed the ambience by letting off an almighty fart nearby which you could actually taste. The Hey, Ma material went down a storm and the songs had become like familiar friends to us all. During 'Gold Mother' the backdrop showed a montage of the best dancers of the evening that had been recorded earlier, I was sure that my big screen debut would be shown but to my dismay and disgust it was left on the cutting room floor whilst my friends who had performed the most laborious dance routine in the world spent an eternity on the screen! I was tormented by the twelve foot high figures of my friends doing what looked like the 'hand jive'; they of course found it highly amusing and slapped me on the back in celebration, I smiled politely at them even if I was full of jealousy, anger and contempt. Well, that's probably a bit too strong really but it was MY BAND, MY SHOW! They were simply GUESTS! Arghhh!!!!

James performed a new song called 'Porcupine', it sounded excellent and reminded me of the classic B-side 'Building A Charge', from the 'Sometimes' single, the song featured a wonderful violin part by the enigmatic Mr Saul Davies which finished off the song beautifully, I looked forward to hearing a recorded version. The rest of the set passed by in a blur and featured audience pleasers 'Born Of Frustration', 'Sit Down', 'Sound', 'Out To Get You', 'Sometimes' and finally 'Laid'. A great show, pure magic even if it had felt and at times smelt like we were stuck inside a giant sweaty sardine can for the majority of it.

On the 19th of December I once again headed westbound across the Pennines for my final gig of the year at Manchester Central, the first of two nights that the band would be performing there. I was no longer living in Tingley and had recently moved to the quiet town of Otley, it felt like the older I was becoming and the further my hair was receding the less rock and roll I was becoming, heck, I hadn't even been to the Leeds Festival that year, the very pinnacle of rock and roll good times vibes that a festival experience can bring you for a couple of hundred pounds. This sadly meant that I'd missed out on experiencing The Fratellis, The Wombats, One Night Only, and Plain White T's, what a complete tragedy.

Manchester was drowning in a sea of rain, the pavements were full of drenched young professionals leaving work and heading towards the nearest tapas and wine bars, it took an awful lot of patience and determination to avoid bumping into them. I'd prearranged to meet up with some of the oneofthethree crew at a local pub and I was warmly greeted by Lisa, Graham and Kay amongst others. Beers were bought, photographs were taken and conversation became slurred and intoxicated. When we eventually left and headed to the venue the rain had stopped and we joined the drunken throngs of people who'd been revving it up with it being the last Friday before Christmas and all that. I'd never been to the venue before and was slightly overawed at the size of it; it had once in a past golden age been a train station and it had the familiar curved roof a lot of old main stations have such as York and London Kings Cross. A group of men gaily dressed as female flight attendants greeted us just to camp up the mood; I tried to ignore them and just gave them a friendly but manly nod of the head. It felt strange being at an indoor venue which had burger vans indoors serving culinary delights that mainly comprised of cheap cut meat served in a bun. I had visions of somebody biting into one and being scalded as they burst a large hot boil of fluid encased inside the meat. I bet when Morrissey played at such huge venues it was vegan or vegetarian options only. Due to our late arrival there was no way we were going to be able to get too close to the barrier so Lisa, her friend and I ended up standing stage left whilst Dave Brown and some of the others squirmed their way forward into the central pack.

The support for the evening came from the woeful Athlete and they received a fair few heckles of abuse from the crowd. A half hearted petition had even been set up to have them removed from the support slot by some of the online James fans, the band were clearly aware of the animosity they were receiving except perhaps from the odd loved up couple who were in attendance who had bought most of their music from supermarkets or petrol stations. Nice lads I'm sure and I quite like the song 'Wires', it's a sweet yet sad little number. The rest of the songs though were utter turkey.

The atmosphere inside the old train station was hot and excitable with just a hint of animosity in the air due to the largely intoxicated audience. I knew that I shouldn't have bothered with having a few drinks though prior to the gig when I went for the first of my scheduled toilet breaks, the queue was horrendous and I feared for my bladder, I'm not the kind of person who'll just go for a wee in a pint glass and then drop it on the floor or heaven forbid throw it into the air particularly after having been on the receiving end of a full pint of wee thrown by some idiot during a performance by Faithless at one of the V festivals. For a brief but unpleasant moment in time I felt just like Meat Loaf must have felt at the Reading Festival in the late eighties.

The area where the toilets were based had a bit of an underworld dodgy feel, lots of people hanging around staring you out whilst speaking to mysterious people on the other end of their mobile phones, or maybe I was just feeling a bit paranoid and my imagination was running away a tad. The music being played on the sound system was reverberating and sounded delayed due to the toilet area being behind the stage area. I headed back to where Lisa and her friend were stood and we chatted and waited, Dave Brown and his brother made brief appearances and were joking and larking about, Dave kept venting about Athlete being the "Spawn of Satan" whilst I tried to interject with lighter subjects such as Global Thermo Nuclear War.

The music stopped, the lights dropped and the audience started to cheer and applaud. It was strange but for a home coming gig a week before Christmas and with an audience that was very drunk the atmosphere was flat and subdued, the Leeds crowd had sounded so much more up for it. Tim and Larry started the gig in a similar fashion to how they had in Leeds with an acoustic rendition of 'Lose Control' sung from the raised disabled area of the arena, it sounded wonderful and even though it was just the two of them performing they filled the large space perfectly. Once the song finished and the two of them regrouped with the rest of James Tim said "Hello" but it was such a poor response that it resulted in him repeating "HELLO!" again just to make sure that James weren't about to play to a crowd of coffin dodgers. And then the band fell into what was to me and a few others familiar territory with a set that was obvious but in no way predictable.

I was annoyed though when I had to nip out for five minutes to use the toilet which resulted in missing what sounded like a manic version of 'Stutter', it sounded ferocious from the toilet cubicle, the walls vibrated heavily and the toilet roll leapt from its holder in sheer alarm. By the time I'd made my way back to where Lisa was the song had finished and 'Born Of Frustration' lit up the arena with every other person pretending to be an American Indian whooping away in unison. 'Porcupine' was played again, yes, it definitely reminded me of 'Building A Charge', Saul appeared on the back of the stage on a raised area similar to what Beyoncé or Nickelback would have at one of their arena shows and he was wearing a pair of angels wings, it was quite sweet and ridiculous in equal measures, in other words it was perfect. We watched the spectacle with smiles upon our faces at the cranky little man playing the most angelic violin piece we'd heard in a long time.

Lisa and I kept laughing at some guy who was stood directly behind us. He was completely off his head or at least appeared to be as his eyes were often rolling into the back of their sockets whilst he performed an intoxicated writhing dance throughout the evening, he was also wearing glittery make up around his eyes and had a side parting the likes of which hadn't been seen in many a year. I couldn't tell if he was simply in ecstasy or was on ecstasy. Still, he looked like he was having a good time so fair play to him I thought. The remainder of the set was played pretty straight although during 'Tomorrow' a smart suited man leapt up to the top of the raised area at the back of the stage, sadly not in a single bound I must add and he used his own form of sign language to play out the lyrics. It was quite hysterical particularly the "I'm just out of your range" lyric as it was signed by the guy pretending to hold a sawn off shot gun at the crowd which was slightly unnerving and I'm guessing that there may have been a few people who soiled themselves due to PTSD flashbacks at that moment.

Tim and the rest of James appeared to have enjoyed the evening too and before we knew it we'd reached the end of the gig via a wonderful and thrilling version of 'Out To Get You' which Mark even had a bit of a boogie too, well not exactly but he leapt down from his Jean Michelle Jarre bank of keyboards, somersaulted and landed squarely with his feet on the ground next to the rest of his mates and then the song ended and that was the end of the show.

Once the band had left the stage I said goodbye to Lisa and then headed towards one of the exits and dragged myself out of the venue purposefully avoiding the expensive merchandise stall before spending fifteen minutes in the drizzle trying to find my wife, my sister in law and her boyfriend who'd spent the evening in Manchester having a few drinks so that they could pick me up post gig. The girls were sober but he was quite the worse for wear after being on the beer since four in the afternoon, he could only communicate by grunting and snorting. And that was the end of the James road trip for another year, I was sure there would be more James action in some form or other the next year; I was already looking forward to it, I'd just have to be patient.

Two thousand and nine

2009/2010

2009 – it was one of my busiest years ever. Within the first five months I'd renovated our new house from top to bottom, completed my nursing degree and was supporting my heavily pregnant (again) wife. Naturally our son kept us very busy. I was also working full time so by the time our new baby emerged I was pretty knackered. Megan was born at home, I'd helped deliver her and it was one of the most life affirming things I have ever done. Then after all of the hard graft of the first half of the year was over I decided to write my first book, just to stop myself from getting bored.

As far as I was aware all was quiet in the James camp, actually this was far from the truth. The band played quite a few gigs throughout the year mainly abroad with a few UK festival performances chucked in for good measure. I wasn't able to attend any of them though, too expensive and too many other things of a greater importance were taking place in my life. From what I'd read though those who'd attended the gigs in warmer climates gave rapturous reviews, James had really caught the attention and love of the Greeks in particular.

Then out of the blue a young lady called Charlotte contacted me via the social network site Facebook who I'd met on the kibbutz back in 1994. You're probably wondering where this fits into the story so I'll tell you. Now you may recall that I'd at one point around that time owned a red/pink James t-shirt with the numbers 1-7 printed upon it, I hadn't really been too keen on the t-shirt but had forgotten as to what had happened to it. Well, during our electronic correspondence she reminded me that I'd "given it to her" (the t-shirt I mean), although the exact details are still a bit hazy probably due to the fact that it had been a very drunken episode of some description or other. So that cleared up the missing t-shirt but the most wonderful thing she said was that she'd given birth to one of her children whilst wearing this item of clothing! I was really chuffed and quite moved by this revelation. I think the t-shirt had been binned afterwards though as child birth can be quite a messy affair.

Rumours began to arise of a new James album. The forum fellowship was naturally very excited indeed at the prospect of new material. 2010 was going to be another exciting year for James fans the world and universe over, the reason was that the band would be releasing two 'mini albums', one in April and one during the summer. It came across as being a bit of a strange move; the band was following up what had been quite a successful album with a spilt release. As *Hey, Ma* hadn't been available to purchase in the supermarkets I guessed the new releases would end up being overlooked as well. Before the end of the year a link went live online where tickets for a tour in April 2010 could be purchased along with the first of the two albums entitled *The Night Before*. Tickets were purchased for Newcastle and Sheffield with a ticket bought for my good wife too as I felt she deserved a half decent night out just for putting up with my weirdness, disgusting table manners not to mention my grubby feet. *The Night Before* was going to be the first of two James mini albums, the second mini album was going to be titled *The Morning After* and it would feature a selection of quiet stripped down tracks compared to the promise of upbeat gay disco numbers that the first release would comprise of. As a James fan the thought of two new official releases was as mental as it could get.

The Night Before started to stir up a bit of interest in the music press; even the bloody NME to much amazement gave the band a brief nod without any insulting comments for once. James fans were given the opportunity to listen to the new songs via a media player on their official website, it was difficult to get a proper feel for them though as I could only listen to them through my tinny laptop speakers, I'm sure there would have been a way to have ripped the songs and burnt them onto a compact disc but that's just not my kind of thing to be honest. I'd rather

291

have the 'real thing', the artwork, the packaging and the pristine shining silver disc emblazoned with the bands name and album title.

An up-tempo shimmering electronic little number called 'It's Hot' opened the album. It was an unusual song and once again sounded like nothing else I'd ever heard before. 'Crazy' followed; once again it was touted as a 'single' although without any kind of promotion, artwork or promo to accompany it. The song sounded a bit like a Doves number which is of course a compliment, it did however feel quite safe and didn't really stretch the band too much. Great lyrics though. 'Ten Below' however blew me away the first time I heard it. The lyrics about the hardships of being sent away to a boarding school were touching without being over sentimental. Tim managed to once again chuck in the "F" word which of course would hamper any potential chance of the song being placed on Radio One's playlists.

I was only three songs into the album and I already preferred it to *Hey, Ma* and I'd seriously loved that album. 'Porcupine' was familiar to me as I'd heard it played live in 2008. Larry's slide guitar made the song instantly recognisable as a James song, there's an awful lot going on in the song, lots of chirrups, bleeps and buzzes and once again there's an epic feel to it. The main problem and it's a big problem is that the wonderful violin part was wiped off the song and instead a pretty shoddy fade out ended the new version. Now, I'm not sure what the reason was but what a tragic waste of potential. 'Shine' was as perfect as a James song could ever be. Again, Larry's guitar made the song stand out from their contemporaries and peers, it's a sublime song, it should have been a single released properly with lots of fanfare and promotion, the record company should have been proud to have had such a wonderful uplifting song amongst their catalogue. What a waste that the song would probably be forgotten about forever as just another album track on an album that only a select few in the know would buy.

'Dr Hellier' had a bit of a nasty vibe running through it, the guitar sounded menacing and hostile, the lyrics sounded like a cross between the script from the sci-fi film *Fantastic Voyage* and a film about the invasion of Afghanistan. Overall I wasn't too impressed with the song;

I felt that the chorus kind of let it down a bit. The final song made up for it though, 'Hero' was on par with 'Shine', the opening accordion like keyboard threw me initially but once Dave's monstrous drums kicked in the song made perfect sense. Tim desperately hollered out the lyrics throughout like a man possessed. Once again it was one of James' finest moments and I was blown away with the fact that the band that I loved so much were still capable of creating such musical gems.

I found *The Night Before* to be excellent, a leap forward from *Hey, Ma* in many ways, the band sounded extremely confident in their abilities and definitely at ease with themselves. Some of the feedback though from the James fans on the forums was slightly damming. Lisa's comment about 'It's Hot' was "It's not", now that certainly made me laugh out loud and the butchering of 'Porcupine' really upset a lot of people too. It would have been interesting to have heard what the record company thought of the album upon its first listen, did they sigh, roll their eyes and say "just sort out the release date and lets move on" or did they wet themselves convinced that this particular release would turn around the alarming decline in album sales due to illegal downloads. The former option is most likely I reckon. Had the album had a few more tunes on it as good as 'Shine' and 'Hero' then maybe the record company would have had more confidence in lavishing the album with a decent release package, sadly and predictably this would not be the case.

The Night Before was going to be released midway through the tour as well. Now personally I'd have thought that it would have been a better idea to have released the album prior to the tour, it would stop the majority of the punters at gigs from chatting during new songs or standing there simply gawping at the band. However, I'm not employed in the music business and as previously mentioned I thought The Spice Girls wouldn't amount to anything so what do I really know.

Another April, with another trip up to Newcastle to see James at the Academy again, the venue felt like a second home. The tour had been dubbed 'The Mirrorball Tour' and there was the promise of plenty of sexy mirrorball tomfoolery from the band. The trip was once again boring and uneventful, I'd set off way too early and ended up pulling over at a service station to browse through the over the top priced music selection and 'pick and mix' sweets. I drove on and eventually found a place to park up in Newcastle, it took several trips around the city via the one way system but within an hour I was stood by the barrier in front of Tim's microphone stand. A petite young lady who was stood next to me struck up conversation, I can't remember her name but she said she'd taken a few weeks off work to attend the entire tour; she'd been to Edinburgh the night previous and raved about it. Kay from the forum was also in attendance and gave me a big wave; I shouted to her that I'd see her after the gig. Kay was the only person I recognised that evening, it felt like the close knit bunch of oneofthethree forum users had kind of disbanded, the fellowship had foundered, or perhaps it was just me and they were all still meeting up with one another, I'm not paranoid, honest! Unkle Bob was the support band, it was a band managed, loved and cared for by Saul. Pleasant enough I suppose, I politely clapped between songs, some lads behind me heckled the band on a couple of occasions and made some crass comments regarding the rather fetching female member of the band, I cringed in embarrassment for her but obviously didn't dare say anything to the lads as they'd have duffed me up.

James played a rather eclectic mix of songs that evening, sadly for me at least the gig didn't really take off until two thirds in when 'Tomorrow' was played. Up till then the crowd had been fairly sober, clapping along conservatively to the new songs which sounded fantastic live, the band had chucked in a few curve balls such as 'Hang On', 'Hup Springs', and 'Walking The Ghost' just to test the crowd but there was a lot of chatter going on which is always a very bad sign at a gig. As mentioned there was a change when 'Tomorrow' was played, I could only describe it as a seismic shift and it felt like the entire audience pushed forward against the barrier and I felt the wind being squeezed out of my lungs. The rest of the set comprised of 'Sound', 'Sit Down', 'Getting Away With It', 'Sometimes' and finally 'Laid'. I wondered if it would have been a better idea to have mixed up the set a bit to please the greatest hits fans but James have always been about challenging the audience and thankfully the days of predictable set lists had been left behind in the nineties.

I have to mention something that baffled me though. I've banged on a bit about various items of James clothing throughout the story and I've always been very impressed with the majority of the shirts that have been for sale. However, the t-shirt for this tour, the 'Mirrorball Tour' was horrendous! It looked like a bootleg shirt and on the front of it was a picture of a cat! It was awful beyond belief! Kay had designed her own James t-shirt, it featured a porcupine on it and it was great fun and cheeky at the same time. Definitely miles better then the official product. My wallet therefore remained unopened that evening.

Two nights later and I was back at the Sheffield Academy this time with my wife, as I'd predicted the flooring was noticeably much stickier than it had been the last time I'd been there. A beer was bought and I dragged my wife over to where I'd stood previously. We had a grand view of the stage and we enjoyed Unkle Bob as much as it was possible to. Come show time and the audience were as expectant as ever. The balcony still looked like a bit of a nightmare for the majority of those who were stood there, the viewing was restricted unless you were stood next to the barrier and the crowd was at least four people deep. Once the house lights dropped and the music finished there was a mighty roar as an acoustic guitar was strummed with the familiar chords of 'Sit Down'. We craned our necks around along with everybody else and just above our heads were Tim and Larry lit up by a spot light whilst they stood on the balcony. The security went a bit mental when Tim then scaled over the barrier and was stood on the lip of the balcony, one security guard was frantically trying to grab him, Tim instead pushed his hands away, the security guard took the hint and backed away. He mouthed something to the other security guard which looked like,

"Leave him, he's an idiot".

Another guy, a punter who was stood next to Tim made me laugh as I thought he was going to wet himself with excitement! A giant grin lit up his entire face and it appeared for him at least to be the greatest moment in the history of time and space. His baseball cap leapt of his head on a few occasions as he shook himself vigorously in time to the song and I chuckled to myself more transfixed by this guy. Tim and Larry made their way around the balcony; those in attendance must have felt like all their Christmas's had come early. The whole room sang the song aloud, it was an absolutely fantastic start to the evening, joyous and triumphant, but how was a band of old men who'd been banging away at this type of malarkey for nigh on thirty years going to improve on such a stunning start to a show I wondered? The song ended and Tim and Larry leapt over the balcony like a couple of salmon on acid, they were delicately caught by those below who then threw the two of them high up into the air where with great skill they managed to land on their feet on the stage to a roar of applause.

(I've made that last bit up).

James indeed lifted the bar somewhat with a stunning performance which was slightly hampered by some muddy sound problems. The new songs continued to sound amazing live, I'd gotten to know them by now and pumped my fists in time to the choruses and the epic moments that each song contained. I felt like the only one though, the majority of those stood near me were as motionless as marble statues. My wife was a tad more animated though thank goodness and she bopped and bounced along to the new music having heard the songs umpteen times at home via the James media player. A massive scary looking Mirrorball was revealed, it was encased in a large plastic transparent box which Tim and Andy scaled a few times during the show, there were also a number of other smaller mirror balls dotted around the stage. It was like being back in the High Harrogate Working Men's Club sometime in the nineteen eighties minus the tinselly curtains.

Towards the end of the main set the band performed 'Sound' which in my opinion simply had to be played each time the band performed live. The bass was so loud that the inside of my nostrils vibrated something terrible; it was actually quite a pleasurable experience if a little bit weird at the same time, I imagine it was probably a sensation that women and some men get when they go to an Ann Summers party and 'demonstrate things' by placing them on their noses, if you know what I mean. (It's something that I've heard about and not actually ever been involved in). We left the venue as happy as the band had appeared during the set, they really did look like they were having the times of their lives, in fact I couldn't remember James looking so at ease and relaxed whilst still remaining so sharp and focused. My wife stated that it had been her favourite ever James gig, it wasn't quite for me but despite the sound quality being a bit hit and miss and the lack of energy from the audience during the new songs it was probably one of my favourite ever James gigs, I was still buzzing when we finally arrived home later that night, the babysitter wasn't so impressed though with our late arrival and she punched herself in the face out of anger.

Promotion for the new album came via a number of different Medias, the oddest yet still quite excellent bit of promotion was when Tim and Jim were interviewed on *Soccer a.m.* The programme was once quite amusing even for non football fans but had become a caricature of itself and it appeared to be listing to one side like a sinking ship. The interview was fine though, quite amusing in fact and when Tim and Jim were invited to take part in some soccer skills Jim set the studio alight by scoring a cracking goal! Whilst the programme was being viewed by me and my two children the postman arrived and hand delivered *The Night Before* which had been ordered some months earlier. It was a good day in our house.

Naturally the album wasn't readily available to buy in the usual outlets such as the supermarkets; it was HMV, an independent record shop or an online purchase only which meant that countless casual and curious music purchasers wouldn't stumble across the album whilst doing their weekly shop in Sainsbury's. The fact that it was cheap to buy would have meant that copies of the album would have been snapped up whilst people bought their toilet rolls, vegetables and Weetabix. For those who enjoyed downloading their music an extra track was available from iTunes in the form of 'All My Letters'. It's a pleasant if slightly throwaway track which managed to name check Jay-Z and Will Smith within its first line or two. Not bad but not great. The album would enter the UK album charts around the number twenty two mark, quite poor after the success of *Hey, Ma*, maybe I should have done another internet campaign. The album was on heavy rotation in our house although I had to be mindful of the bad language in front of the children of course. The nursery had already commented to my wife that Daniel had been "singing very grown up sounding songs"; he'd apparently been singing 'Getting Away With It' to the other children on one occasion and making them cry. A winter tour was hinted at by the band members during interviews, there were also going to be loads of festival appearances throughout the summer in the UK and Europe as well as a US tour, a very busy year in the James camp.

In July we had a family day out to Bridlington, the kids played on the beach and in the sea and a grand day was had by all. On the way home a text came through on my phone from Dinalli.

"JAMES ARE PLAYING BINGLEY, MATE".

'Bingley Music Live' is a Bradford Council organised three day music event, it's not really a festival as all that it has to offer is one stage and a couple of burger vans and a beer tent. However, it always manages to acquire some decent enough bands to play there. There had been rumours the year before that James would play but I laughed them off as preposterous then low and behold a year later it looked like it was actually going to happen! I encouraged my wife to drive home as fast as she could so that I could go online and buy tickets; I was more excited at the prospect of taking Daniel to his first ever James gig though. He'd been to Bingley Music Live the year before with me and had seen Reverend and the Makers where I'd sat him on my shoulders and he'd made everybody in the vicinity laugh with his crazy dancing and hand clapping to the music.

Initially I was going to go to the event by myself but as the weekend of the festival approached and the weather forecast was looking pretty good my wife said she'd go along for the Saturday so that she could see James, naturally it meant that our daughter Megan would therefore be attending her first James gig too. The Friday of the music event is free to attend, I drove down to arrive for the opening of the gates with Daniel and the first act on was Dan Le Sac Vs Scroobius Pip. Their debut album *Angles* had been my favourite album of 2007 and I'd been surprised at the time in the fact that the album hadn't been featured in any of the end of year polls. Their second album *The Logic Of Chance* had been released earlier in the year and although I really liked it wasn't a patch on their debut, possibly a case of 'difficult second album syndrome'. The noise levels for the weekend were going to be quite loud so I'd ordered some kiddie ear protectors from the internet. Daniel was wearing a home made Dan Le Sac Vs. Scroobius Pip t-shirt which had emblazoned across it *"Just A Band"* in reference to the song 'Thou Shalt Always Kill', he looked like a proper little festival goer! I think he was still a bit shocked though when the opening chords of their first song blared out of the sound system as it was very loud. Anyway a great time was had by all even if most of their songs had a fairly dark theme underlying them (self-harm, murder, suicide etc.) The second and final band for us at least was festival legends Dreadzone and then we scarpered off home before all of the scallies turned up and started scrapping with each other.

Saturday was a very hot day. The four of us turned up at about two in the afternoon, the arena was really quiet compared to how busy it had been the year before around the same time. I feared that James hadn't drawn a big crowd; maybe somebody had gotten it very wrong I thought to myself. Daniel was wearing a home made 'Ja-m-es' top with the events date on the back of it, it drew lots of looks and compliments from those in attendance.

"I'm lovin' hiz liddle top mate, well cyute!!" slurred a very drunk lad who was with a lot of other very drunken lads. It was only three in the afternoon!

As mentioned the only problem with Bingley Live is that apart from the main stage there isn't a right lot else to do, the kids soon tired of listening to the music and wrestling with each other. Megan knocked over my full pint of beer which caused much upset as it went all over the picnic blanket and was of course a waste of quality ale.

The afternoon was spent in the company of Frightened Rabbit, Example, Reef, Public Image Limited and finally James. I took Megan down near to the stage to see John Lydon et al with her sat on my shoulders bopping away wearing her pink ear defenders but after a while we headed back to where my wife was and she suggested we went to the kid's playground which is in Myrtle Park itself. In fairness the kids were getting quite restless so away we went weaving in and out of the audience which by then had grown into a massive throng. Not quite every person was wearing a James top but there were enough of them and a variety of designs to make me realise that there was a lot of old school James fans in attendance. Some time was spent watching the kids do somersaults and forward rolls off the play equipment without any serious injuries whilst the heavy dub of Public Image Limited filled the air, the band covered the Lydon featured Leftfield song 'Open Up' and I was suddenly annoyed that I wasn't in the midst of the crowd po-going like a mad 'un.

The temperature was dropping, the music had finished and we encouraged the kids to pack up and head back to the arena.

"I'm tired" said Daniel, my heart skipped a beat.

"C'mon Daniel, we're off to see James, it's going to be great!" I said to him trying to gee him up somewhat.

"Yes Daddy" he said whilst rubbing his eyes with his little hands.

We made our way along the right hand side of the arena near to where the takeaway vans were parked just underneath one of the big viewing screens. I lobbed Daniel onto my shoulders and headed into the audience leaving my wife and Megan somewhere a bit less squashed where she could see all of the action. I managed to squirm quite far in, other kids were on their parent's shoulders and the atmosphere in general was lively yet friendly. From time to time I'd swing Daniel over one of my shoulders to see if he was alright, his thumb was in his mouth but he nodded that he was fine. For me it was a great moment. I was finally getting to share and pass on an experience that meant so much to me and had done for nearly two decades. My son had been named after the band, okay; I didn't have a James tattoo but naming him Daniel James was in my mind at least pretty symbolic of what the band had meant to me for so long.

Showtime, the band marched on stage looking rather dapper to what could only be described as a hero's welcome with at least fifteen thousand in attendance which was probably too large a number for such a small arena. Tim of course dropped in his Bradford linkage and told the audience that he'd been to see his grandfather's grave that day. I just can't think of another rock star who'd ever say something so human and personal on stage and I felt quite moved by his comment. So, a 'festival' appearance, would James freak everybody out by playing a set list of b-sides and *Wah Wah* material? No, of course not, they gave the audience what they wanted. 'Sit Down' opened up the set and every set of lungs sang in unison and in time, some people nearby were in tears. I could tell that Daniel was clapping away in time to the music. I couldn't really clap as to do so would have meant that my young son would have fallen off my shoulders and that would have been the end of his first James gig. I made do with dancing a slow side to side dance in a manner that Jim Glennie would have been proud of.

'Ring The Bells' and 'Hymn From A Village' followed, I sang the latter with much gusto showing those stood nearby that I was a real hardcore James fan as nobody else appeared to know the song! A new song from the as yet to be released mini album was played, it was called 'Lookaway' and I thought it sounded alright. 'Crazy' followed but not before Tim had mentioned that the band was going to play some new material.

"It's important that we're not just seen as a nostalgia act" Tim said to the audience who were probably expecting it to be just hit after hit. 'Crazy' sounded fantastic and was proof to the doubters just how relevant the band was in 2010. 'Getting Away With It' followed. I gained Daniels attention but he'd already recognised the opening bars of the song and was clapping away.

I was tapped on the back by somebody.

"You're little lad's enjoying himself isn't he!" a friendly woman said to me, she was with a large group of people. I explained how he'd been named after the band and they all started to cheer!

"Go on Daniel!!" one of the drunken blokes shouted out, Daniel heard the man through his ear protectors and I could feel him twist around on my shoulders before returning to face the stage again. Once again it was a great moment in time and the song represented a lot to me, "getting away with it" had felt like a mantra regarding my own life for so long. So many times I'd felt like I'd been getting away with it and that one day my mask would slip and those I'd been fooling for so long would catch me unaware.

'Tomorrow' followed, half way through the song Daniel caught my attention by slapping my head and he indicated that he'd had enough. We made our way out of the audience back up to where his mummy and sister were. Megan was sat in a baby carrier strapped to my wife's back and was watching the band on the screen transfixed by Tim Booth's massive bald head. Daniel was knackered, it had been too long a day for him and it had turned dark and was way past his bed time. I held him in my arms and he fell asleep with his head on my shoulder whilst the band powered through 'I Wanna Go Home', a more fitting song couldn't have been played.

By the time that 'Sometimes' was being played we'd decided that we'd all had enough and we left the arena along with quite a few others. It wasn't a case of walking out of a James gig heaven forbid, the kids just wanted their warm milk and beds. As we reached the top of the stairs leading out of the arena I turned around and looked at the spectacle that was the huge audience and I was proud that the band could still draw in so many people with their songs of doubt, failure, mental illness, sex and love. As we walked out of Myrtle Park the noise level lessened until it was nothing more than a dull thudding bass sound and then we finally reached our car and drove back home to Otley.

The Morning After

2010

On the sixth of September 2010 my wife and I drove into Leeds city centre and parked in the rather dilapidated car park behind the market. There was a reason for going which now evades me; however the main reason for heading into the city as far as I was concerned was to buy the new James album *The Morning After*. The album had received favourable reviews across the board. Q magazine even bothered to give it a review after ignoring *The Night Before*. The magazine was aware of the first of the two albums as the review mentioned that the band should have released one album comprising of all of the tracks from both albums, the reviewer appeared puzzled by the bands move to say the least. *The Morning After* was described as being *"quite poignant"* and *"introspective"*, a different beast to its predecessor. I entered HMV and grabbed a copy of the lightly coloured sleeved album and paid the man with the unusual ant hill haircut and then skipped merrily on my way to meet my wife in a shoe shop.

We needed to pick the kids up from nursery so we headed back to the car and I immediately slipped the disc into the car stereo. 'Got The Shakes' emerged like a slumbering beast, its subject matter appearing to focus on a regretful man after an alcohol infused rage the night before. Startling is a word I'd use to describe it. It was a million miles away from 'Destiny Calling' and the melancholy heaving choir that featured during the latter end of the song gave it a very heavy vibe. 'Dust Motes' followed, another character based song that was haunting and desolate in tone, with just the gentlest of piano playing accompanying Tim's vocal for two thirds of the song until the rest of the band fell into place. 'Tell Her I said So', a song written through the eyes of Tim's elderly mother in a nursing home spooked the hell out of me, bleak and resigned lyrics, a disco beat and a children's choir all added up to one of James' greatest and most unusual songs. 'Kaleidoscope' followed, sparse to the point of nothingness, lyrically painful and with a terrible twist in the tale. It's brought me to tears a few times. 'Rabbit Hole' sounded like it had been mashed up from various James songs; it sounded so familiar, comforting and tender with Tim's most beautiful falsetto yet. 'Make For The City' was a bit more up-tempo, it felt like a warm safe song, in the world of James it was nothing amazing but it still blew away their contemporaries. 'Lookaway' I'd heard at Bingley, it was described as the lead song/single of the album but of course this meant nothing without some kind of promotion. Some fans had commented that if 'Lookaway' have been released a number of years ago then it would have been held in the same regards as some of James' other singles, personally I don't agree with this but it's a fine song nonetheless with some pretty strings throughout. The album ended with the wistful 'Fear' which reminded me a little of 'Alaskan Pipeline'. 'Fear' is a song that is just there. No verses, no choruses, no bridge, it just exists and it is beautiful yet unsettling.

Even though we were piling through traffic and dodging the students who insisted on playing 'chicken' with the traffic in Headingley I knew the album was good, in fact it was better than good, it was fantastic. The album sounded much more organic and human than *The Night Before* probably due to the fact that the band had all been in the same room during the recording process compared to the online/cyberspace production of *The Night Before*. Hats must surely be doffed towards Lee "Muddy' Baker as the albums producer; he really knows how to bring out the best in the band. My wife really liked the album, Daniel loved 'Tell Her I Said So' and 'Rabbit Hole' and everyone was very happy in our household. Of course the album hardly set the world alight although it entered the charts one place higher than *The Night Before*. The UK is a funny old place isn't it? The album would be appreciated more so overseas whilst the vast majority of good old Blighty continued its moribund fascination with all things related to Mr Cowell. James would spend the third quarter of the year stateside as well as an appearance in Mexico, a resounding victory lap judging by the blog updates, photographs and reviews that I couldn't understand due to not speaking their lingo, the pictures looked good though.

The end of the year was approaching, another winter tour, tickets would of course be purchased. I bought two tickets for the gig in Leeds, one for my wife and one for moi. We decided to buy balcony seats so that my wife could get a decent enough view, a year earlier we'd seen Ian Brown at the same venue and had sat in the balcony and it had worked out really well. I was surprised that the atmosphere had been as electric as it had been on that occasion and I wondered if seats at gigs were the way forward, well, I'll be hitting forty in a few years time and my back isn't in the best of conditions, along with my legs, my pelvis, my neck and my shoulders. I'm a bit of a wreck to be honest. I really should have kept up with the cod liver oil my mum used to pour down my neck as a young lad.

I bought a ticket for the bands appearance at the Manchester Evening News Arena, well, I had to! Horrific news came in the form that Leeds band The Pigeon Detectives would be the support act. I'd seen them before, the front man wound me up something chronic, all he could do was yelp a lot and throw his microphone up into the air in a Roger Daltrey kind of way before catching it. Impressive to a degree the first time around but when he performed the trick at least thirty four times during the gig (and believe me I was counting) the label 'one trick pony' sprung to mind. Oh well, better than Athlete I suppose. Further good news was announced. Whilst touring the other side of the Atlantic the band had offered a VIP package to fans, for an additional cost you could attend the sound check and have a Q&A session with the band. It had apparently been a resounding success and obviously a good way to bolster income via the tour. In this day and age bands will do anything to survive and pay the bills, some bands will even sell their dignity or mothers at a push. James announced that they'd offer the same VIP package for the UK winter tour, naturally I was ecstatic, when my wife arrived home from work I danced around her like a little lamb with a sore foot whilst telling her the great news, she was mildly impressed but she said she wasn't too fussed in attending particularly as it was an additional twenty pounds on top of a ticket that had already cost nearly forty when you take into account the booking fees and all of that other crap you're forced to pay out for. So, I bought a VIP pass for Leeds, it was the right thing to do and I though that the extra money might pay for a new set of drumsticks for Dave.

Then, a crazy wild idea came into my head. It was time to email Dave Brown........

Now then Dave!

Well, I'm not sure if you can help or advise. I'm off to the Leeds Academy next week, and I'm also off to the VIP thing before hand. Now, if it was at all possible I was hoping that I could bring my little lad along for the sound check as he loves James, but is a bit too young (at 3 1/2) to go to a busy rowdy gig at the academy. He saw them back in Sept at Bingley and really loved it and it would be mega if I could take him along for the sound check as a special treat. (He's called Daniel James, named in ref to the band and GAWI which is of course his favourite track!!) Any idea who I'd need to speak to regarding trying to sort this out at all? He's got some professional ear protectors to protect his little ears so that wouldn't be a problem of course!! Any suggestions would be very much appreciated.

p.s. I'm not sure if you'll be interested but I'm currently ploughing through a James related book at the moment, I've completed about 46,000 words of 100,000. If you want some more info then let me know, but, keep this to yourself if you can in relation to other James fans. I have contacted 'JamesHQ' to inform them but have had no response so far.

Cheers!!

I wasn't sure if Dave would respond, it was quite a cheeky request of course but sometimes in life you need to be a bit cheeky and if you don't ask you don't get as the saying goes. The following day an email arrived in my inbox from Mr Brown himself,

Hi,

Looks like it should be OK – they need to make sure the venue is OK with it.

Dave

Naturally I was over the moon! My son was very excited when I told him that he'd be going to his very own little James gig and that they'd only be playing a few songs because he was only little.

"Daddy, will Tim wave at me?" Daniel asked.

"You never know, he might do!" I replied and he became very giddy indeed at the possibility, in fact he threw up. My wife was as per usual mildly impressed and questioned the actual logistics of the plan. The plan would be as follows.

1. Finish work, drive home, get changed.
2. Drive to Daniels nursery, collect him and then drive to Horsforth train station, park the car.
3. Get on the Leeds bound train, walk up to the venue for about 16:15, and await entry.
4. Enjoy the sound check, leave for about 18:00, head back to the station and catch the train to Horsforth.
5. Drive back home to Otley, feed Daniel, get both kids ready for bed, babysitter to arrive, drive back to Leeds with my wife, attempt to find somewhere to park, head to venue and find some good seats to enjoy the show.

"Sounds a bit full on, are you sure you'll be up for all of that running around?" she questioned. I reassured her that it would be no bother at all and the tiredness would be worth it.

On the 14th December 2010 my son and I attended the sound check at the Leeds Academy as had been arranged, I was very grateful for those involved in making it happen. We arrived outside the venue on a damp and very cold afternoon; I recognised Kay straight away and had a chat with her whilst we stood in the queue which was a lot bigger than I'd expected, probably about fifty people in total, Dave Brown was behind me and I nodded a greeting at him, I'd thank him in person once inside. We waited and waited and waited, the cold crept up through the concrete into my legs and Daniel was fidgeting.

"Daddy, I'm tired".

"It's not time to be tired, you can be tired later on okay? What will Tim think if you're tired?" I said to him which probably came across more like a threat than anything.

Then, just to warm us up the bands coach which we were stood next to suddenly had its engine turned on, the warm exhaust fumes was just what the cold and slightly impatient crowd needed and I suddenly felt quite nauseous.

It wasn't until just after five o'clock when the doors finally opened, my legs had gone to sleep and I staggered in with the rest of the frozen individuals, we were asked to wait in the foyer area, we could clearly hear the band sound checking 'Gold Mother' and our levels of excitement rose further, the coldness and coach fumes were soon nothing more than a distant memory. Time ticked by, some people were starting to become impatient; Daniel was clambering all over me so I plonked him down on a ledge and told him he had to remain still. I was then tapped on the shoulder by a security guard who beckoned the two of us to the back of the queue. I thought that we were going to be evicted in that having somebody so young in the venue was an infringement of the venues policy and nullified their insurance or something. Thankfully the burly bloke said that he didn't want Daniel getting squashed when we were allowed in so he had another entrance ready for us. Stood by the entrance was an older guy I recognised and had spoken to on many an occasion at James gigs, 'Bon' was the only name that I knew him by and he was with his wife, they chatted to us both for a while, as per usual they were attending the entire tour like they did each and every time unless there was a very good reason not to.

Finally, the doors opened and holding his hand tightly Daniel and I entered the large auditorium of the Leeds Academy, there in front of us awaiting our arrival was James minus Larry who had a bad back and was resting it using a variety of medications, some legal, some illegal.

"Oh, we've got a young one here" Tim said in reference to Daniel, "do you need to stand anywhere in particular?" he asked me, I indicated that I'd sit him (Daniel, not Tim) on my shoulders and then I proceeded to dig out his blue ear protectors from my bag and placed them on his head.

"Ah, good idea, it's going to be quite loud!" said Tim. He then kindly arranged for Daniel and I to stand in a segregated area away from everybody else and I sat Daniel down on one of the bands equipment cases. Tim explained that they would play about three or four songs, songs that the band could play without Larry and that there would be a question and answer session at the end.

The sound check commenced with 'Lost A Friend' from *Whiplash*. I'd never heard it live before and I suddenly realised how loud the band was without a full audience there to dampen the sound down. Thank goodness I'd brought Daniels ear protectors. I swayed along to the song whilst my son sat transfixed at the band members as he sucked his thumb. The song sounded fantastic and I felt very lucky to be part of a select few. 'Lookaway' followed, Tim picked up an acoustic guitar which surprised me as I was unaware that he could play any instrument at all apart from the triangle, although I've never actually witnessed Tim playing the simple triangular shaped instrument, I'm just assuming that this is something that he'd be good at. Again, the volume was very loud inside the cavernous room and the bass drum reverberated inside my lungs, as like most of James' songs it made much more sense live than the recorded version. The song finished, the small audience showed their appreciation with a round of applause my son included. 'Five-O' started up, Tim suddenly walked over to the side of the stage near where myself and Daniel was stood, Tim looked down at my son and gave a big warm smile and a wave, I looked at Daniel, at first he didn't know how to respond but then he gave a big wave back to Tim who chuckled, the crowd who'd been watching the spectacle were all smiling, the females cooing and awwing. The money and the journey had all been worth it, it was a memory that I'd savour forever.

After 'Five-O' and a keyboard heavy version of 'Just Like Fred Astaire' the Q&A session started, it was an opportunity to ask some sensible questions that would reveal enlightening answers.

Question 1: "Tim, is 'Stutter' ripped off from 'The End' by The Doors?"

Tim: "Err, no. We were probably more influenced by The Birthday Party to be honest, that probably comes through more so than 'The End'.

The questioner who actually appeared quite drunk tried to argue his point; Tim said that you could sing any song to the tune of 'Stutter' if you tried hard enough.

Question 2: "Tim, can I come and dance onstage tonight?"

Tim: "Err, well it's generally a spontaneous thing to be honest, it isn't something that we plan to do".

Jim: "You can come and dance on stage now if you want to?"

Thankfully he never did.

Question 3: "Tim, on the backdrop of the last tour you had a picture of a woman and I was wondering if she held any significance at all for the band?"

The entire band looked puzzled, nobody appeared to know who the questioner was referring to and I certainly couldn't remember any picture of any woman at all either, the question kind of went unanswered. There was a fair bit of banter going on between Tim, Jim, Saul and the audience. Saul kept turning the air blue with his language until Tim spoke to him.

"SAUL, there's children present here!!"

Saul looked over at the two of us.

"Oh well, I'm sure he's used to it. Judging by the look of his dad, he looks like the kind of man who drinks cans of lager whilst sat on the sofa and swears a lot in front of his kids" Saul casually said.

The place erupted with laughter myself included even if it did give me a bit a complex, I realised that maybe I shouldn't have grown such a big beard and have shaved all of my hair off. Plus my t-shirt looked scruffy and paint splattered when it was in fact quite an expensive Sigur Ros t-shirt and was meant to look like that.

That was pretty much it regarding questions, somebody asked about the long rumoured James box set *The Gathering Sound* that was about to be released but would eventually be once again put on hold for another time. That was it, we were all asked to leave and make our way to the merchandise stall. I called out towards Dave Baynton-Power and asked if it was possible to have a drum stick or two for Daniel but Dave mouthed "no" towards me, I was a bit disappointed particularly as Daniel was getting his first drum kit for Christmas and I really hoped that Dave might have given him some sticks as a souvenir.

I caught up with Dave Brown and said thanks for arranging the session for me, I said goodbye to Kay and with that the two of us headed towards Leeds train station on our journey home. Later in the evening my wife and I returned to the venue where we managed to secure some seats together in an already packed balcony. As we'd arrived late we missed the support band Frazer King that Jim himself had been banging on about for ages regarding how good they were. Without sounding too ageist we were surrounded on all sides by quite a few old crumblies, a couple in front of us looked extremely ancient and even had cobwebs in their hair. The lights dropped, the room was filled with the sound of cheering and applause and James made their way onstage starting the show with 'Lost A Friend', I'm sure it confused a lot of people in attendance, maybe they thought it was a new song.

'Seven' followed and it sounded wonderful. 'Come Home' began and a woman who was sat fairly near to us went absolutely berserk when two girls a few rows in front of her stood up thus obscuring her view. She was screaming at them and shaking her fists in anger. She desperately tried to gain the attention of a security guy to make the girls sit down but he just looked at her instead with a sympathetic look in his eyes. When they eventually sat down on their own accord the cranky old boot performed a sarcastic slow clap and my wife and I almost had hernias from laughing so much. It was becoming apparent that this was one of the best James performances I'd ever witnessed. The band were on top form, the set list was well selected, the new material sounded immense particularly 'Rabbit Hole' and 'Tell Her I Said So', its disco beat making me jostle about in my chair like an electric eel. The highlight of the evening though was 'Out To Get You', I'd become a tad tired of the song but the version the band played that evening gave it new life, Saul's violin work was indefatigable and wild, he took control of the song and the rest of the band followed him. Even Tim stopped his wild dancing and stood staring in amazement at the little guy knocking seven shades of dung out of his string instrument. He kept doing that little motion that all excited violin players do, he'd lift his leg up into the air and hold it there suspended for a short time before placing it back down and then repeating the act. Or perhaps he simply had a bit of cramp.

When the song eventually finished the room erupted with applause. James were already on a high but Saul had definitely increased the energy levels off the richter scale and the rest of the gig was now a feverish whirlwind of emotion and passion. During 'Sound' Mark played a mysterious keyboard line which sounded as if a flying saucer was about to land on top of the venue, The Flaming Lips would have been proud of it. By that point everybody on the balcony was stood up, all except the cranky woman and her partner. She had her arms folded tightly and her lips were pursed. She blatantly couldn't see anything but she refused to join in with the rest of us and then believe it or not she stood up and walked out of the venue with her partner never to be seen again that evening! How sad, what a waste, can you imagine the conversation she had on the way home? I bet she blamed everyone for ruining her evening out.

The band finished their main set with 'Laid' followed by an encore of 'Sit Down' and 'Sometimes' and that was the end of the show. Except it wasn't, the audience showed so much appreciation and love and was just so bloody noisy that the band trooped back on stage and performed a second encore of 'Top Of The World', it was the icing on the cake as far as I was concerned and it was a fantastic ethereal curve ball to end the set on. And then once again they were gone and we left the building and headed back home. Content that we'd witnessed something rather magical.

James Come Home to Manchester

2010

Winter had descended upon the land in an unforgiving manner, weather warnings had been announced days before that the country would be shrouded in deep snow and ice before the weekend and my wife raised her concerns about my journey across The Pennines to see James in Manchester. The gig was taking place on the Saturday, the plan initially had been that I'd set off early afternoon and drop the kids off at her parents house in Northwich before heading back across to Stockport where I'd then meet her brother and the two of us would go to the gig together. He'd never seen James before, in fact he hadn't been to a gig for a number of years so he was curious and intrigued to attend this event at the Manchester Evening News Arena and see the band of now old men that I'd talked incessantly about since the day we'd met some ten years earlier. My wife by the way was travelling to Bath for the weekend to catch up with some of her old university friends hence the reason for dropping my kids off in Northwich.

The bad weather soon turned the weekend on its head though, snow and ice resulted in my wife cancelling her plans meaning that she'd be looking after the kids and instead I'd make the journey across the highest motorway in England straight to Stockport alone. For those of you who've never experienced the pleasure of driving across the M62 as it cuts through the beautiful yet desolate landscape then it's something to try before you die. True, when you're stuck in a traffic jam on a dark, cold wet night then it can be quite hellish but when the weather is clear the views that unfold around the worn tarmac are stunning and on the 18th December 2010 the sky was clear and the sun was prematurely setting in the west. Foolishly I'd forgotten to put any screen wash in my car and halfway through the journey it became quite apparent that I'd put myself in a risky situation due to the low sun, no sunglasses and an extremely filthy windscreen with no way of cleaning it. I spent the remainder of the journey craning my neck to see out of a small area of glass that had somehow evaded the grime and arrived in Stockport with a creak in my neck and an even more nervous disposition than usual.

My wifes brother William was waiting for me in anticipation; we greeted one another, chatted over a cup of coffee and then headed to the train station just in time for an empty train to glide us along the tracks into the city. Conditions in the city were precarious, ice and snow lay everywhere, the last minute Christmas shoppers slid and slipped over one another yet despite the conditions the city was heaving. I suggested we headed towards a bar and before too long we found ourselves in a pretentious drinking hole somewhere in The Printworks which prides itself as a state of the art entertainment complex with drink prices to match. The drink prices were nothing compared to those at the venue though. I suggested that William got the first round of drinks in whilst I used the toilet, when I returned I made a jokey comment about two drinks costing eight pounds. The joke was on me though as it cost exactly eight pounds for two so cold it actually hurt to drink pints of lager. Dismayed and slightly disturbed we headed onto the arena floor to take our place near the front of the already quite busy floor space. The cavernous room took my breath away as I panned my eyes around, it was simply too big a space to be real. I imagined myself sat upon one of the light fixtures way above my head, gazing down at the people below looking like little ants scurrying around the floor.

I noticed Dave Brown doing the rounds talking to seemingly random people, I caught his attention and had a brief chat before he sauntered off to speak to somebody else probably more interesting than I. Kay then made her presence known and we chatted for a while, she told me that she might be able to sort out tickets for the after show party and that William and I should meet her after the show and she'd see what she could do for us. I thanked her in advance before she disappeared off to where her other half was stood. Due to the temperature and cost of the fine ale we sipped carefully and slowly, savouring every last mouth wateringly drop whilst praying that some clumsy fool wouldn't bang into us resulting in a spillage. The lights dropped and an echoing of applause gave the large space a voice. The first support act was the band Jim Glennie had been enthusing about for a while; Frazer King played a bizarre yet wonderful set of punk infused pop that had me jigging along like Captain Birdseye in a set of bell bottoms. I made a mental note to check them out upon returning home. The next support act was The Pigeon Detectives, now I like bands with unusual names but 'The Pigeon Detectives' is just crap. The band themselves played some fairly okay music but the lead singer was still as annoying as a sharp stone inside your shoe. I soon lost count of how many times he threw his microphone into the air before catching it, he'd clearly practiced this act from a very young age in preparation for when he became an international rock star as he was frustratingly very good at it. Not once did the microphone slip from his hand which would have resulted in a loud over amplified thudding sound and stitches to a burst lip.

It was obvious that a lot of people were not going to be attending due to the harsh weather conditions. The James forum had been filled with postings by people who simply couldn't or daren't risk the journey and there were an awful lot of empty seats dotted around the venue. The standing area had filled up considerably though. Nearly ten years earlier I'd stood in exactly the same area of the venue in preparation for what I'd thought at the time would be the last time I'd see James live and space was then at a premium, I'd been wedged into a young sweaty audience and we were all hell bent on having the night of our lives. In 2010 the audience had clearly aged along with me; those in attendance were instead stood politely alongside one another without the merest hint of shove or a push. I knew that the band would probably perform a set of crowd friendly numbers with the odd curio thrown into the mix to test the loyal ones amongst us.

The band wandered onstage, I say wandered but by the looks of it they appeared knackered, the punishing year had clearly taken its toll and Tim announced that various band members had flu and Larry's back

316

was still in a bit of a state. Tim was wrapped up to the eyeballs in a long trench coat whilst balancing a long flowing hat upon his bald head. As ever he was a peculiar looking rock star that didn't fit any kind of mould. I'd watched him change over the years from a tussled haired young man to an aging composed artist who'd long since given up on meeting any preconceived rock star clichés. You had to respect him for this. The rest of James looked as casual as ever save for perhaps Saul who always made that bit more of an effort in his presentation. Not that the rest of the band ever looked scruffy of course, they clearly hadn't started buying their clothes from George at ASDA yet, that time would of course come. They had certain panache but you could have walked past any of them down the street and not batted an eye lid except of course when Andy was wearing one of his lovely dresses.

James played a similar set to what they'd played earlier on the tour, a mixture of crowd pleasing numbers such as 'Born Of Frustration', 'Ring The Bells', 'She's A Star' and 'Sound'. New songs from The Morning After were performed with the backing of a large choir which gave the songs an extra bit of oomph. The version of 'Stutter' they performed was as loud and frightening as Brummie band Napalm Death, Saul and Larry smacking hell out of their instruments with much rage. 'Gold Mother' was performed during the encore, a large organised stage invasion soon saw it swamped with aged James fans staggering and prancing around, their fifteen minutes of fame captured digitally for the Youtube generation. The song dragged on for what seemed like forever, the clattering baggy beat tripping over itself, Andy's trumpet piercing the air with its honking yelps, Jim Glennie's smile couldn't have been any bigger and Mark performed a number of somersaults and other acrobatics whilst playing with his large bank of keyboards. The song ground to a halt, the curfew had been reached, the show had to end but the band somehow managed to squeeze in 'Laid' which probably resulted in them receiving a large fine for breaching curfew.

The band received a well deserved round of applause from the twelve thousand or so attendees. I asked my brother in law if he'd enjoyed the show,

"Yeah, pretty good, not as good as Placebo or Linkin Park though".

I raised my eyebrows slightly exasperated whilst feeling quite humoured and tickled at the same time.

We hung about for a few minutes and eventually caught sight of Kay and her fella. Bad news though, she'd managed to acquire some after show passes for herself but only had one spare one for me. There was no way that I was going to attend the after show without my brother in law. That would have been very rude indeed. I told him to tag along behind me and we'd see what we could do. We made it past the first hurdle and the two of us managed to sneak past the security guard and we sat amongst the hundred or so other people who'd managed to secure a ticket to the best night out in Manchester, apart from the gig itself of course. It was doubtful though that we'd both make it through and sure enough an over militant security guard clocked that my brother in law didn't have a pass and he was ejected from the seating area before anybody else had stood up. Naturally I followed him down to the bottom of the stairs and we waited on the arena floor using an excuse that we needed to speak to somebody who'd be going through to the backstage area.

"Right, everybody have your passes at the ready and follow me" said the same security guard who'd cut short our evenings entertainment. The lucky few made their way down the stairs, their excited happy faces tore into me, sure I could have said goodnight to my brother in law, and I'm sure he'd have been fine about it but I just couldn't do it, I was wiling to sacrifice my pass for him. Salvation suddenly came in the form of two gentlemen, Dave Brown and Andy Diagram. Dave Brown greeted me as he walked past.

"Dave, any chance you can help out? My brother in law hasn't got a pass so they're not letting him through, have you got a spare one?"

Dave looked at the two of us and then proceeded to search through his bag; he then magically found a spare one which was a different colour that would have been used the night before.

"Cheers a lot fella, I owe you a drink" but Dave was already on his way. A security guard had watched what had happened and looked none too happy, thankfully for us Andy Diagram made an appearance, I explained the situation to him and he said it was fine for the two of us to go on through. The security guard said nothing. I took a deep breath. What lay ahead for us I wasn't too sure, a free bar? Free food perhaps? A large room full of fans but no band members? If there was any band members then would I get a chance to speak to any of them? Would I finally get a chance to speak to Tim Booth?

We entered into a large marquee housed inside the bowels of the Manchester Evening News Arena. The moodily lit room was already packed, music was playing and there was an inhumanly large queue for the bar. I managed to catch sight of Kay and her fella, she was sat next to a few people I recognised including Ian and the lad who'd made me chuckle two years earlier at the Manchester Central gig, the one who'd been dancing oddly and wearing a fair bit of eye make up that night, accompanied by a mammoth side parting, he was going for the same look that evening. I thanked Kay for the pass; even she was surprised that the two of us had gotten through when I explained how we'd managed it.

"Are any of the band members here?"

"Dave's knocking about, Mark was here a few minutes ago and I believe that Larry's on his way" replied Kay.

"Is the bar free then?"

"Err, no, and it's *very* expensive".

Great. I was starving, there was no sign of any canapés being passed around and ice cold beers were at a premium, however I couldn't really moan or grumble. We chatted, conversation naturally revolved around the bands performance, everybody agreed that it had been the best James gig in aeons, I personally preferred the Leeds gig due to its intimacy but I agreed that the band had put on a sterling show. It was obvious from his body language that my brother in law wasn't going to be either putting his hand in his pocket or queuing up for a drink so I dragged myself across to the bar and waited at the back of the line.

Being a sociable kind of person I chatted to a few people, they recognised my name from the forums.

"Wow, you've been on there for years haven't you?" an American woman said to me. "Do you know that somewhere in my home in California I've still got your old forum posts from the old James fan forum 'Stutter'!"

I'd used the website along with 'One Fan Clapping' back in 1998 when I was in Australia and had felt very detached from the James story. I eventually reached the bar, for nearly four pounds and fifty pence I managed to purchase two small bottles of coke. I grabbed a couple of plastic glasses in disgust and filled them to the brim with ice just to make sure that I got my moneys worth before returning to the table where Kay et al were sat.

After a few minutes Dave Baynton-Power strolled past I caught his attention and said hello as well as congratulating him on the tour and the year in general. I thought I'd try and crack a joke.

"Hey, Dave, remember when Saul accused me of being the kind of bloke who swears and drinks a lot in front of his kids? Well, Social Services have since been in touch because of his comments".

He gave me a bit of a funny look.

"I think you need to develop a sense of humour mate" he replied deadpan before walking away from me. Okay, well I wasn't expecting that, maybe he thought I was having a go or something which wasn't the case of course. True to form I'd chalked up yet another embarrassing moment it seemed. Oh well. I carried on sipping my drink trying to make it last as long as possible, the guys were all very chatty and I reminisced with Ian about the Leeds gig in 2001 where we'd met and how he'd been blown away by the experience of his first James gig. He'd seen James many times since just like myself, funny looking back to think that at the time we saw it as one of the last opportunities we'd ever have to see this great band and there we were just shy of a decade later sat talking in a marquee in Manchester at the tail end of another winter tour.

My gaze was then drawn towards a bald headed goatee bearded man wearing a rather tight black top; he looked like one of the law enforcers from the film *Logan's Run*. It was Tim Booth and he was talking to some of the guests, I couldn't lip read but it was easy to see that Tim was being congratulated and thanked by those who surrounded him. I didn't have the courage to go and speak to him myself, I knew that I'd lose my nerve and say something stupid or unintentionally stare at him in an inappropriate manner so I resigned myself to watching from a distance instead. That was until Kay got up and made her way over to Tim. I had to do it. If I left the venue without at least trying to say hello to him then I knew that I'd regret it forever. I just had to keep it simple, say "hello" and "thank you" and that would be enough. I got up out of my chair and moved stealthily like a panther towards him and before I knew it I was stood next to him.

Tim was talking to some guy who then conveniently moved away, Kay then made her move and had a brief chat with him. Tim then turned his head towards me and I smiled a nervous smile before stretching out my hand towards. Tim smiled a wary smile but shook my hand nonetheless.

"Hi Tim, it was a great show, thanks very much".

"You're welcome".

"I was at the Leeds VIP show with my son by the way. Thanks very much for allowing him to attend".

"Oh right, no problems, did he enjoy it?"

"Yes he did, he's named after the band by the way".

"That's great", Tim smiled and then walked away.

I winced, I felt that Tim had been cool towards me; I couldn't really blame him though. How many times had he been approached by over excited fans over the years that have made him feel uncomfortable or awkward? I felt that I'd kept myself fairly composed though and at least I hadn't said "ALRIGHT CAPTAIN!" to him. My heart was still racing, there was so much that I could and would have said to him given the chance but I knew that this was never going to be the case. Tim probably met a thousand fans each year anyway and I'd be nothing more than another nameless face to him, soon to be forgotten about. Probably not even that.

I shimmied back to the others and carried on chatting although my mind was still stuck on events from a few moments before, it was probably time to go anyway, it was late and my brother in law and I were due to meet up with some people in a night club on Portland Street. We bid our farewells and I walked over towards where Dave Brown was to thank him for sorting out the opportunity to attend the after show. He was engrossed in conversation with a group of burly men so I caught his attention, waved and gave him the thumbs up whilst he carried on with his conversation. As we were leaving the marquee I had a final look back, the party was in full swing, Mark, Larry and Dave were chatting away, Tim and a woman who I thought must have been his wife were however walking in our direction apparently making their exit.

We walked down the cold concrete tunnel leading away from the after show party, it felt like we were in the insides of a huge concrete beast. We turned a corner and coming towards us was Saul Davies.

"Hey, Saul!" I said loud enough for him to hear. He looked at me with an expressionless face.

"You know what, after your comments in Leeds about me drinking and swearing in front of the kids someone's contacted Social Services!" I was obviously trying to squeeze every last bit out of this joke. Saul pulled a face that simply said "you what?" and then walked past without saying a word. Mortally embarrassed yet again at my foolishness I trudged on with my brother in law in tow. A voice I recognised caught my attention, Tim Booth. I immediately squatted down and pretended to tie my shoelace which meant that Tim and his small entourage walked past me. I stood bolt up right.

"Tim!" I called out. He stopped and turned around; I walked right up to him.

"I just wanted to tell you that I'm writing a book about James you know".

He looked deep into my eyes with just a flicker of confusion.

"Well, good luck with that" he said in a quiet softly spoken voice.

"Yeah, it's obviously going to be an unauthorised book, it's kind of a fans journey, a fans perspective on James".

"Okay, well good luck with that, good luck with that" he said in that same softly spoken voice.

I was struck with paranoia. Was he annoyed with me? Did he think I was serious? Was he even interested? I couldn't tell from those eyes and before I knew it he'd turned around and was walking away from the two of us. I stared at the back of his head for a few moments wondering what the future held for James, myself, in fact for all of us. And with that final thought my brother in law and I walked towards a large door that had an exit sign on it, pushed it open, walked out into the arctic blast of air and headed towards Portland street via snow and black ice covered pavements and roads.

Destiny Calling

February 2012

I must have searched about a billion record shops looking for *One Man Clapping*. Okay, a billion is quite clearly an exaggeration but places I actually searched certainly included every town and city within the UK when I happened to be visiting as well as some of the weird and wonderful places I'd visited on my travels around the world. Whenever I was abroad I'd search and quite literally scour every inch of the dusty racks of the music shops, at times I knew the search was clearly pointless such as inspecting the material that the record shop at Tel Aviv bus station had for sale but search I did. I even managed to find a teeny weeny record shop in Dahab Egypt, obviously the album wasn't there but I was mightily impressed that they had a *Parklife* poster next to a Glen Medeiros poster on their breezeblock wall.

I obviously had and hopefully still have an optimistic outlook on life, the search for *One Man Clapping* in places like Penguin in Tasmania, Avarua in Rarotonga and Las Vegas in America was fruitless but somehow still great fun. Okay, so my search never came up with the goods I craved but from time to time I'd find another little beauty such as *Somewhere Soon* by The High in Wellington New Zealand. Sometimes I'd even find rare That Petrol Emotion remixes whilst rummaging through local car boot sales. Happy memories. I was resigned to the fact that I was never going to find it despite desperately praying to God each and every night that I would.

However, I did own *One Man Clapping*....

Back in 1994 I'd been out for the night, a Sunday night spent at Jimmy's nightclub and bar in Harrogate, it's where me and Steve used to hang out drinking half price cocktails watching and enjoying Jason Feddy and his band. I awoke the next day with a horrible hangover; I'd clearly fallen asleep on the sofa upon arriving home the night before the morning after. I yawned and stretched, something caught my eye. It was a cassette box; its spine was facing me. In scrawled biro were the words *One Man Clapping*. I stared at it for a minute or so wondering if I was still dreaming, I wasn't and I reached out and grabbed the plastic box.

The track listing was included. Hmmm. But where had it come from? I got up, entered the gloomy kitchen and placed the tape into the stereo. I experienced something akin to a carnival of noise, light and airy songs I'd never heard before. I won't break the album down song by song though. All I'll say is that it's a fabulous album, I'm sure I'll find an original version of it one day probably just down the road in the second hand shop in the quiet market town of Otley. As for where the tape had come from, Richard who'd attended the York gig with me and Steve had recorded it for me in a student flat in Salford. He'd called around the evening before and handed it to my mum. It was a nice gesture from a guy who'd drop out of my life forever a couple of years down the line. I believe he's quite a successful business man in London now.

So, James eh! A funny old bunch if ever there was. Always a step out of touch from the rest of the world yet this in itself is what probably draws us all to them. That's certainly been the case for me anyway. A bunch of awkward misfits who've purposely and consistently driven against the grain creating some of the finest music this country has ever produced, and just think about that if you will. The Beatles, The Rolling Stones, The Smiths, Joy Division, Cabaret Voltaire, Blur, the list just goes on and on and James deserve to be recognised for creating music that sounds like no other, their musical references are almost undetectable. Sure, Tim talks about Patti Smith and Iggy as huge influences but that is what they are, influences only. They've never set out to recreate the sound of The Velvet Underground despite covering 'Sunday Morning', 'Sit Down' may have been written as a thank you to Patti Smith and Doris Lessing but you'd never really guess that from the music or the lyrics, well, not to the casual listener anyway. All those nights in Josephine's nightclub listening to 'Sit Down' on the 10p a pint nights, the punk poet and author were probably a million miles away from the minds of those attending. All we wanted to do was dance and let go, that's what Saturday nights are really for, escapism from the routine of sleep-work-sleep.

As I've read back through my story I've discovered the fact that something can swallow you whole and wrap itself around you so much to the point that it almost becomes suffocating rather amazing really. It's a funny relationship to have, for the majority of us the band will have no real idea of our individual existence yet without us bands and musicians wouldn't have a career if you can call being in a band a career. In fact, once it starts to become a career it's probably best to throw in the towel and get a proper job. I believe you should never be boring; never do what's expected of you otherwise you'll lose your identity and what motivated you in the first place.

In 2011 Tim Booth released another album, *Love Life* a self-financed project which was another light and airy collection of pop songs, the kind of pop songs that only Tim Booth could ever come up with. The accompanying tour was a tour de force, the Manchester gig I attended is easily one of the best gigs I've ever had the pleasure to experience. I managed to give Tim a friendly slap on the chest as he walked passed me through the audience, even the often referred to as grumpy Saul who was playing in Tim's band gave me a half friendly nod of the head. Fingers are fiercely crossed in the hope that there will be further releases from the great man himself.

So, what does the future hold for James? At the time of writing the band are preparing for a number of live dates including the Coachella Festival in California which I was hoping to attend. Sadly Mr Bank Manager says I can't go even though I sold the idea of attending on the back of the "Experience of a Lifetime". I'm sure they'll blow the crowd away and reap the seeds that they sowed many years ago during their success in America with the *Laid* era. I can see the headlines now,

"Lost British band make a triumphant return at Coachella"

Manchester band 'James' reminded those in attendance at this weekend's Coachella Festival that they remain one of the most exciting live acts in the world. Despite the fact that the festival is in the dessert the band played during a deluge of rain to a massive audience that enjoyed a set comprised of their rich catalogue of beautiful and at times haunting songs. Frontman Tim Booth commented to the crowd that they'd brought the Manchester weather with them as a treat. However, the rain only added to the atmosphere and a more appropriate song couldn't have suited the occasion any more than the galloping 'Sometimes' with its "Come on thunder" lyric……..

The long awaited, much delayed and at times rather controversial box set *The Gathering Sound* will also hopefully be ending up in our mitts, (although I've still yet to order it). I'm guessing that new material will make an appearance at some point too and James will continue to demonstrate that they're far from a spent force, some of their best material is only a couple of years old, well, that's what I think anyway.

So why write about them in the way that I have? It's simply because I wanted to piece together a story that has threaded its way through some of the most interesting years of my life. James has taken over my whole outlook on life, they've become embedded into who I am, the way I think and the way I interact with others. Sure, there are more passionate and obsessed fans out there. Maybe we should all write a book or at least a short story about how our lives have been moved by this folk rock stadium power beat combo from Manchester and then we can put them all together and Ta Dah! we'll have another 'James' book on our hands! Proceeds from the sales can go towards promoting the next album perhaps.

Thank you for journeying with me over the past twenty years. I hope the adventure was as interesting for you as it was for me. I should probably end with a lyric or two shouldn't I? Hopefully I won't end up being sued for breaching copyright.

"Don't believe the adverts, don't believe the experts, everyone will sell our souls (I always thought Tim was saying "arseholes").Get a little wiser, get a little humble, now we know that we don't know. Tell us when our

time's up, show us how to die well, show us how to let it all go. Here we come, this is our destiny calling, we're freaks, this is our destiny calling, unique, this is our destiny calling now........"

Now that's pure poetry!!!

(Well, at a pinch).

And Michael, thanks again for *Mickey B's*, best compilation tape EVER!!!

John Ormond. March 2012. Otley, West Yorkshire, England, Earth. (mostly).